USING NATIVE PLANTS
TO RESTORE COMMUNITY

IN SOUTHWEST MICHIGAN AND BEYOND

Rebirth of a Monarch   Etching with drypoint and aquatint   Ladislav Hanka

"I cast my lot with the cycles of nature—in regeneration and transformation"

—Ladislav Hanka, "On Primitive Art"

Using Native Plants to Restore Community

in Southwest Michigan and Beyond

By
Nancy Cutbirth Small
and Tom Small

Gratitude to Plants, the sun-facing light-changing leaf
and fine root-hairs; standing still through wind
and rain. their dance is in the flowing spiral grain
in our minds so be it.
—Gary Snyder, "Prayer for the Great Family"—

We cannot in fairness rail against those who destroy the rain forest or threaten the spotted owl when we have made our own yards uninhabitable. Yet how quickly we could grow this land, spangle it with blazing stars, stripe it with red winterberries and white summersweet, let it wave again with grass!
—Sara Stein, *Noah's Garden*

ISBN 978-0-615-52993-6

To order copies of this book, send a check or mail order to Kalamazoo Area Wild Ones, for $25.00 plus $10.00 for shipping and handling.

The entire proceeds from sales are for the benefit of
the Nancy Small Memorial Fund and educational projects of
the Kalamazoo Area Chapter of Wild Ones, a nonprofit organization.

Wild Ones

"For the Children," by Gary Snyder, from *Turtle Island*, copyright ©1974 by Gary Snyder. Reprinted by permission of New Directions Publishing Corp.

Design by Linda Judy
Cover drawing and watercolor by Amelia Hansen
Printed by Cushing-Malloy, Inc.—Ann Arbor, Michigan

For Nancy, who brought love and new life

A thing of beauty is a joy forever:
Its loveliness increases; it will never
Pass into nothingness.

—John Keats, *Endymion*

and

For Sara Stein, who showed us the way
For Steve Keto, who gave us the means
For Doug Tallamy, who provided the proof

CONTENTS

ACKNOWLEDGEMENTS

I like the rare, extravagant spirits
who disclose to me new facts in nature.
—Ralph Waldo Emerson, *Journals*

I am grateful to so many friends and associates who have both encouraged me and given generously of their time and spirit in careful reading of parts of this book and in helping with its preparation.

I am especially grateful to Tyler Bassett, Eleanore Chadderdon, Ken Dahlberg, Ann Fraser, Ilse Gebhard, Nancy Halliday, Ladislav Hanka, Amelia Hansen, Liz Henderson, Jennifer Hopwood, Linda Judy, Mike Klug, Paul Olexia, Pam Rups, and Tom Seiler. Their kindness has sustained me.

For all of those who have provided, over many years, extraordinary kindness, friendship, and indispensable support, for me and for Nancy, I give thanks, and I carry Nancy's thanks in my heart. I cannot convey how important you have been to us.

Steve Allen, Beth Amidon, Amy Anderson, Chris Bartley, Becky Beech, Lucy Bland and Chris Dilley, Louis Bonamego, Leila Bradfield, Richard Brewer and Katy Takahashi, Marilyn Case, Jason Cherry, Matt Clysdale, Marie and Bill Combs, Don Cooney, Becky and Kalman Csia, Judy Dircks, Jenny Doezema, David Dunstone, Nate and Erin Fuller, Jean and Joe Gump, Maryellen Hains, Ruth Harring, Mark Hoffman, Chad and Kristin Hughson, Alice and Bill Howenstine, Celeste and Patrick Jones, Sister Virginia Jones, Shadia and Azzam Kanaan, Ken and Marlena Kirton, Renee Kivikko.

Pam and Lee Larson, Debby Luyster, Marshall Massey, Lois Matthews, Mary Ann Menck, Joe Mills, Catherine Niessink, Sally Olexia, Ruth Pino, Bob Pleznac, Jana Pyle, Stan Rajnak, Lois and Jim Richmond, Sniedze Rungis, Todd Sanford, Russ Schippers, Bill Schneider, Shirley Scott, Bob and Carol Smith, Jerry Stewart, Nancy Stone, Nancy and John Stroupe, James, John, and Nathan Stroupe, Ruah Swennerfelt, Larry Syndergaard, Kim Traverse.

For all those wonderful friends who have not lived to read these words, you live on in Nancy's words and spirit and in my heart.

—Tom Small

PREFACE

To me the meanest flower that blows can give
Thoughts that do often lie too deep for tears.
—William Wordsworth, "Ode: Intimations of Immortality"

This book began in 1996, the year after Nancy and I married and retired from college teaching, the year she read Sara Stein's *Noah's Garden*, which she recognized immediately was to be the crucial discovery and luminous inspiration in our search for what our marriage and our life together would be devoted to. Thus we undertook to live, together, what we both called our "second life," dedicated to saving and restoring some of the degraded and lost biodiversity of southwest Michigan, to creating natural habitat for the distressed creatures of the earth and the air.

Being teachers for most of our lives, we not only began the transformation of our own yard into natural habitat, we began to spread our message by means of talks, slide programs, plant lists, enumerations of the joys and benefits of natural landscaping, essays and notes in environmental journals and newsletters. We became involved with the work of the Southwest Michigan Land Conservancy in maintaining their nature preserves, and then in 1999 we established the Kalamazoo Area Chapter of Wild Ones—Native Plants, Natural Landscapes, the national organization devoted to precisely what we had undertaken as our own

mission. That led to our generating yet more educational materials, for the new members of our chapter. Eventually, a book became inevitable—a book that would be, in itself, a continuing process, of both learning and teaching. And so it has been.

Over and over again, during our life together, Nancy said to me, "We're so lucky, we're so lucky." She felt fortunate and grateful that we had finally found each other and a second life together in a "leading," a mission, that we shared in so many ways and that she believed in so passionately.

I have to say it alone now, for both us. We have indeed been lucky. We're blessed to have found Sara Stein's wonderful book, which inspired Nancy—and she in turn inspired me—to undertake the work of Noah, saving the species of the earth—one small "ark," one suburban yard at a time. Not by ourselves, to be sure. We're blessed to have found so many wonderful friends and associates to work with us in the struggle for a peaceful life, for restoration, and for nonviolence toward the whole Community of Life.

Towards the end of her final struggle with cancer, Nancy expressed great regret that she would have no more chances to tell how grateful she was to those who have been kind to her, and who have helped her to help other people and creatures. She yearned to see the beauty and share the pleasures of the earth, and she desired to help others to see—really to look, to see what's really there—how beautifully complex and simple and how wonderful are all the plants and creatures of the earth. How we must all do whatever we can to save them. She wanted, always, to teach. She leaves behind her all that she has taught and the many lives she touched. In spirit and inspiration, she continues in the hearts and the actions of those who have known her and understood both her fragility and the strength of her spirit and love for all of creation.

The last book Nancy read about the natural world was Lyanda Lynn Haupt's *Crow Planet: Essential Wisdom from the Urban Wilderness*. She loved the book; we bought extra copies to give to special friends. One passage in particular spoke powerfully to both of us:

> There are two Greek words for time. One is *chronos*, which refers to the usual, quantifiable sequential version of time by which we monitor and measure our days. The other word is *kairos*, which denotes an unusual period in human history when eternal time breaks in upon chronological time. *Kairos* is "the appointed time," an opportune moment, even a time of crisis, that creates an opportunity for, and in fact demands, a human response. It is a time brimming with meaning, a time more potent than "normal" time. We live in such a time now, when our collective actions over the next several years will decide whether earthly life will continue its descent into ecological ruin and death or flourish in beauty and diversity.

Nancy loved beauty and cherished diversity. Her second life, dedicated to saving biodiversity, was an opening for both of us. For me, her death, the day after Thanksgiving, 2009, is the kind of shock or crisis that opens the way to yet another renewal.

As teachers, together, of Shakespeare, and then as teachers of what Aldo Leopold calls a "land eth-ic," Nancy and I learned from each other. Only in her death do I begin to realize how much I learned from her, and how much I had yet to learn. We do, however, continue to learn from those we love and lose. This book is part of the continuation and, I trust, the renewal.

During the final year of Nancy's illness—as she realized how little time she had and I was more or less in denial—she over and over again made me promise to "finish the book." I have fulfilled my promise, as best I could. It is nonetheless Nancy's book, not mine. It was her spirit which motivated our work together; it is her insistence on clarity and concreteness which informs the book throughout; it is her generosity in sharing with everyone her reading and observation that generated most of the material in the first three parts of the book; and it is her spirit which has remained with me in this effort to communicate her love and her dedication. During those final months, she worked as hard and as long as she was able to. She did not arrive at a final text; but she had a clear vision—and a rough draft version—of the whole book. Except for my re-ordering of the essays in Part IV and inclusion of one essay we had discussed and reluctantly decided not to include, "Freeing Ourselves From Possessions," the book follows the table of contents she decided on.

My finishing of the book has been a labor that was often painful to perform alone, without Nancy's expertise, her painstaking editorial care, and her guidance. It has also been a labor of love and gratitude. I am both bereft and comforted. Her life continues in the intensity of her vision, in her gardens and her writing, in the lives that she has touched. It continues in my life; she changed the way I see and the way I live.

I have not attempted to change any of Nancy's observations to indicate that she is no longer with me or that she is not speaking, here and now, to the reader. Not only is this book hers, it is her voice that speaks in these words. In all the changes and additions I have made, according to my own judgments or in response to suggestions from others, I have, to the best of my ability, preserved her intention and her voice.

The intended audience remains what it was for us from the beginning. It includes those who want to know what they can do—and why they should do it—to help preserve the wondrous diversity of species that have shared with us human beings the immense and perilous journey of evolution. It includes both devoted and casual gardeners, traditional and unconventional landscapers, suburban and rural property owners, scientists, birdlovers, vegetable gardeners, activists for peace and justice, and all those who may understand that there is a crisis on the land but who simply do not know how they can *make a difference*—a difference that they can *see*.

The "Introduction" to the book stresses how every yard *can* make a difference. Then, in Part I, we provide a series of "Perspectives" on the rationale for natural landscaping and the basis for how to proceed. While the advice is directed primarily to beginners and relative novices, there is much that the two of us learned only over the course of many years and which could be valuable—even if only as reminders—to those of you who consider yourselves well past the "beginner" stage.

Part II, "Particulars," provides plant lists and advice for many different environmental conditions and human intentions. Here, we give particular attention to plant communities that will provide habitat and nurture for the many kinds of pollinators so essential to plant reproduction and yet so stressed and depleted by loss of habitat and by conventional landscaping. Here we also give special attention to trees and shrubs, absolutely essential to fully supportive habitat for wildlife but ordinarily given only casual attention in conventional landscaping and gardening.

In Part III, "Rewards and Joys," Nancy gathered together into three essays many of her close observations of plants and wild creatures. She believed that the whole of the living world participates in the joy of being; and as we observe and cherish the lives of plants and of creatures other than ourselves, we participate in the fullness of their being— and their joy.

Part IV, "Restoring Community," explores more fully the themes and the underlying philosophy of the whole book. Here, we collect many of the essays that we wrote, singly or together, during the 15 years of our marriage and our mission. I've rewritten most of them, sometimes extensively, to bring them up to date, or perhaps, more accurately, simply to continue and extend the conversations between the two of us that brought these essays into being. In some of them, we try to relate local action to "global" issues and contexts. There are by-lines in this section, to indicate the primary authorship of each essay; but they are all of them joint creations.

The final three essays I have rewritten many times over. They raise difficult questions, and I am still far from knowing the answers. Nonetheless, I offer them as provisional truths by which Nancy and I have sought to live.

During our last five years of teaching at the university, Nancy and I team-taught the English Department's undergraduate Shakespeare course. That too was a labor of love. One of my specialties was dramatic literature, and Nancy's was Renaissance literature. We both loved Shakespeare. Nancy especially loved Shakespeare's sonnets; she re-read them closely in her last year of life. I'll close with the final couplet of one of her favorites, sonnet 73:

This thou perceiv'st, which makes thy love more strong,
To love that well which thou must leave ere long.

Kalamazoo, Michigan, September, 2011

INTRODUCTION:
EVERY YARD MAKES A DIFFERENCE

Making amends is the beginning of the healing of the world.
—Paul Hawken, *Blessed Unrest*

One summer shortly after we began landscaping our yard with native plants, a worn, battered monarch butterfly flew into the driveway and started laying eggs on a flat of tiny butterflyweed seedlings that were waiting in the driveway to be planted. That she laid them on such small plants and on a kind of milkweed not preferred for egg-laying—common and swamp milkweed being the preferred species in our area—argues that she was desperate.

She ended up laying about two dozen eggs on about the same number of plants. It was obvious that such small plants wouldn't support even a few caterpillars, so I decided to raise them in the kitchen as my friend Ilse Gebhard had been doing for years. In the wild, a monarch has less than a five percent chance of making it from egg to butterfly; raised in captivity, its chances are much, much better. At first I fed the caterpillars on swamp milkweed from our yard, but, in collecting leaves, found still more eggs. Soon, I'd stripped most of the leaves from our plants, and my husband Tom and I were making trips every other day to the edge of town to collect the leaves of common milkweed for our caterpillars (and in the process acquiring still more eggs). We released a lot of monarchs that summer—though not nearly as many as Ilse did. The last ones were the generation that migrates to Mexico.

After that, we planted a lot more common and swamp milkweed in our yard and never again had to forage on the outskirts of Kalamazoo for leaves with which to feed the caterpillars being raised in the kitchen.

On June 15, 2009, on milkweed plants strung out along the curb in our side yard, we discovered the earliest mature monarch caterpillars we'd ever seen. We took them in, and Ilse nursed them along to butterflies. It's important that this earliest generation produce as many butterflies as possible, in order to make that last generation, traveling all the way to Mexico and partway back, as large as possible. On sunny days in early fall, monarchs bound for Mexico nectar on New England asters in our yard, clinging to the flowers in the wind.

EVERY YARD MAKES A DIFFERENCE—FOR GOOD OR ILL

- Every yard counts, **no matter how small or urban it is**.

- It can link you, and everyone who sees it, more closely with nature and its wondrous cycles OR perpetuate our alienation from the web of life that ultimately sustains us.

- It can help conserve the earth's resources OR damage and waste them.

- It can help limit the spread of invasive alien plants OR help disseminate them.

- It can serve as a stopover site for migrating birds and butterflies, help extend or connect wildlife habitat, and serve as an example to other people; OR it can further fragment or degrade existing habitat and perpetuate conventional—and destructive—notions of landscaping.

- It can help limit climate change and species extinction OR contribute to these calamities.

- It can foster the biological diversity which sustains life on earth OR help suppress it.

YOU CAN MAKE A DIFFERENCE—AND *SEE* IT

Whether our yards bring us closer to nature or divide us from it, help protect or endanger the earth and all its inhabitants, depends on us—and the choices we make. We live in a time of accelerating environmental crisis—vanishing habitat, declining diversity, and climate change—and unless we're actively trying to alleviate the crisis at the level of our own households and yards, then we're part of the problem. "What you do makes a difference," affirms Jane Goodall, "and you have to decide what kind of difference you want to make."

The rewards of landscaping with native plants, of turning your yard into better habitat for wildlife, are quickly and easily visible—and thus almost instantly gratifying—as the rewards of recycling, say, or making your house more energy efficient, are not. These latter activities, to be sure, are essential, no matter how tedious, no matter how remote the result. Reducing the size of your lawn and landscaping with native plants—now that's another matter altogether. Not only will you reduce energy use, water use, and carbon emissions, but also, along with these savings, you will have countless strange and wonderful encounters with the natural world. A butterfly emerging from its chrysa-

lis, a rabbit taking a dust bath on a patch of dry, bare ground, a bird feeding its young—even these minor dramas of the natural world fill us with joy and wonder. We're transported from daily worries and routines to a timeless world from which self-absorption and our need to feel in control ordinarily separate us. Such moments and images can help motivate and inspire us during the great personal and national efforts that lie ahead, if our planet is to remain livable for both its human and its nonhuman inhabitants.

Things weren't nearly so clear to Tom and me when we made a series of choices in the mid-nineties. We got married, agreed to retire in Kalamazoo instead of moving to the country, and decided to turn our yard into a refuge for plants and animals. We'd both had long careers at Western Michigan University, teaching English and American literature, but had no expertise whatever in biology, ecology, or environmental science. We didn't even know very much about gardening, though we'd puttered at it for most of our adult lives. But we knew we loved animals and wanted to help them. Probably another important factor in our decision, though we didn't realize it then, was that as children and young adults we'd both spent considerable time outdoors and even in wild or semi-wild areas.

Two presentations on prairie and savanna wildflowers—the first by "Prairie Bob" Pleznac, one of the founders of the Southwest Michigan Land Conservancy, the other by Steve Keto, for many years a grower of native plants at Van Bochove Nursery in Kalamazoo—got us started. And Steve's electrifying enthusiasm sent us to one of the most important books we've ever read, Sara Stein's wonderfully informative and visionary *Noah's Garden: Restoring the Ecology of Our Own Back Yards* (1993). We read her book in early 1996, and before spring was over, we had started removing lawn from the sunny front corner of our yard and planting wildflowers native to southwest Michigan's prairies and savannas. I don't think we would have actually done it—or done it as soon as we did—without Sara, who saw so clearly and wrote so persuasively that our suburban yards *must* provide the habitat needed by wildlife; and we couldn't have done it without Steve, an accessible and always bountiful source of plants, expertise, kindness, and good cheer. And it was Steve, after all, who put us onto Sara.

Chrysalis   Woodcut   Ladislav Hanka

The Rewards Are Many—and Wonderful

The rewards of shrinking our lawn and replacing it with native plants were immediate; even that first summer black-eyed Susans bloomed on the corner and attracted butterflies, and hummingbirds arrived to nectar at the cardinal flowers (planted in shade next to the house and watered every day). The rewards multiplied as we got rid of more lawn and put in more native plants—plants tolerant of less sun and even (in a small area we dug out and lined) some wetland plants. Rather than telling you here about these rewards, the wonderful encounters we've had with plants and animals and what they've taught us, we're including some stories about them—often mere jottings—in Part III of the book, especially Chapter 15, "Sightings and Insights." We hope these simple observations will suggest how exciting and gratifying the process of turning even a small yard into better habitat is. But I do have to tell you about the Blackburnian warbler that suddenly dropped from the trees one May when I was watering pots on the patio. He then took a leisurely bath in a little pool not ten feet away from me that had formed on the concrete. I just stood there, holding the hose, and trying not to move. Finally, he flew up to a low branch not far away and groomed himself for several minutes.

Another time, I saw from the kitchen window half a dozen young rabbits chasing one another in a circle in the newly-green grass (as if in an illustration in a children's book). Another time, from that same window on a dark and rainy afternoon, I saw a red fox racing through the yard with a rabbit in

Blackburnian warbler   L. Hanka

remnant was nevertheless large enough for a doe to raise three fawns in it.

While you don't know exactly how, or how much, the native plants in your yard are helping wildlife—unless you make a study (and maybe not even then)—you nevertheless do know that they are helping. You see holes in the leaves—holes that you learn to regard not with distaste and dread but with *pride*, as evidence that your plants are supporting something. In summer almost every flower has an insect of some kind nectaring on it: a butterfly; a bee or bee-like insect; a wasp or wasp-like insect; or something less easily categorized—sorry, I don't know much yet about insects. (We've never been stung by anything, though; the insects are too busy feeding.) You know that your yard is helping when American goldfinches flock to composite (daisylike) flowers and prairie grasses, and when the small fruits and berries disappear from your shrubs. You know when birds that ordinarily don't congregate in urban yards—red-winged blackbirds—return to your yard every February, with their wonderful whirring cries, and stay, with their babies, until late fall.

its mouth. I'd never seen a wild fox up close before, much less a wet and bedraggled one, and it took what seemed like a long time (though it must have been only a second or two) to figure out what I was actually seeing.

We know our yard wasn't supporting the fox, at least on a permanent basis; and even the rabbit may have come from someplace else. So how do people know that their native plants are actually helping wildlife, especially when they complicate the situation—as we do—by putting out seed and suet for birds on a regular basis year-round? Our situation is further complicated, too, by the existence of a scrap of degraded woods in the remnant of a glacial kettle at the center of our irregularly-shaped city block. Part of our backyard adjoins the woods though we don't own any of it. Small enough that when the trees are bare we can make out the backs of the houses on the next street, this

Bee   L. Hanka

You're Helping at Times of Stress

It is particularly gratifying to know that your yard is helping support birds that have stayed for the winter—not only by means of the food you put out for them but with fruits and insects that your native plants have produced earlier in the year. Surviving the cold in various stages of development, in crevices in the bark of trees or in brush or leaf litter, these insects form, even in winter, an extremely important part of most birds' diets. Also available to winter birds and returning migrants in the spring are "persistent" fruits, e.g., the berries of Michigan holly and highbush cranberry, that remain on the plant and above the snow. Such fruits are usually bypassed during the fall migration as not yet ready to eat; it will take repeated freezes and thaws to make them palatable. The first persistent berries to be eaten in our yard are usually those from shrubs in the areas of high bird traffic: thickets where birds rest or shrubs that overhang birdbaths. In spring, we see robins eating the remaining fruits. In all seasons, birds rely heavily upon our plants, particularly conifers and tangles of shrubs, for cover.

We felt that we had really "arrived," in terms of our yard being helpful, when Carolina wrens started visiting on a regular basis, summer and winter, because wrens are highly insectivorous, though Carolina wrens also eat fruit and seeds. We sometimes see one or two of them at the seed feeders or on the suet, but more often they seem to be down on the ground in the leaf litter, hunting for insects. This year a pair of Carolina wrens nested between two plastic bottles on a shelf in our garage and raised four young. Perhaps the fact that our garage, which hasn't had a good cleaning in years, is full of spiders accounted for the wrens' choice of location and contributed to their breeding success. Perhaps a rise in the number of insects our native plants are producing and a definite increase in leaf litter also helps account for the increase in

Eastern cottontail rabbit   Amelia Hansen

the number of woodpeckers we're seeing in the yard year round. In the summer of 2008, we saw young downy, young hairy, and young red-bellied woodpeckers—the first time we'd seen the young of all three species in the same summer. Once, this past summer, we saw a female red-bellied feeding a baby almost as large as she was with chunks of suet while he was foraging for himself with some success on a tree a few feet away from the suet feeder.

DO AS MUCH, AS STEADILY, AS YOU CAN

This year, 2009, will be our fourteenth year of landscaping with native plants, and we're still working to get rid of lawn and nonnatives, and to increase the diversity of plants and animals in our yard. Obviously, we didn't change our yard overnight, and you don't have to either. (It's probably impossible, unless you're incredibly energetic and also rich.) The trick is to do as much as you can, as steadily as you can, without getting overwhelmed or coming to regard landscaping your yard with native plants as an ordeal or a burden. Whatever your situation, forget about achieving perfection; the plantings we humans design, however painstakingly, are merely crude imitations of nature's. Don't take your mistakes too hard: they're bound to be an improvement over the lawn and alien ornamentals that were there before; and you're moving in the right direction. Forget, too, about achieving a no-maintenance yard; there's no such thing. Even yards landscaped with native plants need maintenance. For one thing, aggressive, nonnative plants don't give up without a hard fight, and a great many of them (and their seeds) have been introduced since the European settlement of Michigan. For another, natural succession will turn plantings, even when filled with native wildflowers and grasses, into expanses of young shrubs and trees unless they're maintained. But if you've laid the groundwork at all well, there will eventually be less maintenance than in a conventionally-landscaped yard. That maintenance will be less tedious and more richly rewarding than conventional lawn maintenance. It will also be far less harmful to the earth and its inhabitants. And it will almost surely be cheaper, maybe even a lot cheaper.

Tom and I now know a lot more about natural landscaping and the natural world than we did when we started, though we're also increasingly aware of how much we don't—and can't—know. From the first, we've been unusually lucky in the many experts we've encountered—through environmental organizations, conferences, field trips, visits to nurseries—who have so generously and tactfully shared their knowledge with us and continue to do so. Thanks to them, and to a lot of reading, extended trips to natural areas, and "learning by doing" in our yard—that is, making mistakes, correcting them, making new mistakes, and correcting those—we eventually acquired some rough-and-ready expertise of our own. So we've collected some of the thoughts, information and practical advice that we've written up and distributed over the years, revised it all, and included it in this book. Maybe we can smooth your path a little, help you avoid some of the mistakes we've made, save you some time and energy. Time is growing short, experts warn us—and as we can often observe for ourselves—for preserving the diversity of life that ultimately sustains us.

> So the efforts that I find most hopeful are largely the work of individuals, households, and small associations of people. All of these ventures, scattered among thousands of places, add up to a vast ferment of imagination, inquiry, and labor devoted to creating a durable way of life.
>
> —Scott Russell Sanders,
> *A Conservationist Manifesto* (2009)

YOU ARE NOT ALONE

Despite the environmental crisis looming over us, we who are in one stage or another of landscaping our yards with native plants can nevertheless take comfort in a number of encouraging developments. We are by no means working in isolation. Here in southwest Michigan, across the country, and around the world, scientists, nature lovers, students, concerned citizens, indigenous peoples—the list goes on and on—are trying to save wild plants and animals by preserving and restoring their habitat. And we—in our yards—are working in solidarity with them and with each other. There is even a national organization in this country dedicated specifically to helping people turn their yards into better habitat for wild plants and animals: Wild Ones—Native Plants, Natural Landscapes (www.wildones.org). It has three chapters in southwest Michigan: the Kalamazoo Area Chapter (founded 1999), the Calhoun County Chapter, and the River City Chapter in Grand Rapids, plus nine more chapters around Michigan. These chapters offer informative and helpful programs during the winter months and field trips during the growing season, and they're a source of practical advice, companionship, and native plants. Better-known environmental organizations, e.g., the National Wildlife Federation and the Audubon Society, also recognize the need to landscape our yards with native plants for the welfare of the wildlife they seek to protect.

Information about native plants and how to landscape your yard with them has really multiplied in the last several years. Conferences and workshops, books and websites—there are lots more of them than there used to be. (See Chapters 6 and 14 for listings of books and websites; also see the "References" at the end of most chapters, especially in Part II.) There are also—fortunately—more local sources of native plants (see Chapter 5 for the names and websites of growers and consultants in our general area.)

Still another encouraging development is growing awareness among the public in general that an environmental crisis is in progress. Habitat destruction at home and abroad; growing scarcity of water and fossil fuels; spread of aggressive, non-native species; loss and degradation of our soil; loss of biodiversity—these dangers have come to be more familiar and more pressing to people who aren't scientists or amateur naturalists. The human role in climate change has now been acknowledged by most reasonable people, and climate change has become more visible and alarming, in melting Arctic ice and stranded polar bears, rising waters, and unusually severe weather. In this country, individuals, organizations, and even cities and states are now making serious attempts to reduce carbon emissions. Public awareness of these crises makes

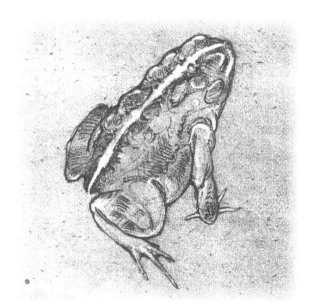

Toad   Ladislav Hanka

While preparing to etch some toads, I experienced the global decline of amphibians directly—not just by reading about changes in distant rain forests, but here where I live. I had difficulties locating the few toads I needed for study. Amphibians depend upon healthy surface waters; they are dying and we should be concerned. —Ladislav Hanka

our attempts to address them in our yards—however peculiar our efforts may look to unaccustomed eyes—at least somewhat easier for people to accept.

And there's more and more scientific evidence to support what we're doing—evidence showing that lawns waste precious resources and actually harm the environment; that the equipment used to maintain a lawn typically emits far more CO_2, when in use, than does a car; that aggressive nonnative plants are destroying our natural areas at a rapid pace; that nonnative shrubs diminish the breeding success of birds; that nonnative plants provide far less support than natives to the herbivorous insects that transfer the sun's energy from plants to animals; and that we *must* share our yards with native plants and animals or lose most of them because there is far too little natural habitat left in our country to maintain the current diversity of wildlife. (See Tallamy, especially Chapter 3, "No Place to Hide," for a summary of this proof.)

DOING THE WORK OF NOAH: GROWING THE ARK

With so much evidence now available and the public's growing awareness of environmental crisis, surely it will become easier to change weed ordinances and convince neighbors not only to tolerate our native landscapes but to join us in helping to provide the ark for wildlife envisioned by Sara Stein and Douglas Tallamy. As Stein puts it so clearly, no one has to do it all:

> We don't have to—indeed, we neither can nor should—each provide all habitats, every sort of food. You plant nut trees and I'll plant spruce, you keep a berry thicket and I'll do the tall grass, or the bog, the woodlot, the crowds of fruiting shrubs and beds of wildflowers. But let us weave them together into something big enough to matter by connecting each patch with others at the corners and along the boundaries. This is the rich, new landscape; this is the new kind of gardener who asks not whether he should plant this ornament or another but which patch is missing from his community, how he can provide it, and how animals will move from his patch to the next. This is the ark (p. 97).

One more thing: a warning about something that has happened to us and may well happen to you. Changing our yard has not been a one-way process. As we've worked on our yard, it has *worked on us* (and continues to do so), greatly strengthening our awareness of and feelings for plants and animals and our gratitude for people everywhere who seek to preserve and restore them. We've come to regard with still more awe and wonder the natural processes that sustain life on earth.

Changing our yard has even changed the way we live: we drive more slowly, especially at night, so that we can stop for animals trying to cross the road or help them across. So far, we've saved several turtles, once with help from a woman who stopped traffic on Howard Street. We eat differently (no beef, pork, or lamb and not very much chicken or fish) and try to avoid coffee that isn't shade-grown and fruits and vegetables that aren't reasonably bird-friendly. That means—just for a start, according to biologist Bridget Stutchbury—buying bananas, strawberries, sweet peppers, grapes, and tomatoes from Latin America *only* if they are grown organically. In Latin America, these crops are likely to receive heavy, unregulated applications of pesticides so harmful to humans and wildlife that they are now banned or closely regulated in the U. S. However, U. S. inspection of of imported fruits and vegetables from Latin America is, at best, perfunctory. We try to buy as much food as possible from local growers, preferably organic but definitely local.

CHANGING OUR HABITS: CHANGING OUR LIVES

When the two of us eat out, we take our own re-usable containers rather than carry home leftovers in containers made of styrofoam, which breaks down into small fragments that are consumed by animals. We try (often unsuccessfully) to use less of everything, including paper, energy, and other resources. If we're not actually using something, we try to put it back into circulation for someone else to use.

When I don't feel like taking the extra time and energy to do something I know I should, e.g., unplugging something, or figuring out how to re-use something instead of just throwing it away, I try to think of animals I might conceivably help, if only in some infinitely small or unlikely way. (Sometimes these are animals that have passed through our yard, sometimes not.) As an incentive to save energy, I often imagine a polar bear swimming for her life, sometimes as far as 400 miles, in search of ice solid enough to hold her up and allow her to hunt. But this Christmas an environmental organization sent me a card showing a young polar bear (maybe a year old) lying on its back with its paws in the air, looking as if it's having such a good time rolling around in the snow. That's going to be my image, at least for a while. That's what I'll try to think of when good intentions, in the yard and elsewhere, flag—as they all too often do.

Landscaping with native plants will probably change your life too. Let it. Let it be a new life for you—and for the earth.

REFERENCES

Stein, Sara. *Noah's Garden: Restoring the Ecology of Our Own Back Yards.* Boston: Houghton Mifflin, 1993.
Stutchbury, Bridget. *The Silence of the Songbirds.* New York: Walker & Company, 2007.
_____. "Put a Songbird on your Shopping List," *National Wildlife*, Dec./Jan., 2008, pp. 14–15.
Tallamy, Douglas. *Bringing Nature Home: How You Can Sustain Wildlife with Native Plants.* Updated and expanded edition. Portland, OR: Timber Press, 2009.

Part I

Perspectives

Our task must be to free ourselves … by widening our circle of compassion
to embrace all living creatures and the whole of nature in its beauty.
—Albert Einstein—

That land is a community is the basic concept of ecology;
but that land is to be loved and respected is an extension of ethics.
—Aldo Leopold—

A thing is right when it tends to preserve the integrity and stability
and beauty of the biotic community. It is wrong when it tends otherwise.
—Wendell Berry—

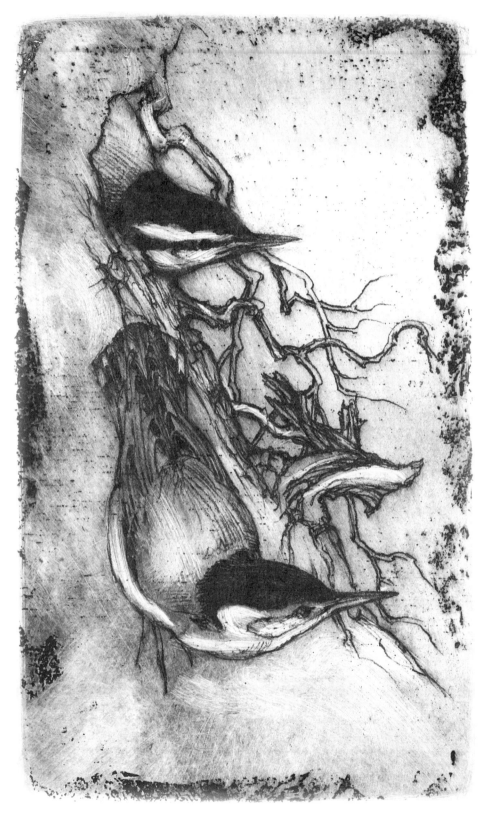

Nuthatches (red-breasted and white-breasted)   Etching   Ladislav Hanka

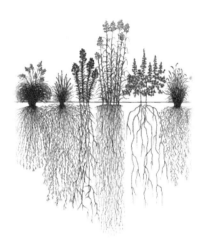

1

WHY REDUCE THE SIZE OF YOUR LAWN?

A lawn is nature under totalitarian rule.
—Michael Pollan, *Second Nature*

Maintaining a big lawn is not only expensive to you personally—in terms of money, time, and energy; it's also costly to the environment—in terms of pollution, waste of natural resources, and waste of space that could be used, quite easily, to provide vitally necessary habitat for the wildlife that we human beings are crowding off the earth. Here are ten of the most important reasons for greatly reducing the size of your lawn.

You'll provide vital support for wildlife. Lawns provide little or no support for wildlife because they're monocultures of nonnative grasses that are not allowed to flower or go to seed. Lawns *are* attractive, however, to Canada geese, which prefer them to taller grasses, which might conceal predators, and to the larvae of Japanese beetles, which feed on lawngrass roots.

You'll prevent lawngrass from invading natural areas. The lawngrass usually used in our area is Kentucky bluegrass (*Poa pratensis*), a cool-season grass not native to Kentucky or indeed to North America. By invading shaded as well as sunny areas, and in the latter outcompeting native prairie grasses and forbs (Czarapata, p. 120), it reduces diversity and degrades habitat vital to wildlife.

You'll provide space desperately needed by wildlife. Lawns already sprawl out over more than 45 million acres in the lower 48 states, and continue to increase by a million acres every year (Holmes,

p. 6). Add to our lawns the space occupied by structures, used for agriculture, and devoted to roads and parking lots, and only 3 to 5 percent of our land area remains as relatively undisturbed habitat for wildlife. Because there is a direct 1-to-1 ratio between the amount of suitable habitat available and species diversity, most of our native wildlife species will become extinct, sooner rather than later. We can still prevent this disaster, however, by transforming our sterile lawns into gardens and groves of native plants capable of supporting wildlife (Tallamy, pp. 28–37).

You'll save water. Lawns consume vast amounts of water, a resource already scarce not only in the western and southwestern parts of our country but even in the Southeast. According to the EPA, watering our lawns and yards accounts for almost 30 percent of residential water use. With an increasing population, the steady drawdown of aquifers and groundwater, and the increasing temperatures that

1

climate change will bring, water will become a still more precious substance, far too valuable to waste on lawns.

You'll save energy. Lawns consume enormous amounts of energy, starting with the energy required to pump water to them. Then there's the gasoline or electricity (probably generated from coal) used by lawnmowers, leafblowers, and other lawn-maintenance devices, to say nothing of the energy used to produce and distribute such devices. Included as well must be the energy expended in the manufacture, packaging, and distribution of lawncare products: the pesticides, herbicides, fungicides, and fertilizers that, along with water, keep lawns green and thick. Oil and natural gas even serve as the major ingredients of some of these products. The enormously energy-intensive process of producing fertilizer from atmospheric nitrogen consumes as much as one percent of the world's power. And the amount of fertilizer applied has more than tripled in the last 30 years and continues to grow. These are just the most obvious energy expenditures on lawns—besides, of course, your own labor. Just think of that extra free time on weekends—time you might even devote to *flowers*.

> I cannot fully appreciate the challenge of a lawn; to force nature, by dint of prodigious quantities of labor, of water, of gasoline, of chemicals, to be the one thing it would never be on its own; monotonous.
>
> —Paul Gruchow

You'll help to reduce climate change. In addition to consuming great amounts of nonrenewable resources, traditional lawn maintenance contributes to global warming, the most immediate culprits being lawn-maintenance devices, which emit carbon dioxide, and fertilizer, which emits nitrous oxide. According to the EPA, a gas-powered lawn-mower, for each hour of operation, emits about 11 times the air pollution of a new car. Other lawn-care devices, e.g., leafblowers, are said to be even dirtier. While lawns absorb some carbon dioxide, the short roots of lawngrass don't absorb anything like as much of this climate-changing gas as natural grasslands or forests do—or nearly as much as yards made up chiefly of native plants.

You may suffer less from seasonal allergies. Kentucky bluegrass, the chief lawngrass of our area, may contribute to your allergy problems. Amy Stewart describes this grass as "the cause of some of the worst suburban allergies" (p. 91).

You won't need chemicals that poison wildlife and us. Though 50 years have passed since the publication in 1962 of Rachel Carson's pioneering work *Silent Spring*, chemicals harmful to humans and creatures other than the targeted "pests" are still being applied to lawns. According to Elizabeth Kolbert, one such chemical still in wide use is the insecticide carbaryl, marketed as Sevin. "A likely human carcinogen, it has been shown to cause developmental damage in lab animals, and is toxic to—among many other organisms—tadpoles, salamanders, and honey bees" (2008). According to the EPA, over 70 million pounds of pesticides alone are annually applied to the nation's lawns. In fact, homeowners tend to apply chemicals to their yards more lavishly and unnecessarily than farmers do to their crops.

You won't be spreading pollution. Just as cigarette smoke endangers not only the smoker but also those forced to breathe secondhand smoke, so the carbon dioxide emitted in the course of lawn maintenance doesn't confine itself to the yard producing it. Rather, it disperses through the air and contributes to the warming of our whole planet and loss of the biodiversity that sustains us all.

Nor do the chemicals applied to our lawns remain in place. The short roots of lawngrass are less effective than the far deeper and thicker root systems of native plants in absorbing stormwater. Moreover, in Michigan most urban lawns grow on glacial till clay soils, compacted by earthmovers during development and subsequently by heavy

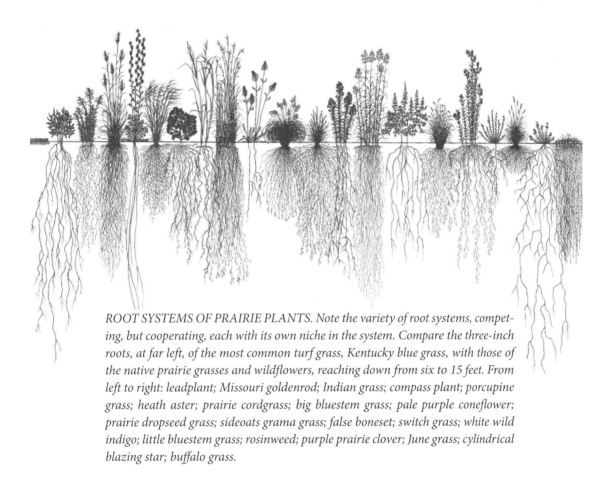

ROOT SYSTEMS OF PRAIRIE PLANTS. Note the variety of root systems, competing, but cooperating, each with its own niche in the system. Compare the three-inch roots, at far left, of the most common turf grass, Kentucky blue grass, with those of the native prairie grasses and wildflowers, reaching down from six to 15 feet. From left to right: leadplant; Missouri goldenrod; Indian grass; compass plant; porcupine grass; heath aster; prairie cordgrass; big bluestem grass; pale purple coneflower; prairie dropseed grass; sideoats grama grass; false boneset; switch grass; white wild indigo; little bluestem grass; rosinweed; purple prairie clover; June grass; cylindrical blazing star; buffalo grass.

mowing equipment. The result is millions of acres of low-permeable lawns that are, hydrologically, the landscaping equivalent of asphalt parking lots. Every heavy rain, therefore, washes pesticides and fertilizers into streams, rivers, and lakes. Some of these chemicals are known or suspected to harm wildlife and humans. Those which are nutrients, e.g., the nitrogen and phosphorus in fertilizers, cause the growth of algae in surface waters and harm aquatic life, ultimately poisoning vast hypoxic "dead zones" in the oceans.

Many of the chemicals applied to our lawns do, however, stay more or less in place and percolate down through the soil; they directly harm soil organisms and may also contaminate groundwater.

The blast, buzz, and whine of power mowers, leafblowers, and weedwhackers is still another form of pollution that travels a long way, with the result that one can hardly step outdoors, even early in the morning, without hearing one or more of these machines in operation.

> Our parks and lawns of sprayed Kentucky bluegrass might as well be Astroturf, except that Astroturf would be safer for the groundwater—and use a lot less of it.
>
> —Robert Michael Pyle,
> *The Thunder Tree: Lessons from an Urban Wildland*

You'll be a more responsible member of the community. There is, to be sure, both personal and community value in maintaining a level, uniform expanse of greensward: it gives us a sense of control, tidiness, well-being; and we have the approval of our neighbors. It's difficult to change values and routines we're accustomed to. But the times, they are a-changing—fast. Whatever sense of expansive well-being that lawn provides is quite deceptive. Maintaining a big lawn wastes vital fossil fuels that are becoming more expensive, difficult, and destructive to produce and that must be shared among a growing, energy-hungry world population. A big lawn also wastes water that must be shared not only among humans but with wildlife. Conventional lawn care also spreads many kinds of pollution that adversely affect all the creatures of the earth. To help save ourselves, our fellow creatures, and our planet, we need to stop using chemicals on our lawns and either eliminate them entirely or reduce them in size until they can be mowed with a push mower. Take those first steps that the next few chapters describe, then continue resolutely on the same meandering path; you'll gain a new sense of well-being and joy from contributing and belonging to a much larger, more vibrant, more essential community of life.

REFERENCES

Czarapata, Elizabeth J. *Invasive Plants of the Upper Midwest: An Illustrated Guide*. Madison: Univ. of Wisconsin, 2005.

Holmes, Hannah. *Suburban Safari: A Year on the Lawn*. New York: Bloomsbury, 2005.

Kolbert, Elizabeth. "Turf War: Americans can't live without their lawns—but how long can they live with them?," *The New Yorker*, July 21, 2008. On-line at www.newyorker.com/arts/critics/books/2008/07/21/080721crbo_books_kolbert.

Pollan, Michael. *Second Nature: A Gardener's Education*. Dell Publishing, 1992. See especially Chapter 3, "Why Mow?"

Stewart, Amy. *Wicked Plants*. Chapel Hill, NC: Algonquin Books of Chapel Hill, 2009.

Tallamy, Douglas. *Bringing Nature Home: How You Can Sustain Wildlife with Native Plants*. Updated and expanded edition. Portland, OR: Timber Press, 2009.

2

WHY LANDSCAPE WITH MICHIGAN'S NATIVE PLANTS?

The wild garden is the spiritual core of the modern landscape.
—Janet Marinelli, *Stalking the Wild Amaranth*

Each of Michigan's native plant species belongs to a dynamic community of plants and creatures that evolved, together, over millennia. Most of us are only beginning to understand and appreciate the complexity and value of these communities, even as they are disappearing from the land around us.

Even for those people who are beginning to understand this, changing an ingrained cultural mindset may not be easy. For years, Tom and I both eagerly anticipated the winter's fresh crop of nursery-industry catalogs, enticing us to order new, strange, arresting cultivars and species, assembled from all over the world for our delight. True, they never grew for us like the picture-perfect ones in the catalog or the garden center; and some of them, quite unsuited to our conditions, didn't grow at all. But we kept trying. It's hard to resist the allure, isn't it?

In most ways, our awakening was slow: we learned to recycle; we tried to live more simply; we became interested in helping to preserve and restore more or less wild lands in our own area—because we like plants and animals. Then, seemingly quite suddenly, with vital help from Sara Stein, Steve Keto, and Wild Ones, it dawned on us. Nature isn't something "out there"; it's right here, just beyond the front door. We can preserve and restore our own yard. We can plant Noah's Garden at home. Sud-

denly, we had a mission. Not only could we make a difference; we *had* to make a difference. The nature preserves, important though they are, won't be enough.

We realized that unless many of us, together, bring these wonderful plant communities back into the urban and suburban spaces from which we banished them, most of our native species will be lost forever; and the communities which they—and we—are part of will simply disintegrate. Here, then, we share a few of the most important reasons why, for our own good, we must all change our landscaping practices.

Michigan's native plants are beautiful and extremely varied. Assembled in gardens or restorations that seek to replicate, in a modest way, the prairie, woodland, or wetland communities of their origin, native plants offer a dramatic and ever-changing spectacle that nonnative ornamentals cannot match. When present in some quantity and variety in yards and other spaces, native plants and the wildlife they support bring us and our families ever closer to the natural world. Plant-watching is a very rewarding pastime; it lifts and calms your spirit. As Ralph Waldo Emerson observes, "Every hour has its morning, noon, and night."

Beautiful mortals of the glowing earth
And children of the season crowd together
In showers and sunny weather
Ye beautiful spring hours
Sunshine and all together
 I love wild flowers.

—John Clare, "Wild Flowers"

Native plant communities are part of our natural heritage. They're what grew here naturally before European invasion and settlement and should be preserved for our descendants rather than allowed to disappear. By one estimate, 25 percent of Michigan's plants will be extinct by 2050, as the result of development and invasion of natural areas by aggressive nonnative plants. (This estimate doesn't include the possible devastating effects of climate change.) By cultivating native plants in our yards and other spaces, we can help preserve and spread the remaining diversity of native vegetation as well as the wildlife that depends on it for food and shelter.

Native plants thrive without chemicals or extra water. Unlike plants from Europe and Asia and even other regions of our own continent, natives are well adapted to poor soils and to Michigan climate, including its extremes of weather. Once they've established their deep, extensive root systems, they'll thrive even during drought, long after nonnatives have withered away. In fact, as parts of their extensive root systems routinely decay, native plants are constantly improving the soil, including its ability to retain stormwater. Because many native plants have both quite short and very long roots, they can absorb moisture both from a very light rain and from deep groundwater.

Native plants provide better food and shelter for wildlife. Native plants and wildlife evolved together, over thousands of years. Research increasingly shows that by landscaping with native plants, we offer birds and other animals exactly the foods that they or their offspring need at exactly the times they need them—for example, host plants for insect larvae; nectar and pollen for adult insects; and insects and fruits suited to birds' seasonally changing activities, whether these be breeding, migration, or wintering. Even the branching structure of native shrubs fosters greater breeding success among birds than that of nonnative shrubs.

Recent research also shows that native plants greatly surpass nonnative plants in their value to plant-eating insects such as caterpillars. For rankings of native and nonnative plants in terms of their abilities to support the caterpillars of butterflies and moths, consult the very valuable website **http://copland.udel.edu/~dtallamy/host/index.html**. Plant-eating insects—roughly 37% of earth's animal species—perform the crucial task of transferring the sun's energy from plants to higher levels of the food web, e.g., to other kinds of insects, spiders, amphibians, birds, and other creatures. The fact that almost all terrestrial bird species in North America feed large quantities of caterpillars to their young helps indicate the importance of supplying these herbivorous insects with the food they need.

[Animals] are not brethren, they are not underlings; they are other nations, caught with ourselves in the net of life and time, fellow prisoners of the splendor and travail of the earth.

—Henry Beston,
The Outermost House

Native plants support food crops. Native bees and other pollinators, under siege from development and deadly chemicals, are essential for pollinating wild plants and also supplement the work of nonnative honey bees in pollinating commercial crops. Native plants attract and support not only the native pollinators, but also the many beneficial insects and other arthropods that help to protect crops by preying on or parasitizing plant-eating insects such as caterpillars, thus helping to control populations of "pest" insects, without heavy use of pesticides. Using strips or rows of perennial, deep-rooted native plants to protect crops or vegetable gardens, instead of nonnative annuals such as coriander, dill, fava beans, and sweet alyssum, is easier and cheaper. Moreover, native perennials, since they don't require fertilizer and extra water, are more likely than nonnatives to develop extensive mycorrhizal and other microbial associations and thus establish better soil conditions and relationships. Since natives, through vigorous root systems and extensive mycorrhizal associations, take up available nutrient quickly and efficiently, they help to suppress weeds, many of which require more available nutrient than do natives.

Landscaping with natives slows spread of nonnatives. While most nonnative plants don't threaten or destroy our remaining natural areas, some have been shown to do so, e.g., purple loosestrife, garlic mustard, common and glossy buckthorn, and autumn olive (see Chapter 12 for a full list). Other aggressive nonnative plants less widely recognized by homeowners as invasive include English ivy, Norway maple, and Dame's rocket (*Hesperis matronalis*), whose four-petaled pinkish-purple, pale lavender, or white flowers people sometimes mistakenly call phlox. Even the popular nonnative shrub Buddleia (*Buddleia davidii*, known as butterfly bush), whose nectar is so attractive to butterflies, can invade natural areas. The closer we live to a natural area, the easier it is for nonnative plants in our yard, some of them invasive or potentially invasive, to escape into and damage native ecosystems.

Landscaping with native plants improves water quality. The short roots of lawn grass do little to slow down stormwater and filter out the pollution it

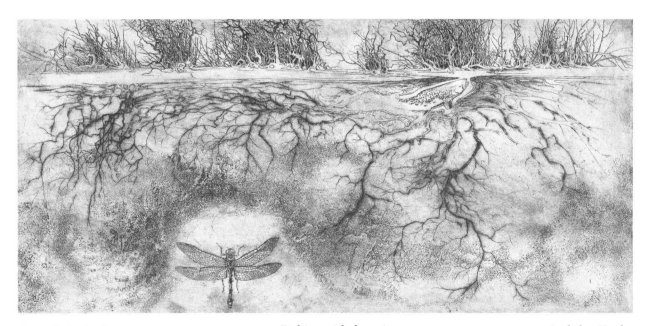

Beneath the Surface   Etching with drypoint   Ladislav Hanka

carries. The deep root systems of native plants, however, are able to absorb, hold, and gradually release this water—water that would otherwise rush into nearby creeks and rivers, eroding their banks and delivering a load of pollution, instead of recharging the groundwater we all drink and depend on.

Native plants help to reduce global warming. Many of our native prairie plants are able to store carbon in their deep and extensive root systems, thus permanently removing it from the air. Well, semi-permanently. Cyclically. Virtually everything *breathes*: soil organisms are constantly respiring CO_2, and roots are continuously decaying and regrowing, releasing and re-storing CO_2. Nonetheless, soil itself and root systems, if left undisturbed, sequester enormous amounts of carbon. The greater the biomass of a root system, the more carbon storage; and a single clump of big bluestem grass (*Andropogon gerardii*), for instance, can have a mass of roots and rootlets that, if stretched out end to end, would extend thousands of miles. There aren't many

nonnative plants to match that, and turf grass, with its very shallow roots, is *puny* by comparison. Also, a yard in which native plants have replaced all or most of the lawn uses less fossil fuel and produces less carbon dioxide than a conventional yard, whose upkeep requires frequent use of power equipment and petroleum products. Gasoline-powered yard-care equipment emits enormous amounts of carbon dioxide, and most conventional pesticides and fertilizers derive from fossil fuels and consume an immense amount of energy in their manufacture and distribution.

With our natural areas under attack and our native plant and animal species being driven to extinction from rapidly increasing development and invasion by aggressive nonnative plants—which rising levels of carbon dioxide seem to stimulate—our yards and similar spaces in the community become absolutely crucial to the survival of the native plant and animal species that all of life depends upon.

Prairie Ronde township, Kalamazoo

L. Hanka

3

Landscaping for Biodiversity: What You Can Do

… a garden can be like the First Garden,
the whole place where we live.
—Sara Stein, *Planting Noah's Garden*

In saving as much biodiversity as we can, we are practicing the art of healing: together, we strive to heal some portion of the earth from the massive wounds inflicted on it by urbanization, industrial agriculture and manufacturing, and ruthless exploitation of natural resources. We must begin with the basic principle of healing: first, do no harm. Then, we do our best to employ nature's own methods to help in healing nature's wounds.

First, Do No Harm

If your property is something other than a conventional yard, if it consists of or contains woods, an unplowed field, or an area that is wet for all or part of the year, seek expert advice before doing anything at all. Natural or semi-natural areas may contain protected plants or animals or be subject to other kinds of regulation (as wetlands are). In any case, such areas provide important habitat for wildlife and should be kept as unfragmented as possible. Before disturbing such an area, consult an expert in order to find out exactly what plants (native and nonnative) are present on the site and what animals live on or frequent it. (For sources of expert advice, see Chapter 5, "What Should I Plant in My Yard?")

> If you don't know what it is, don't fool with it. Don't use it carelessly. Don't destroy it.
>
> —Wendell Berry,
> *The Gift of Good Land*

When in Doubt, Leave it Alone

- Resist "cleaning up" a woods unless you really know what you're doing. Dead trees still standing, fallen branches, and leaf litter provide habitat for wildlife and help a woods

9

regenerate itself. Dead trees provide nesting cavities for birds, and dead wood, whether standing or fallen, provides nesting areas for insects, including native bees.

- Don't plant nonnative plants in or near a natural area. (See Chapter 12 for a list of invasive nonnative plants, some of them mistakenly regarded as native wildflowers.) People are occasionally tempted to "neaten up" a woodland or woodland entrance or edge by planting ground covers such as English ivy or lily-of-the-valley or myrtle. These are invasive nonnative plants that choke out native wildflowers and tree seedlings and, once established, are almost impossible to eradicate. Don't plant anything at all in a natural area unless you have some expertise in restoration.

- Don't remove the natural vegetation next to a body of water in order to improve your view. This vegetation serves important purposes, such as helping prevent erosion and filtering out pollutants. Lawngrass, short-rooted and regularly mowed, can't perform these services.

- Don't be in a hurry to plant trees in overgrown fields or open areas. Such areas may include remnant prairie or be suitable for restoration as prairie. Large treeless areas are vital to the survival of grassland birds such as bobolinks and meadowlarks.

- Preserve persistent native vegetation of value to wildlife, such as patches of violets in your lawn, a large box elder in the corner of the backyard, or common elderberry shrubs in a ditch. Incidentally, don't be in a hurry to remove non-invasive nonnative plants that are being used by wildlife; remove them only as you are able to replace them with similarly useful or even better native plants for your wildlife. Our birds deserted their favored cover of a nonnative forsythia hedge only as it was gradually replaced by viburnum and elderberry; now they scorn a couple of remnant forsythia shrubs.

Next year, no more forsythia. (Forsythia is a host plant for *one* species of Lepidoptera; viburnums, comparable in their landscaping functions to forsythia, support 104.)

- Don't get rid of poison ivy except where you absolutely have to. Its berries provide valuable food for birds.

- **Avoid tilling the ground** in preparing it for planting, whether a flowerbed or overgrown field. Tilling the ground destroys the structure of the soil and releases stored carbon, in a gigantic CO_2 belch. Use some no-till method to prepare planting sites.

> Much soil carbon has been lost through traditional ploughing, which really is a declaration of war on biodiversity—the farmer rips out all life before planting a monoculture which is kept 'pure' with pesticides and herbicides.
>
> —Tim Flannery, *Here on Earth*

Don't Endanger Natural Areas

- Don't remove native plants from the wild unless you are rescuing them from imminent destruction. Even small disturbances such as digging up a couple of plants for your yard on a friend's property may make that spot more vulnerable to invasion by aggressive, nonnative plants. Buy native plants from reputable growers.

- Don't leave invasive nonnative plants in your yard any longer than you have to, lest they spread to nearby natural areas, whose ecosystems are vulnerable to invasion and degradation by exotic plants. The second greatest threat to native species and ecosystems, after loss of habitat to development, is loss of habitat and diversity to invasive nonnative species. Even if they don't spread to other areas, they will spread in your yard and take up space and nutrients that could be used by plants more beneficial to wildlife.

- **Avoid pesticides, herbicides and fungicides**, except as a last resort, and maybe not even then. That includes Bt and other so-called "organic" and "natural" products, which kill many more species than the ones currently bothering you. Native plants will help to attract the predators and parasites that will keep herbivorous insects such as aphids or caterpillars under control. Most of the "damage" and losses that you find distressing will be limited and will last for only a while; then healthy soil and a diverse planting will, without your intervention, restore the balance.

If you *must* save a plant under attack, try old-fashioned remedies: remove insects by hand, use blasts of water from a hose, or concoct homemade sprays featuring garlic and red pepper. Kill weeds that come up through your brick patio by pulling them, pouring boiling water on them, or spraying them with vinegar diluted with water. There are other old-fashioned (and comparatively harmless) remedies for situations you simply can't stand, and the ingredients are readily available: soap, garlic oil, baking soda, crushed eggshells, diatomaceous earth, vegetable oil, onions. Consult any good book or web site on organic gardening for tips and recipes. And remember, even homemade "natural" deterrents and insecticides act on more than just the target creatures; use them sparingly and carefully.

- **Avoid conventional fertilizers**, which are likely to contaminate surface and ground water. They contribute, for example, to the blooms of algae in ponds and lakes that are so unattractive and kill aquatic life. More and

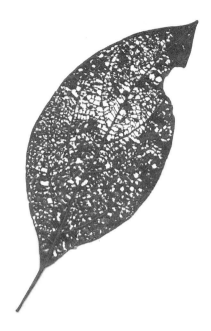

Transformation, from leaf to humus:

This sassafras leaf, used by our friend Stan Rajnak as decoration on a notecard, shows the first two levels of predation: first, an insect uses the living leaf for food (the segment cut from its edge); after it falls, numerous microbes, fungi, and tiny arthropods—all dwellers in decaying leaf litter—consume the soft flesh of the leaf, rich in nitrogen. Then would come specialists to digest the tougher lignin in the leaf's veins and stem. Then the earthworms. Finally, only rich humus would remain, slowly releasing nutrients.

CREATURES AT WORK. DO NOT DISTURB!

more cities and counties are banning or controlling fertilizers containing phosphorus; but non-phosphorus commercial fertilizers still contain heavy doses of nitrogen, and nitrogen pollution in the soil, the water, the air, and our food, is probably a more devastating long-range problem than CO_2 emissions. Instead, use leafmold or compost to enrich your soil; they build humus and thus stabilize soil, releasing nutrients slowly and steadily instead of in a quick addictive "fix," with all the unabsorbed excess polluting the soil and the water.

- Keep sidewalks, driveways, and street gutters free of grass clippings, leaves, and other refuse that may be washed into nearby streams and lakes, polluting and causing blooms of algae. In the fall, don't rake leaves into the street until the night before pickup. (It's a lot better to save and use those leaves, though.)

- Don't contaminate your compost pile with weed seeds (unless you're sure it's hot enough to kill them) or the hulls of sunflower seeds that accumulate below birdfeeders. The latter

contain a chemical that inhibits the growth of other plants, as do some invasive exotic plants, e.g., spotted knapweed (*Centaurea maculosa*). Bag up and throw away aggressive nonnative plants that you've pulled.

- **Don't be greedy in gathering seed** to sow in your yard or germinate for later planting; take only small amounts, even where particular species of plants are abundant. Don't take any unless you have permission.

REDUCE THE SIZE OF YOUR LAWN

For many reasons, you should be aiming for a lawn small enough to mow with a manual lawnmower. Gasoline-powered lawn equipment emits vast quantities of CO_2. Lawns waste valuable resources: the water necessary to keep them green and the fossil fuels (plus your own energy) consumed in maintaining them. They also contribute to pollution of other resources: stormwater traveling through lawngrass, which can't absorb it, carries pollution of all kinds into lakes and streams. Finally, lawns contribute almost nothing to the support of wildlife.

In getting rid of lawn, start slowly and work gradually toward permanent change. Within whatever lawn remains, encourage patches of violets and other native wildflowers that have taken hold. Don't try to get rid of moss, which is used by birds for lining their nests and which maintains soil moisture, enriches the soil, and provides microhabitat for many tiny creatures.

- One way to get started is simply to enlarge and connect existing plantings, while gradually introducing native plants. I list various strategies for widening beds, increasing the number and variety of foundation plants, making hedges wider, etc., in the next chapter, "Welcoming Native Plants into Your Yard."

- Then proceed to create new planting areas. Again in the next chapter, I describe some strategies for doing this.

- Whether expanding existing beds or creating new ones, try to use something like nature's own methods. Tilling the soil not only breaks up the essential soil structure, it will leave roots from which lawngrass can regenerate itself. Another method to avoid: "frying" your lawn by covering it for months with huge sheets of dark plastic—or clear plastic. These sheets (produced from oil and thus environmentally expensive) will kill your lawn all right, but they'll also kill valuable organisms in the soil.

If you're impatient, you can get rid of lawngrass quickly by removing the sod manually or mechanically. That's hard labor, though, and it stirs up weed seeds. Slower is better: try smothering lawngrass with at least a couple of feet of heaped-up dead leaves held down by a thin layer of soil or some branches. Along with dead leaves you can use grass clippings and half-finished compost. Another slow method is to kill the grass with sheets of cardboard or layers of newspaper (about a dozen sheets) covered with a thin layer of soil. The slow methods usually take at least several months. If, however, you put at least six inches of soil—or soil mixed with partially decomposed yard waste—on top of the newspapers, you can put small plants into the new bed right away. In addition to suppressing the lawngrass, you've retained yard waste, enriched the soil, and fed essential soil organisms. So, be pleased with yourself.

- Whether removing the sod or smothering it, don't work the soil below, even to incorporate the remains of the leaves with which you've smothered it; you don't want to destroy the soil structure.

> Nothing in nature is exhausted in its first use
>
> —Ralph Waldo Emerson, *Nature*

- Don't enrich the soil at all before planting prairie plants; they don't need it. Many of them prefer nitrogen-poor soil. Before planting woodland plants, though, a couple of applications of heaped-up dead leaves or composted leaves may be necessary—with enough time allowed for these to break down into soil.

LANDSCAPE WITH NATIVE PLANTS TO PRESERVE BIODIVERSITY

Our native plants and animals have evolved together over thousands of years. As a result, native plants provide much better support for all kinds of wildlife—insects, reptiles, birds, mammals—than nonnative plants are able to. In addition, they're adapted to our climate: they thrive without fertilizer or pesticides, and, once established, need less water than nonnatives. With their extensive root systems, they deal with stormwater and sequester carbon more successfully than lawns and most other nonnative plants do. Besides, native plants are very beautiful. They perform, quietly, beautifully.

> Healthy organisms and ecosystems are diverse, unpredictable, redundant, and adaptive.
>
> —Paul Hawken,
> *Blessed Unrest*

Sara Stein compares a traditionally landscaped yard to a clock that's nothing but a "pretty ornament." It doesn't keep time, not because it's broken but because it never worked to begin with; it had only "a fraction of its parts" (p. 55). Why not have a yard that's landscaped with a true diversity of native plants—an ecosystem that performs its function? A beautiful clock that does work, that tells the time of day, of the year and season, Nature's own time or tune, which is the time we must live by and dance to. The music of time. It's got rhythm.

So here's what you need to do.

- Use plants whose value to wildlife is as high as possible. For ranked lists of native woody and herbaceous plants that support herbivorous insects, e.g, caterpillars, which play a crucial role in transferring the sun's energy up the food chain to other insects, reptiles, birds, and mammals, see http://copland.udel.edu/~dtallamy/host/index.html. For rankings of the value of native trees and shrubs to wildlife other than herbivorous insects, see Chapter 11.

Give careful attention to these various rankings if you have limited space; otherwise, aim for *diversity*.

- Buy native seeds and plants from *local* native plant growers rather than from garden centers or big-box stores. Membership in the Michigan Native Plant Producers Association guarantees that a grower provides seeds and plants that are native to Michigan, were grown in Michigan, and originate from Michigan genotypes. (See Part II for lists of plants native to southwest Michigan.) If in doubt about whether a particular species is native to your home area, consult the county-by-county distribution maps in Edward Voss, *Michigan Flora* or *Michigan Flora Online* (see Chapter 6).

- **Use wild plants** rather than cultivars. The latter have been bred for special traits that may not favor wildlife, and traits that do favor wildlife may have been lost along the way. In fact, in many cases, the cultivar has been bred specifically to *discourage* wildlife. Other cultivars have been bred to satisfy not the needs of wildlife but our own desires for novelty or showiness: an orange, white, or "Ruby Giant" Echinacea, or a double-flowered cultivar, showy but possibly sterile and therefore fruit-

less and seedless. Moreover, the straight wild species, because it evolved with local conditions, is more likely to resist a broad variety of environmental conditions, diseases, and insect predators. If your local nursery carries only cultivars and exotics, *nag* them to carry native plants in their wild form.

- Be aware that some native plants, e.g., many perennial sunflowers, are aggressive ("opportunistic" is the term our friend and native-plant grower Bill Schneider prefers) and should be planted sparingly, if at all, where space is limited. Consult the plant list and guide provided by a local or regional native-plant nursery, such as Prairie Moon Nursery (Minnesota), which provides a valuable "Catalog and Cultural Guide" (www.prairiemoon.com) or—closer to home—Bill Schneider's Wildtype Native Plant Nursery, in Mason, Michigan (www.wildtypeplants.com).

- If you don't like an informal or "wild" look, native plants, if you choose them carefully, can adapt beautifully to just as formal, or casual, a planting as you like. Don't worry much about colors. Native plants blend naturally; they don't clash with each other, as some showy exotics might.

AIM FOR MAXIMUM DIVERSITY OF FOOD AND SHELTER FOR WILDLIFE

Start out with plants whose needs (in terms of soil, light, and water) match the conditions of your site pretty closely; then start pushing the envelope. Many native plants are surprisingly adaptable. Don't be wasteful, but do keep experimenting. If your space is limited, choose plants carefully, not just for your own enjoyment but because, as Douglas Tallamy puts it, "for the first time in its history, gardening has taken on a role that transcends the needs of the gardener. Like it or not, gardeners have become important players in the management of our nation's wildlife. It is now within the power of

individual gardeners to do something that we all dream of doing: to make a difference. In this case, the 'difference' will be to the future of biodiversity, to the native plants and animals of North America and the ecosystems that sustain them" (*Bringing Nature Home*, p. 11).

For the sake of saving species in a time of extinction, **seek greater diversity**:

- the greatest diversity of **species** your site will support;

A rock pile provides shelters and storehouses for numerous creatures, as well as home for lichens and mosses. Slowly, ceaselessly, lichens, bacteria, and plants break down stones to provide soil and nutrient. As Sara Stein observes, "Plants eat stones." So feed them.

- diversity in plant **height**, **shape**, and **density**, including both evergreen and deciduous trees and shrubs—a diversity of tree species will foster greater biodiversity in general;

- diverse **food sources** for wildlife throughout the year: host plants for insects and nectar for pollinators throughout the growing season; fruit and berries that persist on trees and shrubs during the lean times of winter and spring as well as in summer and fall; nuts and seeds for all seasons;

- diverse **shelters** for wildlife (in addition to living trees and shrubs): dead trees (standing or fallen); tall grass, vines, shrub thickets and corridors (rather than isolated shrubs); a brush pile; groupings of rocks and a rock pile;

- diverse **amenities** for wildlife: a pool or pond (in addition to water year-round in birdbaths); some bare soil for dust baths (small mammals,

birds) as well as for ground dwelling bees; warm rocks and a mud puddle for butterflies; damp corners for toads.

Making a Difference

It is now within the power of individual gardeners to do something we all dream of doing: to make a difference. In this case, the "difference" will be to the future of biodiversity, to the native plants and animals of North America and the ecosystems that sustain them.

—Douglas Tallamy

COLLECT AND SAVE WATER

Once established, native plants suited to your site will require less water than lawngrass and other nonnative plants. Bear in mind that, on the average, around one third of the water used by an American household is devoted to lawn and garden, as much as 50 to 60 percent of that amount is usually wasted, and the total amount so used just keeps on growing.

- Capture as much as possible of the rainwater that falls on your property by means of deep-rooted native plants, mulch, rain barrels, rain gardens, and bioswales. Dead tree branches and stumps, especially good-sized ones, are virtual sponges, holding and slowly releasing water; use stumps as pedestals or seats, branches as borders for beds and paths.

- Don't water your lawn. During drought, it will go dormant, not die; and rain will bring it to life again. If you don't cut it short, it will stay greener longer (and store more carbon).

- Group together plants that may need extra water.

- Mulch woodland plants with leaf litter in order to protect them from drought and extremes of temperature. Spaces between plants in a prairie planting can be filled with mulch or, better, prairie grasses, whose roots hold water for the whole community. Mulch shouldn't touch the stalk or basal leaves of the plant.

- Improve your soil with organic matter from yard waste and compost. The more organic matter it contains, the more moisture and nutrients it will retain and thus help to protect plants against the probable effects of climate change, e.g., higher temperatures and less rainfall. Be aware, however, that many native plants—especially some prairie plants— evolved and thrived in poor, dry soil. Too much water and nourishment may "improve" them to death. The cultural guides provided

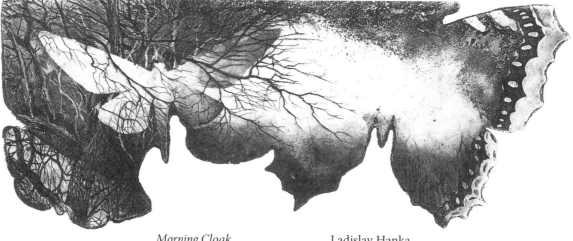

Morning Cloak   Ladislav Hanka

The mourning cloaks are the first butterflies to appear on sunny March days, when they emerge into the light from crevices and woodpiles where they wintered over as adults. "Spring ephemeral" moths, holdovers from the Ice Age, also winter over as adults and emerge in March. Your brush piles and rock piles are essential winter shelter for these harbingers of spring's gathering fertility, breeding skunk cabbages and bringing redwinged blackbirds, even amid the last, wet snows.

in native-plant nursery catalogs will help you identify plants that insist on dry conditions.

- Use water to help native plants get established, but once they're established, let them fend for themselves except in times of extreme drought. Excess water keeps prairie plants from putting down their characteristic deep roots. They're no dummies; they won't waste energy reaching for water as long as you shower them with it.

- Trees and shrubs surrounded by large beds of native wildflowers rarely need special water-ing. They receive water through the extensive root systems of the native wildflowers which, unlike the very short roots of lawn grass, are able to absorb, channel, hold, and eventually release stormwater.

- When you must water your plantings, do it in the early morning. It wastes less water and is better for the plants. Evening or night water-ing is also thrifty (although that may encour-age mildew and slugs). Using drip irrigation or soaker hoses rather than sprinklers is very helpful.

SAVE ENERGY AND CUT DOWN ON GREENHOUSE GAS EMISSIONS

- Try to eliminate use of all lawn equipment powered by gasoline or electricity: lawnmow-ers, leaf blowers or vacuums, hedge-trimmers, weed whackers, shredders. Use a push mower to cut grass and shred leaves for mulch. Rake the leaves off your lawn, but leave them in your flowerbeds for winter protection. If, in the spring, they are too thick, lift them off the emerging plants and use them to suppress more of your lawngrass or put them aside to form leafmold, which you can then use as mulch.

Leaf litter from last fall provides winter shelter for insects and food for returning migrants like this white-throated sparrow. They appear to hop backwards as they scratch at leaves with both feet, turning up food.

- Position native trees and shrubs around your house with a view toward saving energy. Ever-green trees on the north and northwest sides will shield the house from winter winds; de-ciduous trees on the south and southwest sides will shade the house in summer and allow sunlight to warm it in winter. While vines on well-placed trellises can provide insulation in summer, evergreen shrubs planted next to the house (foundation plants) provide insulation year-round. For more tips, see http://www.energysavers.gov/your_home/landscaping/in-dex.cfm/

- **Plant long-lived native trees**, e.g., oaks, so as to lock up as much carbon as possible for as long as possible.

- Return unneeded plant containers and trays to the nursery or garden center where you got them.

- Use recycled materials for structures in your yard, e.g., decks, sheds, compost bins, bird feeders, trellises. Avoid new bricks, concrete, and composition "stone," because they require huge amounts of energy to produce and there-fore have a large "carbon footprint." Recycled bricks are just fine; and broken concrete slabs from old structures or pavings can be used creatively for many purposes. Stone walls or borders provide mineral enrichment for the soil and a variety of niches for plants and wildlife.

- **Think and ask questions before buying anything for your yard**. What is it made of, where did it come from, and how is it produced and transported? Such reflections may inhibit your purchases, particularly of items that you can produce yourself, e.g., fertilizer from compost, mulch from compost or fallen leaves, even plants from seed.

Imitate Nature In How You Use Yard Waste

By keeping yard waste on your own property, you save the energy involved in, and the carbon emissions resulting from, its transport to a landfill. You also help reduce the amount of methane, a powerful greenhouse gas, produced by the landfill. But don't use machines to chop up leaves and branches; that causes carbon emissions (not to mention a lot of racket). By recycling dead vegetation as nature itself does, you help wildlife, e.g., by creating homes for insects, and enriching the soil without releasing additional carbon. You also save yourself lots of composting labor by letting the soil microbes, the fungi, and the invertebrate decomposers compost the material *in place*.

Leaving It Where Nature Put It

- Leave flowerstalks and grasses, standing or fallen, until spring. During the winter, they provide food and shelter for birds, small mammals, and insects—possibly including bumblebee queens, hibernating in thick mats of native grasses, and such beneficial insects as ladybug beetles and lacewings, overwintering in the crowns of grasses, not to mention the moths and butterflies overwintering in pupal or chrysalis stage or as adults, sheltered under leaves and plant detritus.

- Leave grass clippings on your lawn to provide it with nutrients.

- Leave small twigs and stems on your lawn for nesting birds.

- Leave sticks and some leaf litter in your plantings for the mosses, lichens, and fungi—and for the countless organisms that live in the soil. Fertility—and human life—depend on these organisms.

> Say that the leaves are harvested
> when they have rotted into the mold.
> Call that profit. Prophesy such
>   returns.
> Put your faith in the two inches of humus
> that will build under the trees
> every thousand years.
>
> —Wendell Berry, "Manifesto: The Mad Farmer Liberation Front"

- Leave fallen fruit for butterflies, bees, and beetles.

- Leave some portion of dead trees standing for the sake of wildlife (but don't endanger people or structures). Dead trees are particularly valuable to birds, providing food in the form of insects and homes for cavity-nesters, as well as homes for native bees. Such trees are also useful as the central core of thickets for birds or as trellises for vines.

- In the fall, don't rake up leaves that fall directly under trees and shrubs, for they mulch and nourish the plants' roots. They also shelter insects over the winter, including such spectacular species as the polyphemus and luna moths, which spin their cocoons within folded leaves that fall from the host tree in autumn and remain on the ground through the winter, waiting for metamorphosis (unless you stuff them into trash bags or ship them off to the landfill).

In the spring and summer, you can begin turning these areas of leaf litter under your trees, where the grass is now dead, into beds of shallow-rooted woodland plants extending out as far as the larger plants' driplines.

- In the fall, don't rake leaves out of beds, for they help protect plants over the winter and slowly release their nutrients.

- By leaving some dead leaves between your foundation plants and your house, you'll provide winter shelter for insects and food for insect-eating birds.

Using It Nature's Way

- Heap up fallen leaves, removed sod (grass side down), or even incompletely rotted compost in order to kill grass and start nutrient-rich new beds.

- Use thin layers of dead leaves as mulch. Shred them, if you like, by running a manual lawnmower over them a few times. They discourage weeds, offer protection against drought and extremes of temperature, and return nutrients to the soil. Leaves break down faster than woodchips do and draw less nitrogen from the soil as they do so. Maple leaves are especially good as their pH is more or less neutral, and their thinness allows them to break down quickly. Mulch of any kind should be applied in thin layers and should never touch the stems or trunks of the plants. If plants seem to have trouble emerging through this mulch of dead leaves, or if it inhibits the growth of new plants, remove some of it.

- After cutting down grasses and flower stalks in spring, gather or rake them into neat bundles along the edges of the beds, thereby enlarging the beds, inhibiting their invasion by lawn grass, providing the soil with nutrients, and preserving the insects which have overwintered, in various stages, on or within these stalks.

Nature uses everything; nothing goes to waste. Follow nature's method: line your paths and garden beds with downed branches and last year's stems; cover your paths with wood chips. As Ralph Waldo Emerson observes, "in nature's heaps and rubbish are concealed sure and useful results."

We built our brushpile very carefully, starting with two layers of old wooden pallets, then three crisscrossed layers of sizeable tree branches. We finished it off with a loose "thatch" of brush. The result is an open latticework, or three-dimensional labyrinth, or thicket, with a thatched roof (capped with snow in winter). Over the years, the brushpile grows as we add trimmings, or diminishes as we use brush to hold down leaves, for suppressing lawngrass and enriching soil. Winter and summer, birds and other creatures flit back and forth, in and out, using it as a perch or shelter: juncoes, wrens, sparrows, finches, cardinals, chipmunks, toads, rabbits, butterflies. It's almost always in use, and after more than 12 years it still retains its structure, providing openings, passages, and pockets for all manner of creatures.

- Use dead and downed branches to edge or delineate beds. Chopping them up for mulch emits carbon. Dead wood provides nesting areas for insects, including native bees. It also provides a fascinating, often beautiful variety of mosses, lichens, and fungi, all serving to decompose the wood and enrich the soil. In short, constant, slow recycling of wood is important for biodiversity.

- Use dead and downed branches to build a loose brush pile that will provide shelter for small animals, birds, and insects. Keep this small-mammal shelter some distance from the large-mammal shelter (your house).

- Prop up your old Christmas tree (and your neighbors' Christmas trees) near your feeders to provide winter shelter for feeding birds.

- Compost appropriate yard and kitchen waste to create fertilizer that can be used for many purposes.

PROTECT WILDLIFE THAT DEPENDS ON YOUR YARD

- Make sure that clean water is always available in receptacles with gently sloping sides, so that small birds and insects can drink safely.

- **Keep your cats indoors** and strongly encourage your neighbors to do the same. Feral and domestic cats kill millions of birds and other creatures annually.

- Don't use fertilizers, herbicides, or pesticides until you've tried everything else, particularly waiting to see whether the problem resolves itself. Then use old-fashioned remedies and natural products.

- Wash and sterilize bird feeders frequently. Keep them filled during winter months when times are hard for many birds—especially for the lovely, talkative chickadees, who, lacking a crop, can't store food and must eat small meals pretty much all through the day, in order to survive through a frigid night.

- Take measures to keep birds from flying into the windows of your house. Dark hawk-like silhouettes on the windows work pretty well. The cute little transparencies sold in wild bird centers may be inconspicuous and decorative, to please us; but they have little value for birds.

- When you mow whatever lawngrass remains in your yard, mow slowly, so that toads and other creatures can get out of the way.

- Turn off indoor and outdoor lights when not needed so as to avoid distracting nocturnally-active insects from feeding or mating.

- Buy a copy of Laura Erickson's *101 Ways to Help Birds* (Stackpole Books, 2006). Birds not only delight us but help to keep under control the mosquitoes and other insects that are actually pests.

BE A GOOD ADVOCATE FOR NATURAL LANDSCAPING

- **Tell your neighbors what you're doing** in your yard, and try to enlist their support. Visit a meeting of your neighborhood association. You might even try an occasional modest newsletter for the neighbors.

- Don't inconvenience or endanger your neighbors.

- If necessary, keep an attractive buffer between your yard and theirs.

- Assure them that goldenrod doesn't cause hay fever, that tall grasses don't attract rats. It's ragweed, with tiny flowers and light, wind-

blown pollen, that causes allergies, while goldenrod, dropping its heavy pollen to the ground but blooming brightly at the same time as the ragweed, takes the rap. Rats are attracted by garbage, not tall grass.

- Make sure your wild plantings look cared for, not neglected.

- Share plants, information, and enthusiasms, e.g., sightings of uncommon birds and butterflies. Practice the art of "show and tell." Your neighbors' children might be especially interested—even become allies.

- **Provide signage** that makes clear the helpfulness to wildlife and the environment of what you're doing in your yard.

Wild Ones and other organizations provide signs that help your neighbors to understand and accept what you're doing. Shop at www.wildones.org/store/

ENJOY THE WILD PLANTS AND ANIMALS IN YOUR YARD

- Make natural landscaping, and the enjoyment of it, a family project and pleasure, bringing you all closer together as part of a natural community. No children in history have spent less time outdoors than our children do. The "increasing divide between the young and the natural world" endangers, according to Richard Louv, not just the health of our children; the "health of the earth is at stake as well" (pp. 2–3). By having a working, ever-changing ecosystem, however rudimentary, right at your door, you can help your children to observe and appreciate nature. You'll be passing on to them a lasting legacy of skills and values as important as instilling in them a love of reading. In fact, observing the processes of nature is a kind of reading that everyone should be able to do. Make space and take time for it—time for work, time for play and quiet enjoyment. Both you and your children will benefit immensely. (For further observation on how to help overcome what Louv calls "Nature Deficit Disorder" among the young, see Chapter 28.)

- Learn as much as you can about the wonderful history and heritage of our native trees, shrubs, wildflowers, grasses, and other plants—their uses in past times, by both Native Americans and settlers, for food, medicine, ritual, and story.

- Observe your plants throughout the seasons, not only when they're flowering but from earliest spring through the winter. They are always changing and always interesting. Note the fall and winter beauty, for example, of grasses, flower-stalks, and seedheads.

- Quietly observe the fascinating behavior of the insects, birds, and other animals who live in and visit your yard. Not only is this one of the rewards—and a rich one it is—for making your yard more hospitable, you will also learn

> Where will all the conservationists come from when kids no longer have a patch of ground that they can truly call my space?
>
> —Robert Michael Pyle

how to make your yard still more supportive to wildlife.

- Take pictures of the whole process of landscaping your yard, so you can see what you've done and so you can show the process to other people interested in doing the same thing.

- Keep records of plants' year-by-year behavior: when they come up, when they bloom, what insects and other animals visit them, etc. Such information can be reported to the National Phenology Network where scientists keeping track of climate change will welcome it.

- Keep a list of the creatures that live in and visit your yard and a journal describing their behavior and your own feelings and insights. (Later on, you'll be awfully glad you did.)

- Gather seeds and grow still more native plants. You'll learn a lot about them, and you'll take great pleasure in fostering their growth.

ALWAYS REMEMBER
(NO MATTER WHAT THE DISCOURAGEMENT)

- The human species has been on what the naturalist Loren Eiseley calls "The Immense Journey" over millions of years with all the other species of the earth, seen and unseen, and we share the earth with them.

- We have entered into the sixth great age of extinction (the first one caused by *us*), and we must, as in all efforts to put things back together, save as many of the pieces as we can.

"If the biota, in the course of aeons, has built something we like but do not understand, then who but a fool," inquires Aldo Leopold, "would discard seemingly useless parts? To keep every cog and wheel is the first precaution of intelligent tinkering" (p. 177).

- **You're making a difference**. A small one, yes. But you can *see* it—and *feel* it.

The extinction of a species, each one a pilgrim of four billion years of evolution, is an irreversible loss. The ending of the lines of so many creatures with whom we have traveled this far is an occasion of profound sorrow and grief.

—Gary Snyder,
The Practice of the Wild

REFERENCES

Eiseley, Loren. *The Immense Journey*. New York: Vintage Books, 1956.

Flannery, Tim. *Here on Earth: A Natural History of the Planet*. New York: Atlantic Monthly Press, 2010.

Leopold, Aldo. *A Sand County Almanac*. New York: Oxford Univ. Press, 1966.

Louv, Richard. *Last Child in the Woods: Saving Our Children from Nature-Deficit Disorder*. Updated and expanded. Chapel Hill, NC: Algonquin Books of Chapel Hill, 2008.

Pyle, Robert Michael. "Pulling the Plug," *Orion*, Nov.–Dec., 2007, pp. 64–65.

_____. *The Thunder Tree: Lessons from an Urban Wildland*. Boston: Houghton Mifflin, 1993.

Stein, Sara. *Noah's Garden: Restoring the Ecology of Our Own Back Yards*. Boston: Houghton Mifflin, 1993.

HELPFUL BOOKS ON KEEPING A JOURNAL

Hinchman, Hanna, *A Trail Through Leaves: The Journal As a Path to Place*. New York: W. W. Norton, 1997.

Johnson, Cathy, *The Sierra Club Guide to Sketching in Nature*, new edition. San Francisco: Sierra Club Books, 1997.

Leslie, Claire Walker, and Charles E. Roth, *Keeping a Nature Journal*, 2nd ed. Pownal, VT: Storey Books, 2003.

from "THIS COMPOST"
by Walt Whitman

Behold this compost! behold it well!
Perhaps every mite has once form'd part of a sick person—yet behold!
The grass of spring covers the prairies,
The bean bursts noiselessly through the mould in the garden,
The delicate spear of the onion pierces upward,
The apple-buds cluster together on the apple-branches,

The resurrection of the wheat appears with pale visage out of its graves,
The tinge awakes over the willow-tree and the mulberry-tree,
The he-birds carol mornings and evenings while the she-birds sit on their nests,
The young of poultry break through the hatch'd eggs,
The new-born of animals appear, the calf is dropt from the cow, the colt from the mare,
Out of its little hill faithfully rise the potato's dark green leaves,
Out of its hill rises the yellow maize-stalk, the lilacs bloom in the dooryards,
The summer growth is innocent and disdainful above all those strata of sour dead.

What chemistry!
That the winds are really not infectious,
That this is no cheat, this transparent green-wash of the sea which is so amorous after me,
That it is safe to allow it to lick my naked body all over with its tongues,
That it will not endanger me with the fevers that have deposited themselves in it,
That all is clean forever and forever,
That the cool drink from the well tastes so good,
That blackberries are so flavorous and juicy,
That the fruits of the apple-orchard and the orange-orchard, that melons, grapes, peaches, plums,
    will none of them poison me,
That when I recline on the grass I do not catch any disease,
Though probably every spear of grass rises out of what was once a catching disease.

Now I am terrified at the Earth, it is that calm and patient,
It grows such sweet things out of such corruptions,
It turns harmless and stainless on its axis, with such endless successions of diseas'd corpses,
It distills such exquisite winds out of such infused fetor,
It renews with such unwitting looks its prodigal, annual, sumptuous crops,
It gives such divine materials to men, and accepts such leavings from them at last.

Published in *Leaves of Grass*, 1856, as "Poem of Wonder at The Resurrection of The Wheat."

4

WELCOMING NATIVE PLANTS INTO YOUR YARD

Above all, the alliance forged in native-plant
gardening is with nature—nature as teacher, guide
and eventually, as our knowledge expands, partner.
—Lorraine Johnson, *Grow Wild!*

FIRST, SOME WORDS OF CAUTION

- **Don't take on too much at once**. If you do, you're likely to feel overburdened, even resentful, and may soon abandon the whole project. Adopt a gradual but steady approach that allows you time to learn, plan, and enjoy what you're doing. The knowledge that you're supporting biodiversity and reducing stress on the environment will lighten tedious tasks and provide better motivation than simply trying to prettify your yard or avoid offending the neighbors. Remember that as long as you keep establishing native plants in your yard—and maintaining them until they can take care of themselves—you're making progress in your effort to help sustain the planet and its biodiversity.

- Don't tear out *all* your nonnative plants—at least not until you know how you're going to replace them. Some of them you probably need to keep, at least for a while, e.g., the hedge that screens you from your neighbors. Just widen and diversify it with native shrubs and small trees and with wildflowers and grasses at the margins, to make a truly diversified biohedge. As its nonnative shrubs die out—or you manage to dig up a couple of them now and then—replace them with natives. Keep the big copper beech you're so fond of, but use the area below it as a bed for shade-loving native wildflowers. Do, however, remove invasive, nonnative plants as soon as possible. Buckthorn, honeysuckle, autumn olive, oriental bittersweet, garlic mustard, and other aggressive aliens—such plants easily spread into natural areas, where they immediately begin to outcompete native plants. And remember that the nonnative plants in your yard are taking up space and consuming nutrients that could be put to better use by native plants, which support wildlife far better.

- Don't start out by attacking well-established alien groundcover such as English ivy or myrtle in order to create space for native plants. These are invasive, nonnative plants very difficult to get rid of and all too likely to rush back and swallow up the new plants while your back is turned. Much better to start a brand new bed or two on what was formerly lawn because lawngrass is less tenacious than most nonnative groundcovers. Such plants are often nearly impossible to eradicate completely, though they can be brought under control and eventually overgrown and outcompeted by mature wild plants; at least that has been our experience in our yard.

- Don't be too eager to fill up spaces liberated from annuals, lawngrass, or nonnative ground covers with native ground covers. A mixed planting is always better than a monoculture, even when the monoculture is native; it's more natural and more helpful to wildlife. There are places, however, where it's hard to get anything to grow, such as under a Norway maple, so deep is the shade it casts, so greedy are its roots. If all you can get to grow there is Virginia creeper (*Parthenocissus quinquefolia*), so be it. Get rid of the Norway maple as soon as you can: it's an invasive, nonnative plant and a real destroyer of natural areas or areas being restored.

- Don't be in too great a hurry to get plants in the ground. Give every plant the best possible chance for survival. If you're planting plugs or potted plants, be sure not to mound up soil around the stem or root crown; leave a shallow depression around the plant, to aid in wa-

> Although skillful work may help, all healing ultimately depends on the self-renewing powers of nature. Our task is to understand and cooperate with those powers as fully as we can.
>
> —Scott Russell Sanders,
> *A Conservationist Manifesto*

tering—shallow so that water won't wash soil into the depression and cover the root crown. Pack soil carefully to remove air pockets, and water generously, as soon as possible. If you're planting bare rootstock, don't expose the delicate root hairs to air; they dry out quickly and probably won't recover. Carry them in a bucket of water or wrapped in wet cloth. Be sure the hole is big enough to spread out the roots, and fill the hole slowly enough to keep them spread out.

- Keep newly-planted areas weeded. Weeding can be a chore, but it can also be fun and educational. Crouched down in a miniature wilderness of wildflowers, grasses, and weeds, you can't help seeing more than you usually do: the delicate colors, shapes and textures of early stems and leaves; growth patterns; the insects buzzing around the plants. Don't be in a big hurry. You have to learn to distinguish one seedling from another. From careful observation of native plants and the wildlife they attract, through the seasons, you'll start to see things you'd never noticed before, and beauty in things you'd never considered beautiful—and this keeps on happening. It's very gratifying.

You also learn how to protect those tender seedlings. When weeding, try not to shake or otherwise disturb the roots of desirable plants, especially plants such as wild lupine that are *very* sensitive to root disturbance. If necessary, flatten your hand firmly against the ground, fingers spread around the stem, to keep a plant steady as you pull a nearby weed; or use scissors to cut the weed down to the ground. Water seedlings right after weeding them, and don't weed at all when the ground is very dry, or compact the soil when it's very wet.

BEGIN BY ADDING TO WHAT'S THERE

Replace and Diversify

- The easiest first step is simply to replace annual bedding plants with perennial wildflowers in existing beds. Instead of planting beds of tulips or other bulbs, to be filled in each year with the same old impatiens, begonias, or petunias, fill beds with mixtures of native wildflowers and grasses that are helpful to wildlife as well as pleasing to you.

- Increase and diversify your foundation plantings with native plants. Under windows or along a porch or deck, plants should ordinarily be fairly low, but elsewhere along the house they can be taller and more varied in shape. Evergreens with needles help insulate the house, but they must be combined with bushy deciduous shrubs and small trees in order to soften sharp edges and make large blank surfaces interesting. The corners and ends of a house, in particular, need softening.

Enlarge and Diversify

- Then, enlarge existing beds and planting areas, thus reducing the size of your lawn and diversifying your yard with native species at the same time.

As you widen existing flowerbeds, put tall native plants behind nonnative perennials already in place or short native plants in front of medium-tall or short nonnative perennials. You might even create variety among the nonnative perennials already in place by inserting a few unaggressive native plants or clumps of well-behaved native grasses among the established plants or a few tall, slender native plants among short, nonnative ones.

As you widen beds at the expense of lawn, you can make your unnaturally right-angled house and property lines look more natural by giving the beds curved edges, or more informal wavy edges.

- Extend existing beds around trees, killing grass with thin layers of dead leaves—thin so as not to keep water and air from reaching the trees' roots—and then seeding native wildflowers, or carefully inserting small plants, around the trees. Under trees, plants should be fairly short. Keep the ground lightly mulched, with natural leaf fall.

Researchers at Kansas State University have shown recently that turf grasses greatly inhibit tree growth; trees surrounded by natural mulch (shredded bark or leaves) had significantly better root growth and branching and double the stem diameter of trees surrounded by lawn.

- Widen and diversify existing hedges and fill the corners of your yard with a variety of native shrubs and small trees helpful to wildlife. Irregular, or slightly wavy hedges made up of different kinds of plants look more far more natural than straight, single-species hedges only one shrub wide. Hedges make good backdrops for beds of shorter plants, e.g., native wildflowers and grasses. As Sara Stein advises, "bring the hedgerow forth into the lawn with native grasses and meadow wildflowers."

> I like surprises in a garden. It's all very well to sit on a lawn and enjoy a vista up the meadow or over the pond, but it's more exciting if the view suggests, by dark openings and glinting curves of paths, that secrets lie hidden out of sight.
>
> —Sara Stein

Soon, as you extend, widen, connect, and diversify, you will have "a continuous, meandering growth of copse and thicket punctuated by taller trees and lower bursts of flowers," drawing yourself and your visitors through a landscape that is always unfolding and changing, as is nature itself (*Noah's Garden*, pp. 49, 220).

Extend and Diversify

- Extend your foundation plantings further into the yard by means of beds of native wildflowers and grasses, for which the house and foundation plants will serve as a background. Such extensions flow most naturally from the house and foundation plants at entrances and along sidewalks or paths. An occasional taller plant, e.g., a small tree or dramatic forb such as compass plant (tall but not dense), will provide welcome contrast to lower ones. However, too many tall and dense plants in entry areas or close to the sidewalks and paths that issue from them will block your view of the yard and may make the house seem forbidding. On the other hand, plants that are tall but not too dense, e.g., grasses and tall, somewhat finely-textured wildflowers, standing right next to a sidewalk or path, may give the visitor the sense of having magically stepped from the urban into the natural world.

Connect and Diversify

- Use mulch, which will kill the grass, to connect isolated trees and shrubs into larger plantings. These mulched areas can then be planted with additional trees and shrubs, in order to create groves of trees or thickets of shrubs, or left more open and planted with small shrubs, wildflowers, and grasses.

- If possible, connect your plantings to those of your neighbors. You can do this even without

Essential parts of a natural system, snags provide homes, perches, and food. In a woodland garden, they "anchor" the understory and harbor an everchanging community of life as the "dead" tree slowly enriches the soil.

their permission. Use the sides of their hedges that face you as a background for small trees, shrubs, and wildflowers, thus increasing the width of the hedge you share and its value to wildlife. Turn the tree in the corner of your neighbor's yard into a planting of trees and shrubs in the adjacent corner of your own yard.

- If you live next to a natural area, try to extend it or connect your yard to it with native plants that will replicate and enhance the natural area's ecosystem. Be sure to coordinate your efforts with those of the owners or managers of the natural area.

Utilize Difficult or Dead Spaces

- Use a dead or dying tree, especially if it has low-hanging branches under which it's hard

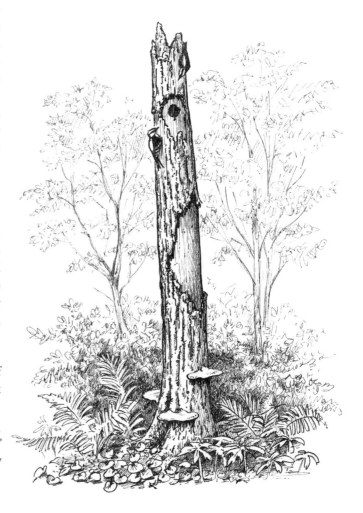

to mow, as the basis for establishing a thicket of native shrubs, small trees, wildflowers and grasses. Birds will love the food and cover provided by the resulting "tangle" and occupy it year-round.

- Utilize the borders and corners of decks, porches, patios, walkways, even driveways, by filling pots and containers with native, rather than nonnative, plants. Some of these could provide food for you as well as for other, wilder life, e.g., blueberry bushes which, because they require extra water and special soil, might be difficult to maintain in your planting beds.

Create New Planting Areas

Now you're ready to venture beyond the "enlarge and connect" approach to create brand-new planting areas, often thereby eliminating sizeable chunks of lawn and doubling your sense of satisfaction.

New Beds in Obvious Places

- Take over your curb lawn, or city strip, or tree lawn, or whatever you call the strip of lawn between the sidewalk and the street that belongs to the city. In the country, use the ditch often found next to the road; you may, however, first have to deal with the weeds already growing there. (The lawngrass on the curb lawn will probably have given the soil underneath some protection from weeds and weed seeds.)

Plant this area with tough but attractive plants that won't get very tall: small shrubs or wildflowers and grasses or even a combination of native groundcovers.

- Use obvious backgrounds for new plantings. Foundations, walls, fences, and hedges, all provide convenient backgrounds and usually some protection for plants. Other natural places for beds are along walks, paths, and driveways, and around entryways, porches, patios, and decks.

- Use the shade cast by structures for shade-loving plants. A friend and grower of native plants maintains that there's no such thing as "dry shade," a difficult situation in which to grow plants of any kind. Six to eight inches of composted leaves, dumped on the difficult area, should ease the problem of dryness. The additional organic matter will hold more water and make it easier to grow shade-loving plants there.

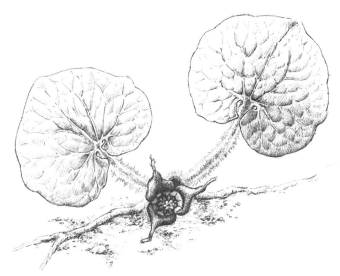

With midday shade and moist soil, wild ginger (Asarum canadense) *will form a low, dense groundcover. Its low, dark red flowers are pollinated by ground insects, such as ants. Its roots may be used as seasoning, much as Asian or European ginger.*

- Likewise, use the shade cast by deciduous trees and shrubs. Start by not raking up the leaves they drop in the fall or by smothering the grass around them with thin layers of leaves—thin, so as not to block water from above to roots below, which are near the surface. (Keep added leaves or other mulch at least 6 inches away from the base of trees or shrubs.) Seed the new soil you've created with native, shade-tolerant wildflowers, or put in small plants which will not disturb the larger plants' roots.

Trees and shrubs will benefit, first of all, from not having to compete for space, water, and nutrients with lawngrass. Also, the root systems of the wildflowers growing underneath them will absorb and hold more water than lawngrass does and slowly release it to the larger plants. Best of all, the leaves dropped from the trees each fall will nourish and protect the smaller plants below as well as the larger ones above, while providing shelter for wildlife, for example, overwintering insects, just as in natural woodlands. The larger the bed around a tree, the less likely that the soil around the tree (and over its roots) will become compacted from walking or mowing.

- Create islands or berms to break up large, featureless areas of lawn or to screen your house from the street or road. Islands or berms can be any shape—round, rectangular, levee-like, free-form. Planting at least a few trees or shrubs on their highest, flat surface, to anchor them, might be a good idea. These islands or peninsulas can be used to take advantage of spots of sunlight or shade, to create special conditions for plants (special soil conditions, a raised area for better drainage, or an "isolation" area for plants that are very aggressive or that don't tolerate much competition). You may find that just a few inches difference in elevation will eventually result in different mixes of species as each plant finds its "niche."

New Beds in Unusual Places

- Round off sharp 90-degree corners for a softer, more natural look. Such corners occur where sidewalks meet or cross; where a sidewalk meets a street, a driveway, or the entrance to a house; and where a driveway meets a street or road. These, too, are natural places to start beds, and such beds can be easily enlarged.

Rural mailboxes are often located in these corners, between the homeowner's driveway and the road or street; and what could be more attractive and welcoming than a bed of native wildflowers and grasses surrounding (actually, mostly behind and along the sides of) the mailbox? This is also a good place to put some signs from national organizations advertising that you are landscaping your property with native plants in order to support wildlife—especially if your plantings aren't visible from the street or road.

> There is something quite preposterous about our devotion to the landscape styles of the seventeenth, eighteenth, and nineteenth centuries at a time when we must address the future of our landscape.
>
> —Leslie Jones Sauer,
> *The Once and Future Forest*

- Then there's the narrow grassy strip that is sometimes found, at least in older suburban neighborhoods, between your cement or asphalt driveway and your neighbor's. Sometimes the strip is surrounded, or partially surrounded, by a low curb. If this strip is on your property, or even if it isn't, perhaps your neighbor will agree to letting you convert it from lawngrass to a planting of short native plants that will bloom in succession.

- What about those areas of lawngrass hard to mow, such as slopes, or places where grass doesn't grow easily, such as under trees? Surely, they're begging for conversion to native plantings. Mowing under trees compacts the soil and may damage a tree's roots, so give up all that endless re-seeding and mowing and, in the autumn, let the leaves of the tree lie where they fall, perhaps adding a few more. Soon, you'll be able to seed or plant the area with wildflowers and grasses. For steep slopes, you'll need to select plants that thrive in rather dry soil.

Save Water, Energy, Species

- Use native plants to slow down and catch rainwater that runs through or pools in ditches, swales, and low areas on your property, or create raingardens in order to trap it.

- Use native plants to improve the weatherization of your house. Put additional conifers (native) on the north and northwest sides of your house to protect it from winter winds—and a few native deciduous shrubs or small trees in front of them. As you look out your windows in winter, the bare branches of the latter will look elegant against the dark green conifers. Put in a few additional deciduous trees (native) on the south for shade if too much sunlight in summer is a problem.

Plant life is organized into layers, or strata, most obvious in forests but found in virtually all plant communities. Below the woodland canopy, the understory trees, shrubs, wildflowers, grasses, sedges, ferns, mosses, and leaf litter form several distinct layers of foliage. More layers extend down among the roots and "soil horizons." Each layer—and every "niche"—supports a different community of creatures.

- Select and arrange native plants carefully to form a biohedge, which is a hedge meant to provide wildlife with a maximum of food and cover. It can incorporate existing trees and shrubs or be started from scratch. It can also serve as a screen between you and the neighbors or as a windbreak. It should incorporate conifers as well as deciduous trees and shrubs and a diversity of perennial wildflowers and grasses, in a series of vertically stepped layers. It should include plants that are valuable as host plants as well as those valuable for their nectar, fruits, nuts and seeds. Native oaks (*Quercus* spp.) are particularly valuable both as host plants for herbivorous insects such as caterpillars and as producers of acorns (nuts), essential food for birds and mammals. Ideally, a biohedge should provide food for insects, birds, and small mammals year-round: berries in summer; fruits in autumn to fuel birds' fall migration; and nuts, seeds, and persistent fruits for wildlife that doesn't migrate as well as for migrants returning in the spring before other food is plentiful. In a biohedge, every few inches of difference in height and mix of plant species, from the soil and leaf-litter right on up to the treetops, provides a different niche or habitat for wildlife, resulting in the greatest possible diversity in a relatively small space.

Native wildflowers and grasses can be planted on both sides of the biohedge as well as among the larger plants. See Chapter 7 for a list of plants, arranged according to bloom times, of plants valuable for their nectar. Wildflowers particularly valuable for their seed are the daisy-like flowers of composites, e.g., asters, blazing stars, coneflowers, perennial sunflowers. Native grasses, similarly, provide valuable seed and cover for wildlife in winter. Chapters 8, 9, and 10 provide plant lists arranged according to height.

BEING GOOD NEIGHBORS

- Try to make the neighbors your allies or at least keep them from complaining to people in authority, whether the neighborhood association or the city administration. (Also see "Be a Good Advocate for Natural Landscaping," in Chapter 3, and "Sharing the Garden with the Whole Community," Chapter 19.) In the 15 years that we've been incorporating native plants into our yard, we've had very little trouble with the neighbors or the authorities even though we haven't always been careful not to offend them. The signs Tom has made identifying those plants in our prairie garden that are now extinct, threatened, or of special concern in Michigan have probably helped

It's fun to do the research and easy to print signs for your plantings. Laminate them and tape them to sticks with duct tape. Add pictures if you like. Passersby stop to read them; sometimes they ask a question. Maybe you've made a friend, even a convert.

COMPASS PLANT
Silphium laciniatum

One of the most impressive of prairie plants, it grows to ten feet tall, with massive roots at least that deep. Our plants took four years to bloom.

Since most of the large, deeply cut leaves are always within ten degrees of north-south alignment, it could be used as a "compass" on cloudy days.

William Bartram observed in 1788 that southern Indian tribes used the resinous sap as chewing gum. The powdered root was used to treat pain and head colds.

A member of the aster family, it wants sun, and its large, yellow composite flowers are much favored by butterflies, especially Eastern tiger swallowtails.

THREATENED SPECIES

suppress complaints, as have signs identifying the area as a "native prairie planting" and a "wildlife refuge."

Signage from national organizations is very helpful, as a way of letting neighbors and passersby know that you're trying to help wildlife and not just letting your yard go wild.

- *Maintain the illusion of neatness* to help pacify those who may not be in sympathy with your efforts. Turn every planting—whether grove of trees, overgrown thicket, island of wildflowers and grasses—into a bed with some kind of edging, and keep the lawngrass in between the plantings quite short. (In our yard, this lawngrass serves as paths.) We use downed branches for edging, which gives our yard a rustic look we like, perhaps too rustic a look for some of our neighbors. Bricks would be more formal and more intimidating. Even the stiff plastic edging with a rounded edge that you have to shove into the ground will do (but we don't recommend it). And it might be a good idea to spread a little bark mulch between the edging and your plants where the neighbors and passersby can see it. Mulch makes it look as if you're trying hard.

Neighbors are perhaps more likely to be distressed by the late summer and early fall "wilderness" look of a native planting than they are by its spring and early summer "flowerbed" look. Emphasize to them nature's *profusion*; and of course embrace it enthusiastically yourself. As a planting develops and matures, so will your relationship to it—and thus your sense of *yourself.*

- Give your neighbors cut flowers from native plants and starts of native plants (if they'll take them), and invite them over to look at native plants in full and glorious bloom or at wildlife in your yard. If you think there's any chance they'll read it, give them Douglas Tallamy's book, *Bringing Nature Home: How You Can Use Native Plants to Sustain Wildlife* (Timber Press, 2009). This lovely, very readable book explains why people who care at all about wildlife *must* fill their yards with native plants.

Finally, Take Some Time

Having done what you can do to welcome native plants and wildlife into your yard and your life, *take time to enjoy and appreciate* what you've done, and how nature has responded to your hard work. The pleasure is mutual, I'm sure.

Gardening with natives is no longer just a peripheral option favored by vegetarians and erstwhile hippies. It is an important part of a paradigm shift in our shaky relationship with the planet that sustains us—one that mainstream gardeners can no longer afford to ignore.

—Douglas Tallamy

5

WHAT SHOULD I PLANT IN MY YARD?

And because it is we who decide what plants will grow in our gardens,
the responsibility for our nation's biodiversity lies largely with us.
—Douglas Tallamy, *Bringing Nature Home*

We began without any overall plan. We had read Sara Stein. We knew we wanted to create habitat for wildlife, we had a local grower of plants who provided some advice and lots of infectious enthusiasm, and we started where we had the most open space and sun. After that, for the next 15 years we just kept doing what seemed to come next, and we kept on learning —from books, from conferences, from knowledgeable friends, from volunteering with the local conservancy, and from our own mistakes (we made lots of them). Sure, some books told us to lay out a plan first—a design. But we didn't. You probably won't either. All that measuring and careful plotting of what goes where, laid out on graph paper—it just doesn't seem consistent with natural landscaping (which "bloweth where it listeth").

Still, there are things that we wish we'd known earlier, and things we knew but didn't take quite seriously enough. So I'll try to share what we've learned so far and what we believe is crucial to success in saving the biodiversity of plants and creatures that are disappearing from the wild—and from the earth. I'll begin with a few "don'ts," but I'll move along quickly to what you should be keeping in mind as you make your choices and create your native-plant gardens and landscapes.

STOP PLANTING NONNATIVE PLANTS

- Nonnative plants aren't, in fact, neutral or benign. Many of the nonnative plants used in landscaping are capable of invading and degrading natural ecosystems, and few nonnative plants actually serve wildlife all that well. Even the most beautiful and least invasive nonnative plants take up space and nutrients that native plants could be using, and the food web that sustains wildlife—and, in the end, us humans too—rests on native plants. Thanks in large part to Douglas Tallamy, experimental evidence is mounting that the herbivorous or plant-eating insects that make the sun's energy available to other wildlife greatly prefer native to nonnative plants. Tallamy reports as well that the ornamental plants favored by the

37

horticultural industry are "not a random sub-set of plants that have evolved on other continents but instead are attractive plants *selected specifically because they are particularly well defended against insects*" (p. 82—emphasis added). Even native bees, whose role in pollination of flowering plants becomes increasingly important as nonnative honey bees decline, have been shown to greatly prefer the nectar and pollen of native, as opposed to nonnative, plants. In fact, Laura Tangley, Senior Editor of *National Wildlife*, advising on "How to Plant for Pollinators," urges selection of as many native plants as possible because, when it comes to nectar and pollen, "many ornamentals have been specifically bred to produce little or none of these essential foods" (p. 45).

- Remove invasive plants **as soon as possible**. Landscaping your yard with plants native to our region doesn't mean you have to rip out *all* your nonnative plants right away, or ever. It does mean, however, that you need to get rid as soon as possible of nonnative plants capable of invading and degrading natural areas, including many past and present garden favorites such as exotic honeysuckles, Japanese barberry, buddleia or butterfly bush, winged euonymus, myrtle, and English ivy. Once you've removed and destroyed such plants, avoid planting any other invasive nonnatives in your yard. Consult Chapter 12 for a list of nonnative plants found to be invasive in the Midwest and a bibliography of useful books. Elizabeth Czarapata's excellent *Invasive Plants of the Upper Midwest* helps you identify these plants, describes them in detail, and outlines methods of removing them.

CHOOSING ALTERNATIVE NATIVES

- Substitute native plants for invasive exotics. Of the books that suggest attractive native substitutes for nonnative plants, perhaps the best are C. Colston Burrell's *Native Alternatives to Invasive Plants* and Carrol L. Henderson's "Plant Substitutes for Invasive Non-Native Species," in *Lakescaping for Wildlife and Water Quality* (see Chapter 12). Be aware that some invasive plants do provide important food and shelter for wildlife—perhaps not the best food and shelter but nonetheless important in degraded habitats where the alternatives are few. For instance, if you remove invasive autumn olive, consider replacing it with dogwoods and other plants that provide nutritious autumn fruit; if you're fighting buckthorn, consider adding hawthorn for birds that prefer a thorny shrub to nest in. If you're taking out spotted knapweed or purple loosestrife, replace it with summer flowers that provide good nectar for the bees.

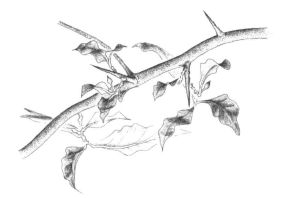

Autumn olive (Eleagnus umbellata) *is an invasive species that takes over from natives in fields, wooded areas, lowlands—just about anywhere. Many property owners have planted it, expecting lots of edible fruit or deer and game birds for hunting. It may bring all three, but it also forms thickets and spreads for miles around, far from its original planting (seeded by birds). If you have it, even a little, and your aim is true diversity, on your own property and in local natural areas, make its eradication and its replacement with another fruit-bearing shrub or tree **a top priority** (see Chapter 12).*

Some nonnative plants may seem hard to replace, for example, annual bedding plants such as impatiens or petunias and perennials such as daylilies (*Hemerocallis* spp.). The advantages of nonnative annuals are obvious: they're colorful (if boring) and bloom all summer; they provide some nectar for wildlife, though at a time when nectar is plentiful. But their environmental costs, though not immediately obvious, are considerable, including, for instance, starting them in heated greenhouses. Daylilies have their advantages too. These sturdy, undemanding perennials will tolerate a lot of shade and have attractive orange flowers on tall, slender stalks borne above the leaves. Their soft, graceful foliage, so capable of filling up space and thus concealing both a multitude of sins and many years of neglect, makes them quite useful in landscaping. This foliage, however, apparently doesn't support even one species of Lepidoptera, whose caterpillars play such a crucial role in transferring the sun's energy from plants to animals. And the orange-flowered daylilies (*Hemerocallis fulva*) growing along roadsides in southern Michigan and often mistaken for wildflowers are aggressive nonnative plants that crowd out virtually everything else and invade natural areas.

- Replace traditional monocultures of nonnatives with *mixed beds* of natives. Combinations of attractive native wildflowers and grasses have far more value to wildlife than nonnative monocultures, of annuals, daylilies, or other nonnative herbaceous plants. A mixed planting of fairly short native wildflowers and grasses can provide nectar for pollinators from early spring to late fall as different species come into bloom, followed by fruits and seeds for wildlife. Such a planting also provides host plants for a significant number of butterflies and moths, as nonnatives cannot. Plant lists provided in Part II of the book will help you assemble mixed plantings of native wildflowers and grasses for different locations.

If you must resort to groundcover (a monoculture) rather than a mixture of wildflowers and grasses, at least use a native groundcover helpful to wildlife, e.g., Canada violets or Virginia creeper under an invasive nonnative Norway maple that you just haven't gotten around to removing.

There are native plants for every horticultural purpose—not just trees, shrubs, wildflowers, and grasses, but also vines and groundcovers and plants whose fruits and nuts you can eat. Many native plants do well even in containers.

Many native violets provide delicate blossoms, fragrance, and nectar in early spring. As they spread slowly through whatever lawn grass you may still have, delay mowing them down because they serve as host plants for many fritillary butterflies.

CHOOSE PLANTS NATIVE TO
YOUR OWN LOCALE AND REGION

- The most authoritative list of which plants are native to our state and region—even to particular counties—is Edward G. Voss's splendid *Michigan Flora* (see Chapter 6). An updated version is now available online; but even so, since the cost of the three volumes is extremely reasonable, everyone with even a moderate interest in native plants should own a copy (I do enjoy holding a book in my hands). This indispensable work provides an enormous amount of useful information even to the nonbotanist. It indicates, for example, whether a plant is native to Michigan and if not, where it originates; exactly where in Michigan a plant grows naturally; often the kinds of areas in which it grows, and what it looks like. These volumes are extremely well indexed, by plants' common as well as botanical names.

  Another official list, this one in a single volume (paperback) and based on Voss's list, is the *Floristic Quality Assessment*, for short (for full citation, see References below). Here, plants found growing in Michigan are listed alphabetically by botanical names (common names are also given), and the wetness or dryness of the area in which they usually occur is indicated. Also indicated, among other things, is whether they are native. Much of this information is now also available online, as part of the updated version of *Michigan Flora*.

- Unofficial lists can be quite helpful. The plant lists or catalogs of local growers of native plants or seeds who belong to the Michigan Native Plant Producers Association (mnppa.org) serve as unofficial lists of the plants native to our region or state and suitable for landscaping, as well as guides to the cultural requirements of the various plants. Nurseries in or near west Michigan include Hidden Savanna Nursery (Kalamazoo), Mary Ann's Michigan Trees and Shrubs (Paw Paw), Native Connections (Three Rivers), Sandhill Farm (Rockford), and Wildtype Native Plant Nursery (Mason). Most of these growers have, in addition to their extremely helpful websites, paper catalogs, often with photographs, that are handy for quick reference (for web addresses, see References below).

- **Beware of more general lists.** Lists of plants covering several states or a large region such as the Upper Midwest have their drawbacks as not all the plants listed are native to Michigan, much less to southwest Michigan. Check such lists against the *Floristic Quality Assessment* or, still better, Voss's *Michigan Flora* and its plant-distribution maps. Lists that don't indicate which communities individual plants belong to, or what kind of growing conditions each requires, aren't very helpful.

CHOOSE PLANTS COMPATIBLE WITH CONDITIONS OF YOUR SITE

It's impossible to overemphasize that just because a plant is native to southwest Michigan doesn't mean it will grow in your yard. Trying to grow native plants completely unsuited to your site is a waste of plants, money, space, and effort.

Nonetheless, like most people who love plants, we have tried hard to grow plants quite unsuited to our site (in our case, a yard of less than half an

acre, neither wet nor dry but mesic). It's taken us a long time to realize that the effort required to keep such plants going just isn't worth it; maybe trying to grow plants that aren't sustainable is a stage we all have to go through. Oh, you can fudge a little and sometimes get away with it, at least for a while; but sooner or later the plants inappropriate to your site will probably die out.

Stubborn to the end, we don't repent our mistakes and unsuccessful experiments. We learned a lot from trying to grow cardinal flower, a wetland plant which needs a steady supply of moisture and is therefore quite unsuited to our mesic yard: locate such species close to the house so you can more easily give them the special care they demand, in this case, water every day; and be sure to put them where you can see and enjoy them from indoors—*while they last*. (Enjoy them we did, especially when a hummingbird used to arrive in late afternoon and work its way up and down the flowerstalks.) We also learned that it's hard to generalize about plants: while cardinal flower needs to be kept wet, other wetland plants, e.g., swamp milkweed, can tolerate periods of dryness. The latter plant flourishes in our yard, even in its driest, sunniest area. Finally (and very important), field trips to natural areas and volunteer work on native plantings elsewhere in the community (such as community projects maintained by the Kalamazoo Area Wild Ones chapter or preserves managed by your local conservancy) allow you to enjoy and work with plants that require significantly wetter or drier conditions than those found in your own yard, without all the personal and environmental stress of special care.

- **Analyze your site**. The more you know about your site the better, but it will take time to get thoroughly acquainted with even a small site. You must quickly find out enough about it, though, to recognize and preserve remnants of its original vegetation and give even the first native plants you put in a good chance of success. What is the site's topography? How much sun or shade does it receive? Would you classify its soil as basically sand, clay, or loam—a mix of sand, clay, and silt? What about the soil's pH? How wet or dry is the site most of the time? Do growing conditions vary within the site? Fortunately, as you'll have seen from lists of native plants offered for sale by growers of native plants, many native plants can tolerate a wide range of conditions. Experiment,

but recognize that even native-plant tolerance has its limits.

As soon as possible, classify the plants growing on your site, to establish your priorities. Which ones are invasive nonnative plants to be removed as soon as possible, lest they spread, possibly by seeds carried by animals, into natural areas? Which are nonnative but not particularly invasive? Which are native, and, still more important, might be remnants of the vegetation that grew on your site prior to European settlement?

Cardinal flower (Lobelia cardinalis)

KNOW YOUR PLANT COMMUNITIES

• Determine what plant community was once present on your site. To find out what grew on your property before the European settlers arrived, vestiges of which—if you're lucky—may still be growing there, consult the *Atlas of Early Michigan's Forests, Grasslands, and Wetlands* (see References below). Because this work superimposes a grid of county roads and streets upon a pre-settlement vegetation map of each of Michigan's counties, you can easily locate your property and find out what kind of plant community it once supported and may still support. The atlas identifies and describes over two dozen plant communities in the state of Michigan, from open-water wetlands such as bogs or muskegs through prairies and open woodlands such as mixed-oak savannas to closed-canopy forests. Fascinating and helpful as these descriptions are, they don't include extensive plant lists and sometimes mention only the major trees of a forest community.

The country [around Kalamazoo] was what is termed 'rolling' ... with some fancied resemblance to the surface of the ocean ... the trees, with very few exceptions, were ... 'burr-oak' ... and the spaces between them, always irregular, and often of singular beauty, have obtained the name of 'openings' ... The [tallgrass prairie] grasses are supposed to be owing to the fires periodically lighted by the Indians in order to clear their hunting grounds.

—James Fenimore Cooper,
The Oak Openings: or, The Bee-Hunter (1848), a novel set in southwest Michigan's mixed-oak savannas in 1812.

Some works that identify plant communities and describe their members—trees, shrubs, wildflowers, grasses, ferns—in more detail are listed in the bibliography in Chapter 6 under "Michigan's Native Plant Communities," as are guides for identifying individual plants and handbooks for replicating and restoring these communities.

Knowing what plant community or communities are most compatible with your site is extremely helpful, no matter whether these communities still remain or your site has changed in some respects. As I emphasize in the "Aim for Diversity" section below, such knowledge doesn't limit your choices but rather enlarges them.

- Preserve existing plant communities or remnants of them. If part of its original community remains on your site, your course is clear. Preserve and, if possible, extend the original plant community by freeing it and keeping it free from invasive plants while enhancing it with additional species from that same original community or related ones. If your site is overrun by invasive species such as multiflora rose or buckthorn, but the site is otherwise relatively undisturbed, you might be pleasantly surprised by what emerges once you begin clearing away the tangle of invasives.

Native vegetation along streams, rivers, and lakes should always be preserved and extended if possible, for it helps protect these bodies of water and serves as a corridor for wildlife. If your site lies next to a natural area, try to use your site (if at all possible) to extend or buffer the natural area. And finally, *don't fight your site.* In other words, learn to live with (and come to love) the things you may not initially be enchanted with. Beyond these truisms, it's hard to generalize much about how to match your plantings to your site. (Nevertheless, I give it a try, in the paragraphs below.)

- In general, preserve forested areas, but keep open areas open. If the pre-settlement landscape that existed on your site has changed radically, you probably should accept that—don't waste time and money fighting it.

If your site, originally prairie or savanna, is now wooded, then treat it as a woods. Keep it free of invasive nonnative plants and diversify it with shrubs, wildflowers, and grasses suited to the type of forest that it is. Clearing out overgrowth of nonnative trees and shrubs may reveal, however, that your site was formerly a savanna, an open or somewhat open woodland with patches and lower lay-

ers of prairie wildflowers and grasses. Once more light reaches the ground, prairie wildflowers and grasses or some woodland edge species may spring up from the seedbank. If they do, you can cherish them, increase their number, and add other appropriate species; if they don't, you can restore what would have been there before disturbance.

If your site is open rather than wooded, or has sizeable open areas, it makes good sense to restore the open areas as some version of prairie or savanna. Many such ecosystems in southern Michigan have been lost to agriculture and other development or, in the absence of fire, to natural succession. Resist any urges to fill open areas with trees, even native trees, and especially trees of only one or two species. Plantations, or monocultures, of trees of the same species are of very limited value to wildlife. Moreover, it's much easier and quicker to restore open areas as prairie or savanna than to create forest; and grassland birds, currently in steep decline, depend on such areas. The authoritative books for restoring prairies, savannas, and woodlands in this part of the country are *The Tallgrass Restoration Handbook for Prairies, Savannas, and Woodlands* and the new *The Tallgrass Prairie Center Guide to Prairie Restoration in the Upper Midwest* (see Bibliography, Chapter 6).

What Tom and I have done in our small urban yard is to use its fairly open areas for beds of prairie and savanna plants and its more shaded areas for woodland plants. These areas of "high" shade are created by mature trees we couldn't bear to cut down and fairly mature street trees planted by the city. Among the mature trees are a couple of oaks, but they aren't old enough to be remnants of the pre-settlement plant community, "mixed-oak savanna." Developed as a suburb in the middle of the twentieth century, our yard was formerly an apple and peach orchard. (You, too, can probably find out something about the post-settlement history of your site from deeds and other records and longtime residents of the neighborhood.)

Of particular help in matching native plants and plantings to small sites like ours is Mariette Nowak's *Birdscaping in the Midwest* (see Chapter 6). She organizes her book by categories of gardens, each based on a different ecosystem or set of conditions; at least one set of conditions she describes is almost certain to be similar to your own. Nowak's lists of trees, shrubs, wildflowers, and grasses for each garden, e.g., prairie gardens, savanna gardens, maple woodland gardens, oak woodland gardens, pine woodland gardens, lowland woodland gardens, spruce-fir woodland gardens, are very helpful and detailed.

RESTORING OR STARTING ANEW, ALWAYS AIM FOR DIVERSITY

Although the plant communities that originally grew on your site are probably better adapted to it than most other plants, you shouldn't feel limited to them. Nor need authoritative species lists for plant communities inhibit you. Donald I. Dickmann, a highly respected scientist who describes Michigan's various forest communities, makes it clear, in fact, that the lists of plant species in his book merely help characterize different types of forest and don't represent hard and fast boundaries. Most reassuringly, he says, "The trees, other plants, and animals that inhabit Michigan can occur together in an almost infinite array of combinations and permutations" (p. 22). I find this statement, coming from a scientist, extremely liberating, even exhilarating. Yippee! I can plant anything I want wherever I want as long as it's native to my region and its requirements for growth match the conditions of the site. At the same time (sigh), I know I can't do exactly that. It's necessary, for one thing, to watch out for aggressive native plants that would take over smaller and less competitive plants and thus reduce diversity. For another, it's not always easy to introduce young plants into established plantings. For still another, even the most sunloving, drought-tolerant prairie wildflowers— to isolate a relatively small group of plants—are far from being interchangeable or compatible. Finally, the soil or microclimate may vary greatly from one part to another of even a quite small yard. So— when it comes right down to it—I'm free, sort of, to experiment.

By making your plantings as diverse as possible, subject to limitations imposed by your site, you both make the plantings more interesting and attractive to human viewers and provide a greater variety of food and shelter for wildlife. In this age of climate change, a more diverse planting may also have better chances of long-term sustainability than a less diverse one (see Chapter 31).

> Civilization is permeable, and could be as inhabited as the wild is.
>
> —Gary Snyder,
> *The Practice of the Wild*

- Don't exclude members of a native-plant community for trivial reasons. Gardening, like most pursuits, is subject to fashions and fads, and we need to resist whatever encourages us to create native-plant communities without basis in our region or even in nature. Past fads included gardens composed solely of plants with white flowers and, if possible, gray-green or gray-blue foliage. White Gardens were thought very ethereal and romantic. However, to exclude members of a native plant community on account of their color, or their height, or your distaste for them is not only frivolous but a serious disservice to wildlife. Particularly distressing, in my opinion, is the current prejudice in the horticultural industry and among the public against tall plants. Cultivars of native plants, whether shrubs, wildflowers, or grasses, always seem to be shorter than the wild plants. There also seems to be prejudice against native grasses and grasslike plants, whose flowers may be less showy than those of wildflowers but which form the essential matrix of many plant communities. In prairies and savannas, for example, the long roots of grasses absorb scarce rainwater and then slowly release it to the whole community.

DON'T SHUN DIFFICULTY

Do not be too timid and squeamish about your actions. All life is an experiment.

—Ralph Waldo Emerson,
Journals

tremely important to insects as host and nectar plants and to birds for their seed, and should by no means be excluded from prairie plantings. Nor should the big grasses, switchgrass (*Panicum virgatum*), Indian grass (*Sorgastrum nutans*), and big bluestem (*Andropogon gerardii*), all of them extremely valuable to wildlife as food plants and for shelter (including hibernating bumblebee queens).

Big bluestem grass (Andropogon gerardii) *blossoms profusely in July on its "turkey-foot" seedheads held eight feet above the ground, curving gracefully over the prairie wildflowers. It's worth a close look—with a magnifying glass—for the delicate purples and yellows of its flowers.*

- Love *aggressive* native plants too. Under the right circumstances, many plants, native or nonnative, sun-loving or shade-loving, tall or short, can be aggressive. However, excluding plants that may become aggressive will result in plantings that lack variety and interest and, worse, are much less valuable to wildife than they might be. Find out, before planting them, which plants are likely be aggressive (many native-plant nurseries include such information in their catalogs, or can provide it), and take measures (more about these later) to keep them under control. In our yard, the most aggressive wildflowers have been sunflowers (*Helianthus* spp.), even those that grow in the shade; goldenrods (*Solidago* spp.); some species of coreopsis (*Coreopsis palmata*, sand or prairie coreopsis, and *Coreopsis tripteris*, tall coreopsis); some silphiums (*Silphium integrifolium*, rosinweed, and *Silphium perfoliatum*, cup plant); green-headed coneflower (*Rudbeckia laciniata*); golden Alexanders (*Zizia aurea*); and brown-eyed Susans (*Rudbeckia triloba*). The latter two seed themselves especially profusely. However, these wildflowers, aggressive in our mesic yard, may be less aggressive in yours or under harsher conditions than they enjoy here. In any case, they are ex-

Some woodland and wetland plants are also likely to be aggressive. Among the former, in our mesic yard, Canada anemone (*Anemone canadensis*), and white snakeroot (*Eupatorium rugosum*); among the latter, Virginia waterleaf (*Hydrophyllum virginianum*), appendaged waterleaf (*Hydrophyllum appendiculatum*), and meadow rue (*Thalictrum dasycarpum*). Aggressive vines, in our mesic yard, include virgin's bower (*Clematis virginiana*), Virginia creeper (*Parthenocissus quinquefolia*), and moonseed (*Menispermum canadense*); aggressive shrubs, wild roses and common elderberry. These woodland and wetland plants, too, are extremely valuable to wildlife, especially the woody plants, and especially common elderberry (*Sambucus canadensis*). Gardeners concerned about preserving biodiversity simply have to learn to garden with aggressive and "opportunistic" plants.

Canada anemone (Anemone canadensis) *blooms profusely with lovely white flowers for several weeks in June, forms a woodland ground cover, and provides lots of extras for your neighbors and friends.*

If, however, you have a large site or difficult area, control may not even be an issue. In the right place, aggressive plants may solve some of your problems. Canada anemone, for example, will form a groundcover in a shaded area and compete successfully even with myrtle; and Virginia creeper will tolerate a lot of shade and cover practically anything. Common elderberry likes a little more sun but it too will grow just about anywhere. A combination of tough, aggressive grasses and forbs may be just the thing for an eroding hillside where not much seems to grow. Don't settle for a monoculture, and never give up on a difficult spot! There are wonderful native plants that *thrive* in poor conditions. The Brooklyn Botanic Garden guide to *Great Natives for Tough Places* will get you started (see "References" at the end of this chapter), and native-plant catalogs and growers will help you turn your headache into habitat.

How to Control "Opportunists"

1) Plant **only a few plants** of the aggressive species, and plant them together.

2) Locate the plants in **less than ideal conditions**. If we hadn't planted so many golden Alexanders in the first place, and put them in full sun, they probably wouldn't have been such a problem. A shadier location (or a drier one), for this plant at any rate, might have really inhibited its seed production and spread.

3) Give the potentially aggressive plant some **stiff competition** right from the start. If we hadn't put the Canada anemone in a brand-new bed, all by itself, it might not have been able to establish itself as such a rampant monoculture. If we'd combined it with other vigorous plants, meadow-rue and wood poppy, Canada violets and ferns, it probably would have behaved itself better. To put it bluntly, you can plant a bunch of aggressive plants together, stand out of the way, and watch them duke it out.

In prairie plantings started from seed, the amount of grass seed can be kept to a minimum (though this is expensive) in order to favor wildflowers, or forbs; and the wildflowers, or forbs, can be planted first and allowed to gain a foothold before they have to compete with prairie grasses.

4) **Confine or isolate** plants likely to become aggressive on your site. You can plant them on islands by themselves or, better, in combination with other aggressive plants and grasses. Islands can be defined in various ways: by the amount of sun or shade or water they receive, with borders of stones or branches, by mowing, or by the use of edging that goes deep into the ground. The latter method is particularly successful in controlling plants that clone themselves, as is the practice of planting them in large, deep plastic pots with the bottoms cut out.

5) If, in spite of everything, a plant makes a break for it and threatens to reduce the diversity of your planting, go back to basics and **pull it or dig it up**, or even cut off the offending stalks level with the ground, ideally when the plant is at the peak of its growth. You may not even have to dig up the roots. You can also share your excess with people and groups who want native plants and have appropriate spaces for these species. (There's always someone who wants a native "groundcover"; and there's your opportunity.) You should, of course, warn the recipients of your bounty that these plants are "opportunistic."

BUY FROM GROWERS
SPECIALIZING IN WILD MICHIGAN PLANTS

- Don't remove plants from natural or semi-natural areas. If they're native plants and protected, as orchids and certain other plants are, or state-listed as "Threatened" or of "Special Concern," it is, in fact, illegal to disturb them in any way. Removing plants from wild areas, even digging up a few plants from a friend's property, creates a disturbance that may allow invasive nonnative plants to gain a foothold. If the plants you've admired in wild or semi-wild areas are invasive nonnative plants that you've mistaken for native wildflowers, e.g., dame's rocket, money plant (both of which people mistakenly call phlox), Queen Anne's lace, orange daylilies, bouncing Bet, or wild daisies, you don't want to introduce them into your yard.

- Remove plants from the wild only when they're in imminent danger of being bulldozed. Try to plant these rescued plants in an area as similar as possible to where they came from and then keep a careful eye on them; the seeds of invasive nonnative plants may have come along with them. It's better to put rescued plants in areas that enjoy some kind of official protection rather than in your yard.

- Don't buy plants that seem to have been dug up from wild areas rather than propagated in nurseries. It's often hard to distinguish these plants from nursery-grown plants, but plants taken from the wild may seem to have been stuffed into their pots rather than grown there from seed. Sometimes their pots contain several plants, often of different species.

- **Don't buy plants from big-box stores** or conventional garden centers. You may not be able to tell whether they're cultivars rather than wild plants, which are generally more accessible and more valuable to wildlife than cultivars, e.g., they often provide more nectar. Another problem with plants sold at big-box stores or conventional garden centers is that you don't know where they come from, nor do the store's employees. Biologists have found that some plants sold as native species by large nurseries and garden centers may actually be exotics from other parts of the world, and many more may be incorrectly identified. Even if they are species native to your area, if their origin is North Carolina or Arkansas, they may behave quite differently here, e.g., be less hardy, than plants originating in Michigan.

Remember that specialized cultivars sometimes aren't used by pollinators. Flowers that have been drastically altered, such as those that are double or a completely different color than the wild species, often prevent pollinators from finding and feeding on the flowers. In addition, some altered plants don't contain the same nectar and pollen resources that attract pollinators to the wild types.

—From the excellent series of Regional Guides to "Selecting Plants for Pollinators," available at www.pollinator.org

- **Buy native plants and seeds from Michigan growers certified by the Michigan Native Plant Producers Association.** Plants and seeds raised by these growers come from Michigan stock whose sources are known. While native plants may be more expensive, initially, than nonnatives, they'll end up costing less. First, they are better adapted to local growing conditions and more likely to survive. Also, they'll require less support, e.g., less water and no fertilizer other than perhaps your own compost or compost tea. In addition, most of the native plants on the market are perennials and, unlike annuals, won't have to be renewed every year.

Get As Much Expert Help and Advice As You Can

- Develop friendships with the MNPPA growers who supply your native plants. They are a rich source of knowledge about native plants and informal advice. Make appointments to visit their nurseries when they aren't particularly busy, rather than visiting on sale days, which can be chaotic. Many growers will assess your site at no charge and then (for a fee) design, install, or maintain your plantings. Growers will also be willing to refer you to a professional consultant.

- Other sources of advice besides growers and professional designers and installers include faculty members in the biology, environmental studies, and geography departments of local universities, and organizations dedicated to conservation and restoration. Statewide organizations include the Wildflower Association of Michigan, the Michigan Botanical Club, and the Michigan Nature Association, this last a land trust covering the state. More local organizations are nature centers, local land trusts, and chapters of Wild Ones, Native Plants, Natural Landscapes, a national organization with several chapters in southern Michigan. This organization is dedicated to landscaping yards and other spaces with native plants. The Kalamazoo Area Chapter of Wild Ones offers free site visits to members.

Seek advice right from the start if your site, or part of your site, retains its presettlement vegetation, seems never to have been disturbed, and has not been invaded by nonnative plants. This is especially important if your site is a prairie fen, prairie, or savanna—ecosystems which development has practically erased from southern Michigan. In fact, the Wildlife Division of Michigan's Department of Natural Resources (MDNR) has developed a Landowner Incentive Program that provides assistance to landowners willing to manage their land as habitat for rare species.

- Federal programs designed to encourage landowners to restore former cropland or fallow fields to prairie or savanna include the Conservation Reserve Program (CRP), which is administered through local offices of the Farm Service Agency. A new program, CRP—SAFE (State Acres For wildlife Enhancement), now helps landowners create habitat for pollinators—wild and domestic bees and other insects, even birds—whose services in pollinating crops and wild plants are so essential. Another federal program, the Wildlife Habitat Incentives Program (WHIP), is administered through the Natural Resource Conservation Service (NRCS).

Always Remember: So Much Depends on You

> What we do in the home landscape ... is a reflection of how we see our relationship to the larger natural world.
>
> —Leslie Jones Sauer,
> *The Once and Future Forest*

- Native plants are proven to be more attractive and more sustaining to native wildlife, from the soil organisms to the insects and birds and other animals who *must* have a fair share of the earth's resources if they—and we—are to thrive, or even survive. Since there's not enough undisturbed land to sustain the earth's biodiversity, we gardeners must make up the difference—in our yards.

- **All of the earth's species are under serious stress,** from climate change, exploitation, development, pollution, and deliberate extermination. Many are threatened with extinction, and none more so than many of the insects largely responsible for pollinating and thus sustaining most of the earth's plant species. Those insects depend heavily on native plants. Most species of birds depend on the insects. So they all depend *on our choices*. Choose carefully, thoughtfully, compassionately, with a view to at least the next seven generations.

REFERENCES

Albert, Dennis A., and Patrick J. Comer. *Atlas of Early Michigan's Forests, Grasslands, and Wetlands: An Interpretation of the 1810–1850 General Land Office Survey.* East Lansing: Michigan State Univ. Press, 2008.

Dickman, Donald I. *Michigan Forest Communities: A Field Guide and Reference.* East Lansing: Michigan State University Extension, 2004.

Dunne, Niall (ed.). *Great Natives for Tough Places.* Brooklyn, NY: Brooklyn Botanic Garden, 2009. Since this is an "All-Region Guide," many of the plants listed and described are not native in our area, but usually there are Michigan natives in the same genus or family that will have much the same characteristics.

Herman, Kim D., et al. *Floristic Quality Assessment with Wetland Categories and Examples of Computer Applications for the State of Michigan*—Revised, 2nd ed. Lansing: Michigan Dept. of Natural Resources, Wildlife Division, Natural Heritage Program, 2001.

Tangley, Laura. "The Buzz on Native Pollinators," *National Wildlife*, June/July, 2009, pp. 40–46.

WEBSITES—NATIVE PLANT PRODUCERS

These MNPPA websites and their on-line catalogs contain a wealth of information, and most provide links to other very useful databases:

Hidden Savanna Nursery (Kalamazoo)—www.hiddensavanna.com.
Mary Ann's Michigan Trees and Shrubs (Paw Paw)—www.maryannstrees.com.
Native Connections (Three Rivers)—www.nativeconnections.net.
Sandhill Farm (Rockford)—for information, e-mail cherylt@iserv.net.
Wildtype Native Plant Nursery (Mason)—www.wildtypeplants.com.

6

Helpful Books on Native Plants and Natural Landscaping

I have always imagined that Paradise will be a kind of library.
—Jorge Luis Borges

Landscaping with Michigan's Native Plants

Druse, Ken, with Margaret Roach. *The Natural Habitat Garden.* New York: Clarkson Potter/Publishers, 1994. Beautiful photographs and valuable text.

Nowak, Mariette. *Birdscaping in the Midwest: A Guide to Gardening with Native Plants to Attract Birds.* Blue Mounds, WI: Itchy Cat Press, 2007. A splendid book, with ideas and lists to suit just about every site and objective.

Stein, Sara. *Noah's Garden: Restoring the Ecology of Our Own Backyards.* Boston: Houghton Mifflin, 1993. A wonderfully inspiring and informative classic.

_____. *Planting Noah's Garden: Further Adventures in Backyard Ecology.* Boston: Houghton Mifflin, 1997. Informative essays, plus very detailed instructions.

Steiner, Lynn M. *Landscaping with Native Plants of Michigan.* St. Paul: Voyageur Press, 2006.

_____. *Prairie-Style Gardens: Capturing the Essence of the American Prairie Wherever You Live.* Portland, OR: Timber Press, 2010.

Tallamy, Douglas W. *Bringing Nature Home: How You Can Sustain Wildlife with Native Plants.* Updated and Expanded edition, with Foreword by Rick Darke. Portland, OR: Timber Press, 2009.

Tylka, Dave. *Native Landscaping for Wildlife and People: How to Use Native Midwestern Plants to Beautify Your Property and Benefit Wildlife.* Jefferson City, MO: Missouri Dept. of Conservation, 2002. Focuses, in part, on attracting butterflies and bees.

Recognizing and Growing Michigan's Native Plants

Peterson and Audubon Society field guides depict and briefly describe many of Michigan's native trees, shrubs, wildflowers, and ferns. Particularly helpful in precisely identifying wildflowers (and some shrubs and vines) is *Newcomb's Wildflower Guide* (by Lawrence Newcomb). Also helpful are Stan Tekiela's small-format guides: one to Michigan trees, another to Michigan wildflowers.

The standard guides, however, are not very useful in identifying small seedlings: for help when it comes to differentiating your tender, new treasures from "weeds," see *The Tallgrass Prairie Center Guide to Seed and Seedling Identification in the Upper Midwest*, by Dave Williams (Univ. of Iowa Press, 2010).

Works listed below, however, do more than identify plants. They deal with them in sufficient detail to help people make selections for their yards and grow the plants successfully. Very helpful for specific information on characteristics and sun, water, and soil requirements for various species of wildflowers and grasses, and some shrubs and vines, is the yearly catalog of the Prairie Moon Nursery, in Winona, MN.

Also very informative in such matters are the catalogs for Wildtype Native Plant Nursery in Mason, MI (www.wildtypeplants.com) and for Native Connections, Three Rivers, MI (www.nativeconnections.net). The on-line catalog for Hidden Savanna Nursery, Kalamazoo, MI, provides similar information and important links to other sources (www.hiddensavanna.com). All the members of the Michigan Native Plant Producers Association (www.mnppa.org) will provide specific information in response to e-mail questions.

Michigan's Flora (comprehensive)

Herman, Kim D., et al. *Floristic Quality Assessment with Wetland Categories and Examples of Computer Applications for the State of Michigan*. Lansing, MI: Michigan Dept. of Natural Resources, 2001. A little technical, but very simple once you get the hang of it, this publication's "Michigan Plants Database" provides an assessment of the "quality" (rarity) of each species of Michigan plant (trees, shrubs, vines, grasses, and sedges), whether it's a native or not, and the habitats in which it's most commonly found. You do need to know the botanical name of the species you're interested in.

Voss, Edward G. *Michigan Flora*. Bloomfield Hills: Cranbrook Institute of Science and Univ. of Michigan Herbarium, 1972 (Pt. 1), 1985 (Pt. 2), 1996 (Pt. 3). One needs little or no botanical expertise to begin getting acquainted with and to profit greatly from the drawings, distribution maps, and other features of this *immensely valuable work*.

Reznicek, A. A., E. G. Voss, and B. S. Walters. *Michigan Flora Online*. University of Michigan. Web. 2-14-2011. http://michiganflora.net/home.aspx. **This revised edition of Voss's classic work** is now available online and is quite easy to browse and search. In addition to virtually all the information included in the published *Michigan Flora*, the online version includes the spore-bearing vascular plants (ferns, horsetails, club mosses, etc.), taxonomic and nomenclatural changes, the coefficient of conservatism, the coefficient of wetness, and the wetness index (plus photos in most cases—but **not** the drawings from *Michigan Flora*). It does help to know what you're looking for, and to know either the scientific name, the genus, or some alternate common names: e.g., a search for "rattlesnake master" yields no result, but "rattlesnake-master" gets you what you want.

Native Trees, Shrubs, and Vines

Barnes, Burton V., and Warren H. Wagner, Jr. *Michigan Trees: A Guide to the Trees of Michigan and the Great Lakes Region*. Ann Arbor: Univ. of Michigan Press, 1981.

Cullina, William. *Native Trees, Shrubs, and Vines: A Guide to Using, Growing, and Propagating North American Woody Plants*. Boston: Houghton Mifflin, 2002. Indicates the value of each plant for wildlife.

Hightshoe, Gary. *Native Trees, Shrubs, and Vines for Urban and Rural America: A Planting Design Manual for Environmental Designers*. New York: John Wiley and Sons, 1988.

Smith, Norman F. *Trees of Michigan and the Upper Great Lakes*. 6th ed., rev. Lansing: Thunder Bay Press, 1995.

Wildflowers and Grasses

Brown, Lauren. *Grasses: An Identification Guide*. Boston: Houghton Mifflin, 1979. Includes some sedges and rushes.

Cullina, William. *The New England Wildflower Society Guide to Growing and Propagating Wildflowers of the United States and Canada*. Boston: Houghton Mifflin, 2000. Indispensable if you want to grow plants from seed.

Ladd, Doug, and Frank Oberle. *Tallgrass Prairie Wildflowers*. Helena, MT: The Nature Conservancy/Falcon Press, 1995.

Runkel, Sylvan T., and Dean M. Roosa. *Wildflowers of the Tallgrass Prairie: The Upper Midwest*. Ames: Iowa State Univ. Press, 1996. Handsome photographs, interesting cultural information.

Wells, James R., Frederick W. Case, Jr., and T. Lawrence Mellichamp. *Wildflowers of the Western Great Lakes Region*. Bloomfield Hills: Cranbrook Institute of Science, 1999. Good photographs of wildflowers, arranged by habitat.

(For additional guides to prairie and wetland wildflowers, see the following section.)

Michigan's Native-Plant Communities

A few nursery catalogs describe installing and maintaining prairie plantings in very helpful detail. They include the catalog of Prairie Nursery, in Westfield, WI, a pioneer in prairie restoration (www.prairienursery.com), and that of Native Connections, in Three Rivers, MI (www.nativeconnections.net).

Prairies and Savannas

Kurtz, Carl. *A Practical Guide to Prairie Reconstruction*. Iowa City: Univ. of Iowa Press, 2001.

Packard, Stephen, and Cornelia Mutel, eds. *The Tallgrass Restoration Handbook for Prairies, Savannas, and Woodlands*. Society for Ecological Restoration. Washington, D.C.: Island Press, 1997. This has been the "bible" of large-scale restorationists, but is accessible and useful to beginners.

Smith, Daryl, et al. *The Tallgrass Prairie Center Guide to Prairie Restoration in the Upper Midwest.* Iowa City, IA: Univ. of Iowa Press, 2010. This supplements and to some extent supercedes the above book. It includes useful information for native-plant gardeners.

Swink, Floyd, and Gerould Wilhelm. *Plants of the Chicago Region.* 4th ed. Indianapolis: Indiana Academy of Science, 1994.

Wasowski, Sally. *Gardening with Prairie Plants: How to Create Beautiful Native Landscapes.* Minneapolis: Univ. of Minnesota Press, 2002.

Woodlands

Darke, Rick. *The American Woodland Garden: Capturing the Spirit of the Deciduous Forest.* Portland: Timber Press, 2002.

Dickmann, Donald I. *Michigan Forest Communities: A Field Guide and Reference.* East Lansing: Michigan State Univ. Extension, 2004.

Packard, Stephen, and Cornelia Mutel, eds. *The Tallgrass Prairie Restoration Handbook for Prairies, Savannas, and Woodlands.* (See main entry above, under "Prairies.")

Sauer, Leslie Jones. *The Once and Future Forest: A Guide to Forest Restoration Strategies.* Washington, D.C.: Island Press, 1998. An invaluable book for anyone undertaking extensive woodland restoration, but containing useful information and insights for homeowners.

Wetlands

Chadde, Steve W. *A Great Lakes Wetland Flora.* 2nd ed. Calumet, MI: Pocketflora Press, 2002.

Crow, Garrett E., and C. Barre Hellquist. *Aquatic and Wetland Plants of Northeastern North America.* 2 vols. Madison, WI: Univ. of Wisconsin Press, 2000.

Cwikiel, Wilfred. *Living with Michigan's Wetlands: A Landowner's Guide.* Conway, MI: Tip of the Mitt Watershed Council, 1996.

Henderson, Carrol L., Carolyn J. Dindorf, and Fred J. Rozumalski. *Lakescaping for Wildlife and Water Quality.* St. Paul: Minnesota Dept. of Natural Resources, No date. Includes very helpful charts on plants' cultural requirements.

PART II

PARTICULARS

He who wishes to see a Vision;
a perfect Whole, Must see it in its Minute Particulars.
—William Blake, *Jerusalem* (1820)

Yes. Feet on earth. Knock on wood. Touch stone. Good luck to all.
—Edward Abbey, *Desert Solitaire* (1968)

… let us open our leaves like a flower and be passive and receptive …
taking hints from every noble insect that favors us with a visit
—John Keats, *Letters* (19 February 1818)

Eastern tiger swallowtails, male and female, on cup plant   Amelia Hansen

7

GARDENS FOR POLLINATORS

WITH A SCHEDULE OF WHEN NATIVE NECTAR PLANTS START BLOOMING IN SOUTHWEST MICHIGAN

Is it not reasonable that we attempt to embrace all
life-forms in our gardens in an effort to restore
the balance that the garden, itself, has displaced?
—Eric Grissell, *Insects and Gardens*

Most serious gardeners are familiar with the idea of a butterfly garden or a hummingbird garden, with a selection of plants especially attractive to these colorful and fascinating species. But most such gardens are very limited in their support of even those species they are designed to attract; moreover, they fail to provide support for either full life cycles or any broad spectrum of wild creatures, especially the many varieties of pollinators that all life depends upon.

A TRUE GARDEN IS AN ECOSYSTEM

The idea of a garden for pollinators comes from a brilliant and moving book, *The Forgotten Pollinators*, by Stephen L. Buchmann and Gary Paul Nabhan (1996). In it they discuss the intimate relationships that have evolved between plants and their pollinators and the disastrous consequences of disrupting or severing these relationships. Near the end of the book, Nabhan describes his "pollinator garden" near Tucson, Arizona—a garden intended for bees, birds, bats, butterflies, and moths, complete with host plants for the larvae of the latter two. Gardeners in southwest Michigan and elsewhere would do well to follow his model by designing gardens to help support not only butterflies or hummingbirds but also bees, wasps, moths, beetles, flies, and other pollinators.

Using native trees, shrubs, wildflowers, and grasses, a garden for pollinators provides nectar and pollen throughout the growing season and attempts to meet pollinators' other essential needs as well, such as host plants for butterflies and moths. Such a garden also serves as a happy hunting ground for creatures, including beneficial insects and spiders, that seek insects to prey upon or parasitize. Hummingbirds, in fact, pursue insects as well as nectar: they themselves eat both and, like almost all other terrestrial bird species of North America, feed their young entirely on insects and other arthropods such as spiders. In the process, they pollinate some of the most beautiful plants of our region: wild columbine (*Aquilegia canadensis*) and cardinal flower (*Lobelia cardinalis*).

57

Portrait of a ruby-throated hummingbird.

Few of us fully realize that about 80 percent of flowering plants must be pollinated by animals in order to produce fruit or seed. According to Gary A. Dunn, "bees are probably the most significant and reliable pollinators of plants, and most flow-ering plants would not be able to survive without them" (p. 246). Nor, ultimately, would we humans. While bees are the chief pollinators of wild and cultivated plants, they are by no means the only ones. Other pollinators in southwestern Michigan include wasps and sawflies, which, like bees, are members of the Order Hymenoptera; some fly species (Order Diptera); butterflies, moths, and skippers (Order Lepidoptera); many kinds of beetles (Order Coleoptera); and the ruby-throated hummingbird, the only hummingbird species that usually frequents our region. Although Michigan species of bats, unlike some in the West, don't feed on nectar and thus don't serve as pollinators, they consume large numbers of insects, especially mosquitoes; so give them welcome to your garden. They won't get in your hair.

THE NEED FOR *NATIVE* BEES

The only bees familiar to most people are European honey bees (*Apis mellifera*), the hive-inhabiting, honey–producing bees that guard their hoards from their veiled keepers and are routinely trucked around the country as industrial crops come into bloom. These domesticated insects arrived with early settlers in the seventeenth century and are currently the most important pollinators of our crops. But managed bees are in decline, afflicted by diseases and parasites and most recently by Colony Collapse Disorder—its causes still undetermined. The number of managed honey bee hives in the U.S. is half what it was in the late 1940s, and feral honey bees almost completely disappeared during the late 1980s to mid '90s (Mader, p. 39).

Also thought to be in decline are our wild, native bees, which in many ways are more effective pollinators than honey bees. Tristram Seidler, staff ecologist for the New England Wildflower Society, says that native bees are "at least 10 times more efficient than honey bees." According to him, they fly farther between flowers, thus achieving better cross-pollination, and even visit more plants per hour than honey bees. Bumble bees and some other native bees, through buzz pollination (vibration of their muscles), are capable of shaking loose more

The black and yellow bumble first on wing
To buzz among the sallows early flowers
Hiding its nest in holes from fickle spring
Who stints his rambles with her frequent showers.

—John Clare, "Wild Bees" (1820)

pollen from plants' anthers than honey bees—pollen then carried by the native bees to other plants (Raver, p. D9). Native bees, especially bumble bees, are willing to forage in colder, damper weather than honey bees. Native bees have also been shown to improve crop yields and are considered to be especially helpful in the pollination of many plants grown in our region, including apples, blueberries, cherries, peppers, squash, melons, and tomatoes, increasing the fruit set and size of the latter. A large percentage of honey bees that you see are accomplishing little pollination, perhaps none at all; they're effective only because they can be concentrated, by beekeepers, in such large numbers (Mader, p. 26).

Unlike honey bees, native bees don't live in large colonies or provide us with honey. Of the roughly 4000 species of native bees in North America, 90 percent are solitary rather than social, nesting independently, though sometimes in such close proximity as to form large groups (Mader, p. 27); the others, mainly bumble bees and some sweat bees, are social. About 70 percent of native bees are ground-nesting, needing direct access to the soil's surface. Most of the others nest in dead wood, standing or fallen, often in abandoned beetle tunnels. A few nest in the stems of woody plants which they are able to hollow out. Bumble bees "require small cavities, either in tree boles, underground (often in old rodent burrows), or under clumps of fallen grass, in which to raise their young, as well as undisturbed duff in which queens burrow and hibernate through the winter" (Vaughan and Black, p. 81).

About 300 species of wild bees are native to Michigan, including perhaps as many as 20 bumble bee species. These and other native pollinators suffer from loss, fragmentation, and degradation of habitat, and from pesticide use. Local populations, and some entire species, are simply disappearing, all over the world. Their loss would have a devastating effect not only on human food crops but on the entire food web and whole ecosystems.

Michigan's native bees, even though they don't provide us with honey, deserve our gratitude and respect. Instead, they are often regarded with unwarranted fear, increasingly instilled in children by their parents. In 13 years of gardening with native plants—walking through them, weeding them, and moving them around—my husband and I have never been stung by anything. Maybe the bees in our yard recognize us. Biologist Nigel Raine maintains that honey bees are able to recognize human faces (Whitman, p. 8). However, most native bees are simply unlikely to sting anyone. Indeed, male bees or wasps cannot sting at all (a bee's sting is a modified ovipositor, a structure used to deposit eggs). Most native bees are solitary and, having no colonies to protect, are extremely docile and rarely sting unless they are physically harmed, such as stepping on one with a bare foot. Bumble bees, which do form social colonies, can become defensive around their nests, but when gathering pollen they and other bees have more important things to do than to bother with us (Mader, p. 40).

Wasps can be more aggressive, but we ought to try harder to co-exist even with them. Some species hunt gypsy moth caterpillars. In fact, "among the social wasps, solitary wasps, and ants [also members of the Order Hymenoptera], many different sorts of insect . . . species are harvested from the garden. For this reason . . . the insect order Hymenoptera is considered one of the preeminent forces for insect population control" (Grissell, p. 185).

Amazing—an order so important for both insect control *and* pollination!

And speaking of ants, they're not only helpful scavengers and predators, they're vitally important in both aerating and enriching the soil, mixing in organic debris, and bringing mineral nourishment up from the depths into depleted topsoil.

We Need Them; They Need Native Habitat

One of the many scientists who suggest that a yard can be "something more than [lawn and] a bunch of flowers" is Gordon Frankie, an entomologist at the University of California at Berkeley. He hates turf, plastic sheeting, and very thick mulch—impenetrable barriers to the ground-nesting bees which constitute the majority of our native bees. He also calls domesticated roses "horrible," because their tightly bunched petals keep bees from reaching the nectar and pollen within. In a large experimental garden near the Berkeley campus, Frankie has discovered, among other things, that wild bees prefer native to nonnative plants:

> "We have a really good idea of what works now," Frankie says. Today, the experimental bee garden has a smattering of non-native plants that the bees like, but the team has discovered that *native bees are six times more likely to visit the native plants with which they have evolved* (Jenkins, p. 64—emphasis added).

According to a fact sheet from the Xerces Society for Invertebrate Conservation, however, native plants are only *four* times more attractive than nonnative plants to native bees ("Upper Midwest Plants for Native Bees," www.xerces.org). Whichever the case, there is a clear preference on the part of native bees for the nectar and pollen of native plants. There is also conclusive evidence that native plants serve butterflies and moths, also important pollinators, far better than nonnatives do. In his splendid book *Bringing Nature Home*, Douglas Tallamy demonstrates that the caterpillars of butterflies and moths greatly prefer to eat the native plants with which they evolved rather than the nonnative plants of other continents.

These and other herbivorous insects play a crucial role in transferring the sun's energy up the food web, from plants to other arthropods, amphibians, birds, and small mammals. Tallamy supplements the evidence presented in his book with a website that not only links Lepidoptera with their specific host plants but also ranks individual native and nonnative plants for their usefulness as host plants to Lepidoptera. While his evidence of Lepidoptera-host plant relationships, compiled from scientific literature, is confined to Eastern states, it nevertheless has enormous implications for our region, whose flora is similar in many respects. The website is http://copland.udel.edu/~dtallamy/host/index.html.

> The life-sustaining matrix is built of green plants with legions of microorganisms and mostly small, obscure animals—in other words, weeds and bugs.
>
> —E. O. Wilson, *The Diversity of Life*

There are many advantages to using native plants for pollinator gardens or the more limited butterfly gardens:

- Native plants, blooming in sequence, provide nectar and pollen all season long—nectar and pollen which seem to be preferred by native bees and perhaps by other pollinators as well.

- Recent research demonstrates that gathering pollen from a variety of native plants strengthens the immune systems of bees, increasingly important given the drastic declines in bee populations (Carder, p. 67).

- Crucially important for pollination, most species of butterflies and moths require, or greatly prefer, native plants as the host plants for their eggs and caterpillars.

The list of native plants that follows this essay focuses on plants considered good sources of nectar and pollen. Almost all of them also serve as host plants for at least one species of Lepidoptera, and many as host plants for an impressive number of species. Among the wildflowers, native asters serve as host plants for over 100 different species of butterflies and moths, and native perennial sunflowers for 75 species. In contrast, nonnative *Buddleia davidii* (butterfly bush), a shrub justly celebrated for its nectar and a mainstay of so-called butterfly gardens, is a host plant for *only one* Lepidoptera species. Another problem with this shrub is that it may escape into natural areas and overwhelm native ecosystems.

A POLLINATOR GARDEN CONSISTS OF MANY LAYERS

Generally, we use shrubs and trees in our home landscapes solely for their practical and decorative value to ourselves. Large trees provide our dwellings with shade and protection from weather; smaller trees and shrubs serve us as foundation plants and as single-species hedges and privacy screens, occasionally as a special "specimen" planting or to delineate a special space. Most urban yards, however, contain little or no true understory of shrubs and small trees or, at best, one composed of nonnative species.

Native shrubs and trees, however, are especially important for a complete pollinator garden. Not only can they serve as backdrops and windbreaks for plantings of native wildflowers, they are invaluable as host plants for hundreds of species of Lepidoptera. Among tree species, native oaks, for example, support 534 species of Lepidoptera; native maples, 297; native pines, 201; native walnuts, 129. Among shrub species, native serviceberries support 124 species; native dogwoods, 118 species; arrowwood viburnum (*Viburnum dentatum*), 104; elderberries, 42 (figures from Tallamy's website, 4/19/09). Moreover, a carefully planned understory offers much more than host plants for Lepidoptera; it also provides shelter and nesting areas for birds, caterpillars and other insects as food for their nestlings, plus berries and other fruits as food throughout the year.

The early blooming and fruiting of serviceberry make it doubly important, for early pollinators and for migrants returning when food is still scarce.

Grasses and sedges are also important to pollinators. They are host plants for some butterflies, especially skippers. Bunch grasses such as little bluestem (*Schizachyrium scoparium*) and prairie dropseed (*Sporobolus heterolepis*) are potential nesting sites for colonies of bumble bees and provide overwintering protection for many insects. Such grasses and a variety of sedges also serve as important matrix for the wildflowers that provide nectar and pollen.

As gardeners trying to support wildlife, we must make full use of the extremely valuable information provided by Frankie, Tallamy, and many others as to the needs of insects and birds. Above all, we must share our newfound knowledge, persuading friends and neighbors to join us in creating an ever larger neighborhood of polllinator gardens.

THERE ARE MANY WAYS TO HELP

Avoid Cultivars and Chemicals

It's important to use not only native but also genuinely wild plants, instead of cultivars derived from them. Cultivars are often shorter and more compact than their wild ancestors; or they have more flowers or double flowers or flowers of a different color, shape, or scent; or they bloom at a different time—features that may be confusing to pollinators or make the plants less helpful to them. Some cultivars are reported to have less—or less accessible—nectar than their wild forebears; and shorter plants are likely to make pollinators more vulnerable to cats and other predators.

People concerned with supporting pollinators and other wildlife should avoid the use of pesticides. Neo-nicotinoids, a class of systemic insecticides often used to treat seeds, foliage, or roots, may eventually concentrate in nectar and pollen, poisoning pollinators (Mader, p. 81). Even "organic" or "natural" pesticides, including Bt (*Bacillus thuringiensis*), can be dangerous. Herbicides should be avoided too, for they destroy plants on which pollinators depend for nectar and pollen.

Provide Basic Needs

The basic requirements of native bees have been suggested already: these include water and clay soil (for mason bees, which build their nests with mud); bare, undisturbed ground (a south-facing slope, if possible) for ground-nesting bees; dead wood, including standing trees, stumps, logs,

downed branches, and plants with hollow or pithy stems for wood-nesting bees; and undisturbed leaf litter for bumble bee queens to burrow into for the winter. For the most comprehensive guide to bee conservation, see Eric Mader's *Attracting Native Pollinators*. This extremely readable and useful book, published by the Xerces Society for Invertebrate Conservation, contains detailed information about native bees' nesting habits and how to create nesting areas and nests for them. As the Society's web site emphasizes, even amidst all the news of pollinator declines, there is still good news: "pollinators can survive, even thrive, in small patches of habitat and we can all contribute to their conservation" (www.xerces.org).

Butterflies' basic needs include flowers planted in same-species groups, an arrangement that probably saves energy for every kind of pollinator. Also helpful to butterflies are puddles of water and of mud; a dish of salty water (preferably sea salt—more minerals) and a sponge for butterflies to light on; warm, smooth rocks for basking; stalk and leaf litter in flowerbeds and under trees (winter shelter for larvae and cocoons and helpful to insects in general); and a brush pile for shelter. Too much clean-up in fall or spring may, in our region, mean the destruction of butterfly and moth caterpillars and cocoons on or near the ground. Cocoons of the spectacular Polyphemus moth, for instance, may lie among the fallen leaves of its woody host plants. Indeed, too much emphasis on keeping things neat is not good for pollinators. Those spreading patches of violets in the lawn? They may be harboring some

Many trees and shrubs serve as host plants for Polyphemus caterpillars, including oaks, maples, pines, birches, hawthorns, black cherry, elderberry, blueberries, grapes, willows, hickories, and American sycamore. The Polyphemus is one of our biggest moths, with wingspan of nearly six inches.

overwintering caterpillars of the great spangled fritillary, and they'll provide nectar for early spring azures. Those messy stray tufts of grass? Cocoons of the truly spectacular Cecropia moth may be attached to such tufts of grass at the feet of its woody hosts. The unsightly brush pile you want to get rid of? Probably much more useful for hibernating butterflies than those attractive-looking butterfly houses, which function mainly as garden ornaments. Whatever your questions, you'll find a lot of help in Janet Marinelli's *The Wildlife Gardener's Guide.*

From this rumpled cocoon emerges the largest and one of the most spectacular North American moths, the Cecropia, with six-inch wingspan.

A L-o-o-ong Blooming Season

At the conclusion of this essay, you'll find lists of plants in order of their bloom times in our area. Gardeners and pollinators are agreed on at least one thing: they like to have flowers coming into bloom all season long. Here in southwest Michigan, late-blooming flowers in our yards may be especially helpful to two migrating pollinators (those beginning their journey from our area as well as those from further north as they pass through): monarch butterflies and ruby-throated hummingbirds. You should keep your nectar feeders up until October 15 for the benefit of hummingbird migrants. Early flowers, of course, help awakening and emerging insects as well as hummingbirds, which may arrive in southern Michigan as early as the middle of April. By the time monarchs arrive, in late May, nectar is more readily available. Buchmann and Nabhan illustrate, in harrowing detail, the multiplying dangers that these and other migratory pollinators face as they negotiate increasing development in Central and North America.

Bee experts Vaughan and Black emphasize the importance of providing nectar and pollen for bees *especially at the beginning and end of the growing season*. They first point out that, depending on the species, solitary bees may emerge from early spring to late summer and that bumble bees may be active as early as February and as late as November. They then show how important early-blooming and late-blooming plants are to reproductive success:

> When forage is available earlier in the growing season (such as willow, red bud, maple…), freshly emerged, overwintering bumble bee queens are more successful in establishing their colonies. Also, some solitary bees produce multiple generations each year, so reproductive success in the spring and early summer can lead to larger populations in the mid- to late-summer, when many crops are in bloom … When plants such as goldenrod and asters are in bloom, some native bee species, as well as honey bees, will benefit from the abundant late-season forage. For example,

the next year's bumble bee queens will be able to go into hibernation with more energy reserves than they would otherwise (Vaughan and Black, p. 83).

Provide W-i-i-ide Variety

In addition to providing nectar and pollen throughout the growing season, gardens for pollinators should include a wide variety of flowers. Bees and other creatures in search of nectar and pollen have distinct preferences as to flower scent, color, and form. The bees tend to seek out scented flowers of any color except pure red. They prefer flowers that are radially symmetrical (producing two similar halves when divided through the middle along any axis) and fairly shallow in depth. The flowers may be tubular, as with both the disk and ray flowers of composites, the disk flowers being packed together in the center with the ray flowers forming an outer ring of "petals." These daisylike flowers include asters, coneflowers, and sunflowers, and bees seem to like the sturdy landing platforms they provide. But these "pollinator syndromes," the preferred plant characteristics noted here for bees and below for other pollinators, are by no means rigid requirements. For example, enjoy watching a bumble bee muscle its way into and out of the tubular and almost closed flower of a bottle gentian (*Gentian andrewsii*).

The recent development of the theory of pollination syndromes has helped scientists to better understand how "convergent evolution," the interaction between plants and pollinators, leads to specialized adaptations and greater diversity of both—just one instance of the wondrously complex, interdependent, and ever-changing web of life (Mader, pp. 19–20). For more information about pollinator syndromes, see the table provided by Buchmann and Nabhan, pp. 66–67.

If you should ever doubt the intelligence of bees, consider that despite having a brain about the size of a grass seed, they are capable of very complex calculations as to the most efficient routes between flowers. Unlike human beings, with brains thousands of times larger, *bees don't waste energy*.

The Lepidoptera—butterflies, moths, and skippers—also thrive on variety. As larvae, they make use of the leaves, stems, and other parts of their respective host plants. However, according to Robert Michael Pyle, "very few butterfly species cause significant damage to garden plants" (p. 149); and "only a small percentage of moth species may be considered pests of food and fiber. The rest are benign or beneficial" (p. 205). Adult lepidopterans generally feed on nectar or other liquids, and their favored "butterfly" flowers tend to be brightly colored (red, orange, yellow, or blue), have a deep narrow tube or spur, and occur in clusters, e.g., the flowers of composites or the clustered flowers of milkweeds or *Eupatorium* species (Joe Pye weeds,

Hummingbird clearwing moth on swamp milkweed. Hovering like a hummingbird, it feeds on the wing, with its long proboscis, in broad daylight.

Take Back the Night   Ladislav Hanka

Our obsession with illuminating the darkness causes problems for most moths, which find mates and food under cover of darkness but are attracted and confused by light. Some cultures regard moths as ghostly embodiment for spirits of the dead; to interfere with them is to risk retribution. Let moths take back the night; they help to pollinate 80 per cent of our flora.

bonesets, etc.). Strong "petals," i.e. the ray flowers that surround the disk flowers of composites, and rounded or flat-topped clusters give butterflies a good landing platform. "Butterfly flowers," like those preferred by bees, tend to be scented.

Sphinx or hawk moths—like hummingbirds—are able to hover while reaching with their long proboscises the nectar in deep, tubular flowers. Most are night-flying, though some, e.g., hummingbird or clearwing moths, fly during the day and are so large they're difficult, at a distance, to distinguish from hummingbirds. Most moths, however, use more narrowly tubular flowers than hummingbirds do and favor pale scented flowers of white to green. Smaller moths, though attracted to the same scents and colors, use flowers with somewhat shorter tubes than those used by sphinx moths.

It's unfortunate that most moths, because of their generally drab colors and nocturnal lives, go unnoticed and undervalued. Charles Darwin was the first scientist to notice that moths are important pollinators. There are more than 10,000 species of moths in North America, as opposed to only about 800 species of butterflies; and they're extremely important as both generalist and specialist pollinators. Respect their need for darkness. Unless you want to attract them for study and wonderment, don't confuse them with lots of outside lighting. Motion lights should keep both you and the moths sufficiently safe.

VARIETY IS NATURE'S WAY

Not only is a wide variety of plants necessary in a true pollinator garden, the pollinators themselves come in a great diversity of forms. Many kinds of beetles (Order Coleoptera) cross-pollinate plants as they forage and are consequently considered pollinators. They are said to be attracted to large bowl-shaped, white or pale flowers having lots of pollen and a fruity or spicy fragrance. Plants reported to be popular with beetles include *Oenothera* species (evening primroses and sundrops) and large-flowered *Cornus* (dogwood) species. Maybe these or other flowers will attract fireflies, the charismatic beetles that seem the very essence of summer as they flicker in the darkness of hot, still nights. As larvae, fireflies often prey on the larvae of slugs and snails; and as adults, some species may feed on pollen and nectar.

Pollinators may help in many ways to sustain the diversity of your garden and keep it in balance. In addition to pollinating plants, some wasps and beetles are also considered beneficial insects, i.e. insects that prey on or parasitize other insects and thus help to protect crops grown commercially or in household gardens. Some can even act as biocontrols for invasive plants. According to Anna Fiedler and her colleagues, insect predators, "feeding both as young and as adults," include not only some beetles but also some true bugs, flies, and lacewings. The most common parasitoids, they report, are small wasps (Fiedler, 2008).

> Bugs are not going to inherit the earth. They own it now. So we might as well make peace with the landlord.
>
> —Tom Eisner,
> Xerces Society

Although they feed on other insects, most predatory and parasitoid insects still need a variety of nectar plants because many of them, usually as adults, forage for pollen and nectar, nutrition necessary to increase their life span and ability to lay eggs. According to Janet Marinelli, in her excellent discussion of "A Buffet for Beneficial Insects" (pp.

94–101), predators and parasitoids are often attracted to the small flowers of umbelliferous plants. The most familiar umbelliferous plants—dill, parsley, and other culinary herbs—are not, however, native to our shores. In your native garden, you can provide attractive umbelliferous plants from early to late in the growing season: *Zizia aurea* (golden Alexander—May), *Angelica atropurpurea* (angelica—June), *Allium cernuum* (nodding wild onion—June), and *Eryngium yuccifolium* (rattlesnake master—July). Milkweeds and especially the daisylike flowers of composites—asters, coneflowers, goldenrods, sunflowers—are also reported to appeal to beneficial insects.

Even in a hummingbird garden, a wide variety of plants is important. While the ideal hummingbird flower is tubular, both wide and deep, red or reddish, and unscented, hummingbirds are known to make use of flowers of all different colors, including blue and even white. I've seen them nectar on tall bellflower (*Campanula americana*) and great blue lobelia (*Lobelia siphilitica*), both of which have medium-blue flowers. And I've read that pale flowers—white and blue—are especially appealing to hummingbirds at dawn and dusk, perhaps because they observe the same phenomenon we do, the strange luminescence of these flowers in twilight.

Nor do hummingbirds limit themselves to tubular flowers. If you see them on, for instance, daisylike composites such as black-eyed Susans and coneflowers, they're in search of the small insects and spiders that are part of their own diet and are absolutely essential to the diet of their nestlings, the same as for almost all other terrestrial bird species. And for their nests, hummingbirds make use of soft fibers from *Salix discolor* (pussywillow) and *Osmunda cinnamomea* (cinnamon fern), as well as fluff from dandelions and thistles.

EVEN "POLLINATOR GARDENS" TOO LIMITED A CONCEPT?

To read Eric Grissell's *Insects and Gardens* is to realize that even a "pollinator garden" isn't exactly the right concept. To be sure, it's better than the more exclusive "butterfly" or "hummingbird" garden. But what true garden lacks dragonflies, with their bright bodies and glittering wings? Dragonflies eat vast quantities of mosquitoes, rather than nectar and pollen, so they are definitely beneficial insects, if not to crops at least to us humans. Male mosquitoes, however, feed on nectar and perhaps serve as pollinators in the process. And what gardener would exclude daddy-long-legs or harvestmen, those exquisite angular creatures, technically neither insects nor spiders, that seem to function in the garden as scavengers or predators or both (Grissell, p. 29). Even insect-haters don't despise these compelling and nonthreatening species. As Grissell makes clear to readers by the end of his book, "all insects [and daddy-long-legs and spiders too] should be invited into the garden, if only to take care of each other in their ordinary predator-prey interactions—the natural way, that is" (pp. 279–80).

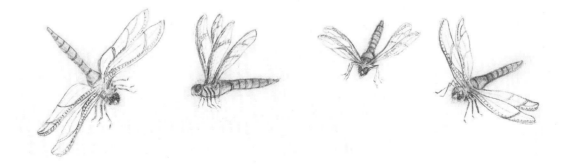

And may your garden, whatever its focus or whatever it's called, be as diverse in native plant species as possible, be welcoming to as many pollinators and other creatures as possible, and eventually take in your whole yard. As well as your whole heart.

Nectar and Pollen for Pollinators all Season Long

Dates when plants bloom in southwest Michigan (and everywhere else) are variable and to some extent depend on weather as well as the plants' immediate situation, e.g., amount of sun, kind of exposure, etc. Consequently, this schedule is meant only to suggest the rough order in which plants usually come into bloom. Under each month, I first list woody plants and then forbs (wildflowers). Sometimes I refer to plants by species, sometimes by genus.

Plants reported to be attractive to hummingbirds are followed by a capital "H"; however, this designation doesn't mean that a plant's flowers are attractive only to hummingbirds and not to other pollinators.

Gordon Frankie recommends deadheading plants—cutting off dead and dying blooms—in order to keep plants blooming (thus supplying nectar and pollen) rather than producing seed—but I've never tried this with native plants. And on the whole I prefer to provide a bountiful variety of species and blooming times and let each plant follow its own natural bent of flowering and seed-forming.

Plants blooming in April (or earlier)

Arctostaphylos uva-ursi	(Bearberry)
Cercis canadensis	(Eastern redbud)—H
Cornus florida	(Flowering dogwood)
Lindera benzoin	(Spicebush)
Pedicularis canadensis	(Lousewort, Wood betony)—H
Polemonium reptans	(Jacob's ladder)
Prunus americanus	(Wild plum)—bloomed very late April, 2009.
Rhus species	(Sumacs)
Salix species	(Willows)
Sambucus pubens	(Red elderberry)—bloomed very late April, 2009.
Aquilegia canadensis	(Wild columbine)—H
Caltha palustris	(Marsh marigold)
Castilleja coccinea	(Indian paintbrush)—H
Dicentra cucullaria	(Dutchman's breeches)
Fragaria virginiana	(Wild strawberry)
Geranium maculatum	(Wild geranium)
Mertensia virginica	(Virginia bluebell)—H
Pedicularis canadensis	(Lousewort, wood-betony)—H
Ranunculus fascicularis	(Early buttercup)—very good early nectar source. Dormant in summer, with possible second bloom in September or October.
R. rhomboideus	(Prairie buttercup)—same as *fascicularis*, but taller (6")
Thalictrum dioicum	(Early meadow-rue)
Viola species	(Violets)

> The rich man is not he who has plenty of money, but he who
> has the means to live now in the luxurious surroundings
> given us by early spring.
>
> —Anton Chekhov

NOTE: Exotic weeds providing early nectar and pollen include dandelions, clovers, wild mustards, and purple deadnettles, so you might not want to remove them unless there are plenty of other sources nearby.

Plants that start blooming in May

Aesculus glabra	(Ohio buckeye)—H
Cornus canadensis	(Bunchberry)
Cornus racemosa	(Gray dogwood)
Cornus stolonifera	(Red-osier dogwood)
Crataegus species	(Hawthorns)—H
Malus coronaria	(wild crabapple)
M. ioensis	(prairie crabapple)
Nyssa sylvatica	(Black gum, black tupelo)
Prunus americana	(Wild plum)
P. pensylvanica	(Pin cherry)
P. serotina	(Wild black cherry)
P. virginiana	(Common chokecherry)
Ribes americanum	(Wild black currant)
Rubus occidentalis	(Black raspberry);
R. strigosus	(Wild red raspberry)

Vaccinium angustifolium	(Lowbush blueberry)
V. corymbosum	(Highbush blueberry)
Viburnum cassinoides	(Northern haw)
V. dentatum	(Smooth arrow-wood)
V. lentago	(Nannyberry)
V. rafinesquianum	(Downy arrow-wood)
V. trilobum	(Highbush cranberry)

Allium canadense	(Wild garlic)
Aquilegia canadensis	(Wild columbine)—H
Caulophyllum thalictroides	(Blue cohosh, papoose root)
Coreopsis lanceolata	(Sand coreopsis)
Erigeron annuus	(Daisy fleabane)
Heuchera americana	(Alumroot)—H
H. richardsonii	(Prairie alumroot)—H
Hydrophyllum appendiculatum	(Great waterleaf, appendaged waterleaf) —biennial, spreads aggressively by seed.

H. virginiana	(Virginia waterleaf)—blooms earlier than *appendiculatum.*
Iris versicolor	(Wild iris)—H
Krigia biflora	(Two-flowered Cynthia)
Lithospermum canescens	(Hoary puccoon)
L. caroliniense	(Hairy, plains puccoon)
Lupinus perennis	(Wild lupine)
Phlox divaricata	(Wild blue phlox)—H
P. pilosa	(Prairie or Downy phlox)—H
Polygonatum biflorum	(Solomon's seal)—H
Scrophularia lanceolata	(Early figwort)—nondescript flowers, rich nectar.
Senecio species	(Ragworts)
Tradescantia species	(Spiderworts)
Zizia species	(Golden Alexanders)

Plants that start blooming in June

Amorpha canescens	(Lead plant)
Ceanothus americanus	(New Jersey tea)—H. A very important and attractive plant for native bees; plant it and they will congregate.
Cephalanthus occidentalis	(Buttonbush)—H
Cornus amomum	(Silky dogwood)
C. rugosa	(Roundleaf dogwood)
Gleditisia triacanthos	(Honey locust)
Liriodendron tulipifera	(Tulip tree)—H
Potentilla fruticosa	(Shrubby cinquefoil)
P. arguta	(Prairie or tall cinquefoil)
Rhus copallina	(Shining or dwarf sumac)
R. typhina	(Staghorn sumac)
Rosa blanda	(Wild Rose) All the native roses are single, fragrant, and lovely. Important for pollinators between spring woodland flowers and later prairie forbs.
R. carolina	(Pasture rose)
R. palustris	(Swamp rose)
R. setigera	(Prairie rose) Vigorous climber. Usually blooms later than others, early July in our yard
Rubus species	(Raspberries, dewberries, blackberries)
Sambucus canadensis	(Black, or common, elderberry)
Symphoricarpos albus var. *albus*	(Snowberry)—H
Tilia americana	(American linden)—H
Toxicodendron radicans	(Poison ivy)—inconspicuous flowers, late May to July. Important fruits for birds, to late November.
Vaccinium macrocarpum	(Cranberry)
Viburnum acerifolium	(Maple-leaf viburnum)
V. cassinoides	(Northern haw)
Achillea millefolium	(Yarrow)
Allium cernuum	(Nodding wild onion)
Anemone canadensis	(Canada anemone)

A. cylindrica (Thimbleweed)
Angelica purpurea (Angelica)
Apocynum species (Dogbanes), esp. *A. androsaemifolium* (Spreading dogbane)
Asclepias exaltata (Poke milkweed) The only native woodland milkweed. Not as vigorous as most others. *All* milkweeds important for pollinators.

A. incarnata (Swamp milkweed) The only native wetland milkweed. Tolerates some dryness. Showy, deep color. Along with *verticillata*, blooms somewhat later than other milkweeds, perhaps not until July.
A. purpurascens (Purple milkweed) Bright, purplish red.
A. syriaca (Common milkweed) Spreads by rhizomes. Vital, along with *incarnata*, for monarch butterflies. Can grow in shade, but won't bloom—nonetheless can serve as a host plant.
A. tuberosa (Butterfly-weed)—H. All milkweeds attract hummingbirds, but bright colored, such as *tuberosa*, are preferred. Dry sun.
A. verticillata (Whorled milkweed) Dry sun. Does not like competition.
Astragalus canadensis (Canadian milk vetch)—H
Baptisia lactea (B. leucantha) (White wild indigo)—H
Blephilia ciliata (Downy wood-mint)
Campanula americana (Tall bellflower)—H
C. rotundifolia (Harebell)—H
Coreopsis palmata (Prairie coreopsis)

Dalea purpurea (Purple prairie-clover)
Echinacea purpurea (Purple coneflower)
E. pallida (Pale purple coneflower)
Eupatorium maculatum (Joe Pye weed)
Heliopsis helianthoides (False sunflower, Ox-eye sunflower, Early sunflower)
Mimulus ringens (Monkey flower)—H
Oenothera fruticosa (Sundrops, Narrow-leaf evening primrose). This species, along with other evening primroses, is important for moths: *O. biennis* (common) is a biennial and a weedy, aggressive species; *O. rhombipetala* (sand or four-point) requires very sandy soil; *O. macrocarpa* (Missouri) and *O. pilosella* (prairie sundrops) are very attractive but native no closer than Illinois.
Opuntia humifusa (Eastern prickly pear)
Penstemon digitalis (Foxglove beardtongue)—H. Important for hummingbirds when not much else is blooming that's accessible to them. And Penstemons are beloved by bumble bees.

P. hirsutus (Hairy beardtongue)—H
Pondeteria cordata (Pickerel weed)
Pycnanthemum virginianum (Mountain mint)
Rudbeckia hirta (Black-eyed Susan)
Ruellia humilis (Wild petunia)—H
Silphium laciniatum (Compass plant)

Stachys hyssopifolia   (Hyssop hedge nettle)—*not a stinging nettle (Urtica dioica)*
Tephrosia virginiana   (Goat's rue)
Verbena stricta   (Hoary vervain)
Veronicastrum virginicum   (Culver's root)

Plants that start blooming in July

Ribes cynosbati   (Prickly gooseberry, wild gooseberry)
Rubus allegheniensis   (Common blackberry)
Spiraea alba   (Meadowsweet)

Agastache nepetoides   (Yellow giant hyssop)
A. scrophulariifolia   (Purple giant hyssop)—H (occasionally)
Anaphalis margaritacea   (Pearly everlasting)
Aureolaria species   (False foxgloves)—H
Cacalia atriplicifolia   (Pale Indian plantain)
Chelone glabra   (White turtlehead)—H
Coreopsis tripteris   (Tall coreopsis)
Dalea purpurea   (Purple prairie clover)—considered
                                 a "must-have" (Mader, p. 292).

Eryngium yuccifolium   (Rattlesnake master)
Eupatorium perfoliatum   (Common boneset)
E. purpureum   (Sweet Joe Pye weed)
Epilobium angustifolium   (Fireweed, Great-willow herb)—H
Helianthus species   (perennial sunflowers)
Heliopsis helianthoides   (False sunflower, Ox-eye)
Hibiscus moscheutos   (Swamp rose mallow)—H
Impatiens capensis   Spotted touch-me-not, Jewelweed)—H
I. pallida   (Pale touch-me-not)—H
Liatris aspera   (Rough blazing star)—H
L. cylindracea   (Cylindrical, Dwarf blazing star)—H
L. punctata   (Dotted blazing star)
L. spicata   (Marsh blazing star)—H
Lilium michiganense   (Michigan lily)—H
Lobelia cardinalis   (Cardinal flower)—H
L. siphilitica   (Great blue lobelia)—H
Monarda didyma   (Oswego tea)—H
M. fistulosa   (Wild bergamot)—H
M. punctata   (Spotted bee balm, Horsemint)
Physostegia virginiana   (Obedient plant, False dragonhead)—H
Polymnia canadensis   (Small-flowered leafcup)
Ratibida pinnata   (Gray-headed coneflower, Yellow coneflower)
Rudbeckia subtomentosa   (Sweet black-eyed Susan)
R. triloba   (Brown-eyed Susan)
Scrophularia marilandica   (Late figwort)—nondescript flowers, *rich* nectar.
Silene regia   (Royal catchfly)—H
S. stellata   (Starry campion)—H
Silphium integrifolium   (Rosinweed)
S. perfoliatum   (Cup plant)

S. terebinthinaceum	(Prairie dock)
Silene virginica	(Fire pink)—H
Solidago juncea	(Early goldenrod)
S. graminifolia	(Grass-leaved goldenrod) Aggressive
S. ohiensis	(Ohio goldenrod)
S. ulmifolia	(Elm-leaved goldenrod)
Thalictrum species	(Meadow rues)
Verbena hastata	(Blue vervain)
Vernonia species	(Ironweeds)—H

Plants that start blooming in August

Aster (Symphyotrichum) species	(asters)
Boltonia asteroides	(False aster)
Cirsium discolor	(Pasture thistle)
C. muticum	(Swamp thistle)
Eupatorium altissimum	(Tall boneset)
Gentiana flavida or *alba*	(Cream or white gentian)
Helenium autumnale	(Sneezeweed)
Helianthus species	(perennial sunflowers)
Lespedeza capitata	(Round-headed bush clover)
Liatris scariosa	(Northern, Savanna blazing star)—H
Physostegia virginiana	(Obedient plant)—H
Solidago caesia	(Blue-stemmed goldenrod) Late goldenrods very important for native bees.
S. flexicaulis	(Zig-zag goldenrod)
S. patula	(Swamp, Rough-leaved goldenrod)
S. riddellii	(Riddell's goldenrod)
S. rigida	(Stiff goldenrod)
S. speciosa	(Showy goldenrod)

Plants blooming very late, perhaps until frost

Aster laevis, now *Symphyotrichum laeve*	(Smooth blue aster)
A. novae-angliae, now *Symphyotrichum novae-angliae*	(New England aster)
Rudbeckia triloba	(Brown-eyed Susan)
Solidago caesia	(Blue-stemmed goldenrod)
S. speciosa	(Showy goldenrod)

REFERENCES
(Works cited in the text above, plus useful others)

Buchmann, Stephen L., and Gary Paul Nabhan. *The Forgotten Pollinators*. Washington, D.C.: Island Press, 1996.

Carder, Maurice. "The New Canaries in the Coal Mine," *Resurgence*, March/April, 2010, p. 67.

Douglas, Matthew M., and Jonathan M. Douglas. *Butterflies of the Great Lakes Region*. Ann Arbor: Univ. of Michigan Press, 2005.

Dunn, Gary A. *Insects of the Great Lakes Region*. Ann Arbor: Univ. of Michigan Press, 1996.

Evans, Elaine, et al. *Befriending Bumble Bees: A Practical Guide to Raising Local Bumble Bees*. Univ. of Minnesota Extension, 2007.

Fiedler, Anna, et al. "Attracting Beneficial Insects with Native Flowering Plants," Michigan State Univ. Extension Bulletin E-2973, rev., Jan., 2008.

Grissell, Eric. *Insects and Gardens: In Pursuit of a Garden Ecology*. Portland, OR: Timber Press, 2001.

Harker, Donald, et al. *Landscape Restoration Handbook*, 2nd ed. Boca Raton, LA: Lewis Publishers, 1999.

Henderson, Carrol L. *Landscaping for Wildlife*. Minnesota Dept. of Natural Resources, St. Paul, MN: Minnesota's Bookstore, 1987.

Hightshoe, Gary L. *Native Trees, Shrubs, and Vines for Urban and Rural America: A Planting Design Manual for Environmental Designers*. New York: John Wiley & Sons, 1988.

Jenkins, Matt. "The Headbonkers' Ball," *Orion*, March/April, 2008, pp. 62–69.

Kress, Stephen W., ed. *Hummingbird Gardens*. 21st-Century Gardening Series. Brooklyn Botanic Garden, 2000.

Mader, Eric, Matthew Shepard, et al. *Attracting Native Pollinators: Protecting North America's Bees and Butterflies*. North Adams, MA: Storey Publishing, 2011. The Xerces Society Guide to improving habitat for native pollinators, in home landscapes and community gardens, on farms, in natural areas, and in urban greenspaces of all kinds. A very readable, beautifully illustrated step-by-step guide to understanding the biology of pollination and pollinators, the stresses and losses that they are suffering from, and the absolute necessity for a "grass-roots revolution" in the way we care for the land and ourselves. An indispensable book, no matter where or how you live.

Marinelli, Janet. *The Wildlife Gardener's Guide*. All-Region Guides. Brooklyn, NY: Brooklyn Botanic Garden, 2008.

Nowak, Mariette. *Birdscaping in the Midwest: A Guide to Gardening with Native Plants to Attract Birds*. Blue Mounds, WI: Itchy Cat Press, 2007.

Pyle, Robert Michael. *The Audubon Society Book for Butterfly Watchers*. New York: Scribner's, 1984.

Raver, Anne. "Humming Praises for the Wild Bee," *The New York Times*, 24 April, 2008, p. D9.

Shepherd, Matthew, et al. *Pollinator Conservation Handbook*. Portland, OR: Xerces Society, 2003. This book is largely superseded by Mader, above.

Tallamy, Douglas. *Bringing Nature Home: How You Can Sustain Wildlife with Native Plants* (updated and expanded). Portland, OR: Timber Press, 2009.

Vaughan, Mace, and Scott Hoffman Black. "Native Pollinators: How to Protect and Enhance Habitat for Native Bees," *Native Plants Journal*, Vol. 9, No. 2 (Summer, 2008), 81–91. This article is largely incorporated into Mader, above.

Wagner, David L. *Caterpillars of Eastern North America: A Guide to Identification and Natural History.* Princeton Field Guides. Princeton Univ. Press, 2005.

Whitman, Maryann, "Grapevine," *Wild Ones Journal*, May/June, 2008, p. 8.

Other sources include publications of the North American Butterfly Association, field guides, nursery catalogs, and observations by various individuals, including myself.

HELPFUL WEBSITES

Bug Guide—**www.bugguide.net**

Cornell Lab of Ornithology—**www.birds.cornell.edu**

Discover Life—**www.discoverlife.org**. An interactive "Encyclopedia of Life" with information and online identification keys on hundreds of thousands of species. Click on the "bee" icon.

Lady Bird Johnson Wildflower Center—**www.wildflower.org**

Michigan State University—**http://nativeplants.msu.edu**. A wide variety of online information about native plants and pollinators, including downloadable publications and powerpoint presentations.

Monarch Watch—**www.monarchwatch.org**

National Wildlife Federation—**www.nwf.org/butterflies**

North American Butterfly Association—**www.naba.org**

North American Pollinator Protection Campaign—**www.nappc.org**

Pollinator Partnership—**www.pollinator.org.** Sponsored by the North American Pollinator Protection Campaign, this is a particularly rich website, full of useful information. Among its most valuable features are guides to selecting plants for pollinators in different parts of the country (www.pollinator.org/guides.htm). The guide applicable to our region is "Selecting Plants for Pollinators: A Regional Guide for Farmers, Land Managers, and Gardeners in the Eastern Broadleaf Forest."

The Lepidopterists' Society—**www.lepsoc.org**

The Xerces Society for Invertebrate Conservation—**www.xerces.org/pollinator-conservation**. Lots of excellent information, free downloads, guides for teachers.

U.S. Forest Service—**www.fs.fed.us/wildflowers/pollinators/index.shtml**. Good information about pollinators, native plants, and pollinator gardens.

Univ. of Calif. at Berkeley—**nature.berkeley.edu/urbanbeegardens**

Wild Ones—Native Plants, Natural Landscapes—**www.wildones.org**

Wildflower Association of Michigan—**www.wildflowersmich.org**

Wildtype Nursery, Mason, MI—**www.wildtypeplants.com/butterflyplants.htm**. Lists host and nectar plants for many Michigan butterflies.

Other websites valuable to vegetable gardeners. Not only can you help native pollinators with native plants, the pollinators and other insects can help you to grow vegetables and fruits without using chemicals harmful both to yourself and to other creatures. See Chapter 13, "Native Plants and Insects They Support Can Improve Your Vegetable Garden," for an annotated list of websites that provide lots of practical information about how to enhance the beneficial relationships between native plants, native insects, and food crops.

8

NATIVE WILDFLOWERS AND GRASSES

FOR SUNNY, DRY AREAS IN SOUTHWEST MICHIGAN

Give me the splendid silent sun with all his beams full-dazzling!
—Walt Whitman, "Give Me the Splendid Silent Sun"

These prairie and savanna plants are native to southwest Michigan unless otherwise noted; however, this is by no means an exhaustive list of southwest Michigan's wildflowers and grasses. Heights are approximate and based on my own observation and various nursery catalogs. Many factors influence a plant's height, including soil, water, location (exposure, amount of sun or shade), and competition.

The smaller a wildflower or grass, the greater the number needed to make an impact—or even be visible—in a planting. Arrange small plants in same-species groups of at least three (ideally, more) and medium-sized plants in groups of three. With larger plants, e.g., cup plant (*Silphium perfoliatum*) you may want only one or two per planting. For the sake of pollinators, you may want larger single-species clumps than I've suggested as large clumps make foraging easier and more efficient for them.

Locate short plants at the edges of plantings or beds and next to paths and sidewalks, so that they will be in somewhat less competition with taller plants. Generally, tall plants belong at the backs of beds or in the center or perhaps at the ends of islands, with short plants at the front edges and medium-tall plants in between the two. But by mixing things up a little, you can make your beds more interesting. Put a rattlesnake master (*Eryngium yuccifolium*) or a compass plant (*Silphium laciniatum*)

near the front of a bed, where its basal leaves won't overwhelm the short plants but its tall flowerstalk will rise well—and dramatically—above them.

Rattlesnake master in flower (Eryngium yuccifolium)

Plants that, once they're established, prefer conditions drier than mesic are marked with an asterisk (*).

To help emphasize the importance of native-plant gardening to preserving biodiversity, I've indicated which species are extirpated (**X**), endangered (**E**), threatened (**T**), and of special concern (**SC**) in the state of Michigan.

Short Plants (2 ft. and under)

Allium cernuum   (Nodding wild onion)

Anemone cylindrica   (Thimbleweed)

*A. patens wolfgangiana   (Pasque flower)—not native on this side of Lake Michigan. Earliest prairie bloomer.

Asclepias verticillata   (Whorled milkweed)

*A. viridiflora)   (Green milkweed)

Aster ericoides   (Heath aster)
   —now known as *Symphiotrichum ericoides*

*A. sericeus   (Silky aster) (**T**)
   —now known as *Symphiotrichum sericeum*

A. ptarmicoides   (Upland white aster)
   —now classified as *Solidago ptarmicoides*   (Upland white or Sneezewort goldenrod)

Blephilia ciliata   (Downy wood mint)

Bouteloua curtipendula   (Side-oats grama)—a delicate grass with minute red flowers. (**E**)

*Campanula rotundifolia   (Harebell)

Carex muhlenbergii   (Sand bracted sedge)

C. pensylvanica   (Common Oak sedge, Pennsylvania sedge)—tolerates both sun and shade. This and other sedges provide a very good matrix for wildflowers.

Castilleja coccinea   (Indian paintbrush)—annual or biennial.

Dalea purpurea   (Purple prairie clover) (**X**)
   —also known as *Petalostemon purpureum*

Fragaria virginiana   (Wild strawberry)

Geum triflorum   (Prairie smoke) (**T**)

Heuchera richardsonii   (Prairie alumroot)—tolerates dry part shade.

*Koeleria cristata   (June grass)—best in sand, full sun. Very attractive.

Krigia biflora   (Two-flowered Cynthia)—adaptable to all but very wet conditions.

*Liatris cylindracea   (Cylindrical or Dwarf blazing star)

*L. punctata   (Dotted blazing star)

L. scariosa   (Northern blazing star)

Lithospermum canescens   (Hoary puccoon)—best in sand.

*L. caroliniense   (Hairy or Yellow puccoon)—best in sand.

*Lupinus perennis   (Wild lupine)—best in sand. Tolerates part shade.

*Monarda punctata   (Spotted bee balm, Dotted horse-mint)—doesn't like tall competition.

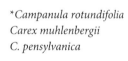

Opuntia humifusa (Prickly-pear cactus)—best in sand.
Packera aurea—formerly *Senecio aureus* (Golden ragwort)
P. plattensis—formerly *Senecio plattensis* (Prairie ragwort)
Penstemon hirsutus (Hairy beardtongue)
Ruellia humilis (Wild petunia)—spreads easily, by exploding its seeds as far as 10 feet.

Phlox pilosa (Prairie or Downy phlox)
Ranunculus fascicularis (Early buttercup)—very low-growing, good early nectar source.

R. rhomboideus (Prairie buttercup)
Sisyrinchium angustifolium (Stout blue-eyed grass)
Sporobolus heterolepis (Prairie dropseed)—the leaves of the grass form a very low cushion; the flowerstalks rise a couple of feet above it, but they are so fine in texture as to be almost invisible. A gorgeous grass, it may be situated as a short plant, despite its taller flowering stems. (**SC**)

Tephrosia virginiana (Goat's rue)—best in sand and full sun. Prefers acidic soil.
Viola pedata (Bird's foot violet)—needs sand.

Somewhat Taller Plants (about 3 ft. or under)

Amorpha canescens (Leadplant)—shrub; may occasionally be somewhat taller. (**SC**)

Anemone virginiana (Tall thimbleweed). Also tolerates shade.
Aquilegia canadensis (Wild columbine)—biennial.
Asclepias amplexicaulis (Sand milkweed)
A. hirtella (Tall green milkweed) (**T**)
A. purpurascens (Purple milkweed) (**T**)
A. tuberosa (Butterfly weed)—prefers sandy soil.
Aster oolentangiensis [*Aster azureus*] (Sky-blue aster).
  —now known as *Symphiotrichum oolentangiense*
A. pilosus (Frost aster).
  —now known as *Symphiotrichum pilosum*
Astragalus canadensis (Canada milk-vetch)—rhizomatous.
Baptisia leucophaea (Cream wild indigo) (**E**)
Carex bicknellii (Bicknell's sedge, Copper-shouldered oval sedge)
Ceanothus americanus (New Jersey tea)—shrub. May be taller when well established.

Coreopsis lanceolata (Lance-leaved coreopsis, Sand coreopsis, Tickseed coreopsis)

Echinacea purpurea (Purple coneflower) (**X**)
Euphorbia corollata (Flowering spurge)
Gentiana flavida or *alba* (Cream or White gentian)
Helianthus occidentalis (Western sunflower)—slender, bare flowerstalks rising over basal rosettes. Tolerates dry conditions, poor soil.

Liatris aspera (Rough blazing star)
Monarda fistulosa (Bee balm)
Potentilla arguta (Prairie cinquefoil)
P. fruticosa (Shrubby cinquefoil)—shrub.

[^] *Penstemon grandiflorus*   (Large-flowered beard-tongue)
                                           —native further west but spectacular.
Rudbeckia hirta   (Black-eyed Susan)
Schizachyrium scoparium   (Little bluestem)—a short, beautiful,
   [*Andropogon scoparius*]   well-behaved grass.
Tradescantia ohiensis   (Ohio spiderwort)
Zizia aurea   (Golden Alexander)

Moderately Tall Plants (at least 3 but not over 5 ft.)

Plants that send up a single flowerstalk or whose flowerstalks rise on more or less bare stems above significantly lower foliage can be successfully combined with shorter plants.

Asclepias syriaca   (Common milkweed)—aggressive, but essential.
Aster laevis—now known   (Smooth blue aster)
   as *Symphiotrichum laeve*
A. novae-angliae—now known   (New England aster).
   as *Symphiotrichum novaeangliae*
Baptisia lactea [*B. leucantha*]   (White wild indigo)—flowerstalks rise well
                                              above foliage. (**SC**)
Cassia hebecarpa   (Wild senna)—may not tolerate conditions
                                              drier than mesic.
Desmanthus illinoensis   (Illinois bundleflower)—native as close as
                                              northern Indiana.
Desmodium canadense   (Showy tick-trefoil)
Echinacea pallida   (Pale-purple coneflower)—native west of Michigan.
                                              Stiff, bare flowerstalks rise well above foliage.
Elymus canadensis   (Canada wild rye)—a graceful, nodding grass
                                              with soft, bristly seedhead. Tolerates dry, poor soil.
E. virginicus   (Virginia wild rye)—also graceful,
                                              more erect. Shade-tolerant.
Eryngium yuccifolium   (Rattlesnake master)—flowerstalk rises well
                                              above basal rosette. (**T**)
Helianthus mollis   (Downy sunflower) (**T**)
Lespedeza capitata   (Round-headed bush clover)
                                              —likes dry, poor soil. Attractive to birds.
                                              Rhizomatous, may form loose ground cover.
Parthenium integrifolium   (Wild quinine)—native in Indiana but not in Michigan.
Penstemon digitalis   (Foxglove beardtongue)
Physostegia virginiana   (Obedient plant, False dragonhead)—aggressive.
Ratibida pinnata   (Gray-headed coneflower, yellow coneflower)
Rudbeckia triloba   (Brown-eyed Susan)
Silene regia   (Royal catchfly)—native in Indiana and Illinois but
                                              not in Michigan. A beautiful plant, rare in the wild.
Silene stellata   (Starry campion)—native to Michigan,
                                              but not to SW Michigan. (**T**)
Silphium integrifolium   (Rosinweed) (**T**)
Solidago rigida   (Stiff goldenrod)

Solidago speciosa	(Showy goldenrod)
Sporobolus heterolepis	(Prairie or northern dropseed)—forms a low cushion from which rise tall, delicate flowerstalks. A most attractive grass. (**SC**)
*Verbena stricta	(Hoary vervain)
Veronicastrum virginicum	(Culver's root)

Tall Plants (over 5 ft.)

In general, these plants are appropriate for the back of the bed or for the middle (or ends) of an island planting. However, placing a few taller plants in an area of considerably shorter plants creates an interesting, dramatic, and natural-looking effect.

Andropogon gerardii	(Big bluestem)—aggressive.
Cacalia atriplicifolia	(Pale Indian plantain)
Coreopsis tripteris	(Tall coreopsis)—aggressive.
Desmodium illinoense	(Illinois tick-trefoil)
Heliopsis helianthoides	(Ox-eye, Early, or False sunflower)—very aggressive.
Silphium laciniatum	(Compass plant)—big leaves only at base, single flowerstalk. Must have full sun. (**T**)
Silphium terebinthinaceum	(Prairie dock)—large, beautiful leaves at base, slender bare flowerstalks. Very deep-rooted, difficult to transplant or eradicate.
Silphium perfoliatum	(Cup plant)—in soil rich in organic material, together with partial shade, may tolerate conditions slightly drier than mesic. (**T**)
Sorghastrum nutans	(Indian grass)—aggressive.

Good manners requires you to get to know the names of the plants and flowers and birds. That's etiquette.

—Gary Snyder

9

NATIVE WILDFLOWERS, GRASSES, AND FERNS

FOR SHADED AREAS IN SOUTHWEST MICHIGAN

… a green thought in a green shade.
—Andrew Marvell, "The Garden"

Native woodland plants, which most of these are, need soil rich in leaf litter, which provides them with nutrients and insulates them from drought and extremes of temperature. Heights are approximate, and based on my own observation and various nursery catalogs. Few of the plants listed grow in really deep shade; most of them benefit from at least two to three hours of filtered sunlight per day. Plants needing a lot of moisture are marked with an asterisk (*).

Ferns and sedges are important components for woodland plantings, providing cover for creatures and matrix for wildflowers. Some sedges are also important as host plants for Lepidoptera.

Since people often ask me what will serve as a native groundcover to replace exotics such as pachysandra or myrtle (*Vinca minor* or *major*), I've indicated, with a plus (+), species of various heights which could suit the purpose.

To help emphasize the importance of native-plant gardening to preserving biodiversity, I've indicated which species are endangered (**E**), threatened (**T**), and of special concern (**SC**) in the state of Michigan.

Wood poppy, Celandine poppy   *Stylophorum diphyllum*

Spring "Ephemerals" (very short)

These woodland plants bloom early, before the trees leaf out fully, and then tend to die down, some disappearing faster and more completely than others. Even if the plants remain above ground, they don't cover the ground very thickly. Consequently, they need to be grouped together and carefully marked, and combined with somewhat larger—but not aggressive—plants with substantial leaves that persist throughout the growing season.

Claytonia virginica	(Spring beauty)
Dentaria diphylla	(Two-leaved toothwort)
D. laciniata	(Cut-leaved toothwort)
Dicentra canadensis	(Squirrel corn)
D. cucullaria	(Dutchman's breeches)
Erythronium americanum	(Trout lily, Adder's tongue, Dogtooth violet)
Hepatica acutiloba	(Sharp-lobed hepatica) —leaves appear after flowering.
H. americana	(Round-lobed hepatica) —leaves appear after flowering.
Isopyrum biternatum	(False rue anemone)
Mertensia virginica	(Virginia bluebells) (**E**)
Trillium grandiflorum	(Large-flowered trillium)

Other Short Plants (2 ft. or under)

Many of the plants in this section bloom in combination with and at roughly the same time (April and May) as the more "ephemeral" plants listed above.

Actaea rubra	(Red baneberry)
Adiantum pedatum	(Maidenhair fern)
+*Anemone canadensis*	(Canada anemone)—a vigorous ground cover for shade.
Anemonella thalictroides	(Rue anemone)
Arisaema triphyllum	(Jack-in-the-pulpit)—we have in our yard what is apparently a taller form of this species that grows to 3 ft. and slightly taller.
+*Asarum canadense*	(Wild ginger)—short and "flat"; possible ground cover in shade or moist part shade.
Aster macrophyllus —now known as *Eurybia macrophylla*	(Big-leaved aster). Rhizomatous, aggressive.
Athyrium filix-femina	(Lady fern)
Caltha palustris	(Marsh marigold)—needs to stay wet.
Carex pensylvanica	(Pennsylvania sedge, Common oak sedge) —very adaptable.
C. sprengelii	(Long-beaked sedge)
Dodecatheon meadia	(Shooting star)—adapts to both sun and light shade. (**E**)
+*Euonymus obovatus*	(Running strawberry, Hearts a-busting) —low shrub or short vine, ground cover. Can be aggressive. Tolerates deep shade but not continuously dry soil.

Geranium maculatum	(Wild geranium)—a beautiful plant that seeds itself generously but not aggressively.
Heuchera americana	(Alumroot)—tolerant of dry shade.
Hydrastis canadensis	(Goldenseal) (**T**)
Jeffersonia diphylla	(Twinleaf) (**SC**)
+*Maianthemum canadense*	(Canada mayflower)—very short, possible ground cover.
*Onoclea sensibilis	(Sensitive fern)—needs moist soil. Rhizomatous, somewhat aggressive.
Phlox divaricata	(Wild blue phlox)
+*Podophyllum peltatum*	(Mayapple)—vigorous ground cover.
Polemonium reptans	(Jacob's ladder) (**T**)
Polygonatum biflorum	(Solomon's seal). There's also a tetraploid variant of this species that grows much taller, 3 feet and more.
Polystichum acrostichoides	(Christmas fern)—evergreen.
Sanguinaria canadensis	(Bloodroot)—leaves unfurl after flowering and increase in size.
Smilacina racemosa	(False Solomon's seal)
S. stellata	(Starry Solomon's seal)
+*Uvularia grandiflora*	(Large-flowered bellwort) —spreads readily and, with its dense foliage, forms something of a low ground cover, suppressing weedy species.
Viola spp.	*Viola* spp. (Violet species)

Taller Plants (often between 2 and 3 ft. but may be somewhat shorter or taller)

Some of the plants in this section also bloom in spring.

Anemone virginiana	(Tall thimbleweed)
Aquilegia canadensis	(Wild columbine)—best as an edge plant, in part sun. Biennial.
Collinsonia canadensis	(Richweed)—blooms summer.
Caulophyllum thalictroides	(Blue cohosh)
Osmunda cinnamomea	(Cinnamon fern)
Penstemon digitalis	(Foxglove beardtongue) —blooms early summer.
Polygonatum biflorum	(Solomon's seal)—apparently a taller form of this species.
Stylophorum diphyllum	(Wood poppy)—spreads readily and tends to form a ground cover.
Thalictrum dioicum	(Early meadow rue)
Triosteum aurantiacum	(Horse gentian)—blooms summer.

Moderately Tall Plants (3 to 5ft.)

These plants bloom in summer or later.

Actaea pachypoda	(White baneberry)—may also be shorter.
Aralia racemosa	(American spikenard)—spectacular, shrub-like forb.
Asclepias exaltata	(Poke milkweed)—the only woodland milkweed. Beloved by deer.
Aster cordifolius—now known as *Symphiotrichum cordifolium*	(Heart-leaved aster)
A. sagittifolius—now known as *Symphiotrichum sagittifolium*	(Arrow-leaved aster, Sword-leaf wood aster).
Campanula americana	(Tall bellflower)—biennial.
Elymus villosa	(Silky wild rye)—tall, graceful woodland grass.
E. virginicus	(Virginia wild rye)—quite tolerant of wet soil; less tolerant of dryness than *E. villosa*.
Eupatorium rugosum	(White snakeroot)—poisonous. Blooms very late. Aggressive.
Helianthus decapitalus	(Thin-leaved sunflower)—tolerates heavy shade, likes moist soil. Aggressive.
+*H. divaricatus*	(Woodland sunflower)—prefers more open shade, tolerates drier soil. Aggressive.
H. strumosus	(Pale-leaved sunflower)—aggressive.
Hystrix patula or *Elymus hystrix*	(Bottlebrush grass)—a lovely, interesting woodland grass that wanders but doesn't take over.
Lobelia cardinalis	(Cardinal flower)—tolerates shade but still must be kept wet. Don't mulch.
L. siphilitica	(Great blue lobelia)—needs less water than *L. cardinalis*.
+*Matteuccia struthiopteris*	(Ostrich fern)—rhizomatous, may be aggressive.
Osmunda claytoniana	(Interrupted fern)
Polymnia canadensis	(Small-flowered leafcup)—spreads aggressively by seed. Strange, interesting leaves.
Prenanthes alba	(White lettuce, Lion's foot)—beautiful leaves and blooms.
Scrophularia lanceolata	(Early figwort)
Solidago caesia	(Blue-stemmed goldenrod)
S. flexicaulis	(Zig-zag goldenrod)

Tall Plants (over 5ft.)

Agastache nepetoides   (Yellow giant hyssop)
Eupatorium purpureum   (Sweet Joe Pye weed)
Thalictrum dasycarpum   (Tall meadow rue)—spreads
                                  aggressively from seed.
Scrophularia marilandica   (Late figwort)—striking tall plant, with
                                  small green flowers. Blooms late into fall.

Vines (vigorous climbers)

Adlumaria fungosa   (Climbing fumitory)—delicate, ghostly-pale
                                  flowers, akin to bleeding heart. Biennial. (**SC**)
Celastrus scandens   (American bittersweet)—dioecious, needing
                                  both male and female plants. The orange
                                  capsules fold back to reveal bright red
                                  berries. Take care not to get Oriental bitter-
                                  sweet, which is highly invasive and persistent.
Clematis virginiana   (Virgin's bower)—clouds of delicate white
                                  flowers, forming wispy seed coverings
                                  that persist through the winter. Attractive.
                                  Aggressive.
Dioscorea villosa   (Wild yam)—a lovely plant, with
                                  corrugated leaves like heart-shaped
                                  fans. Leaves are a rich, dark red at first,
                                  gradually turning green.
*Echinocystis lobata   (Wild cucumber)—needs moist soil.
                                  Interesting cucumber-like fruit, but
                                  not good for your salads.
Menispermum canadense   (Moonseed)—interesting plant,
                                  but very aggressive.

Wild geranium, Spotted cranesbill, Old-maid's-nightcap (Geranium maculatum). A beautiful woodland plant, spreading by seed but not aggressive, with distinctive leaves lingering on through the summer and lovely spent seed caps (on the right).

10

NATIVE WILDFLOWERS AND GRASSES

FOR DAMP AND WET AREAS IN SOUTHWEST MICHIGAN

What would the world be, once bereft
Of wet and wildness? Let them be left,
O let them be left, wildness and wet;
Long live the weeds and the wilderness yet.
—Gerard Manley Hopkins, "Inversnaid"

Some wetland plants, e.g., *Eupatorium perfoliatum* (Common boneset), do well in average soil if grown in partial shade and in soil containing considerable organic material. Others, e.g., *Lobelia cardinalis* (Cardinal flower), demand continuously wet soil or even standing water. Plants most demanding of continuously wet conditions are indicated with an asterisk (*). Most of these plants require sun or at most part shade. Heights are approximate and depend to some extent upon growing conditions.

These are beautiful plants, many of them spectacularly so; by all means grow them if you have the conditions, but don't waste time and space on the ones marked with an asterisk (*) unless you do have wet areas.

Short Plants (3 ft. or under)

Caltha palustris	(Marsh marigold)
Carex bebbii	(Bebb's sedge)—this and other wetland sedges are valuable for "filling in" and providing matrix for other plants.
C. comosa	(Bristly sedge)
C. lupulina	(Common hop sedge)—also grows in shade.
*C. stricta	(Tussock sedge)
C. vulpinoidea	(Fox sedge)
Gentiana andrewsii	(Bottle gentian)
Heuchera richardsonii	(Prairie alumroot)—also tolerates dry shade.
Hierochloe odorata	(Sweetgrass)—aggressive.
Iris versicolor	(Wild iris)
I. virginica	(Southern blue iris)

Juncus effusus	(Soft-stemmed rush)
*Mimulus ringens	(Monkey flower)
Physostegia virginiana	(Obedient plant)
Potentilla fruticosa	(Shrubby cinquefoil)—shrub; grows in wet or dry-mesic soil.
Pycnanthemum virginianum	(Mountain mint) (**T**)
Senecio aureus —now known as *Packera aurea*	(Golden ragwort)
Solidago ohioensis	(Ohio goldenrod)
Zizia aurea	(Golden Alexander)

Moderately Tall Plants (3 to 5 ft.)

Asclepias incarnata	(Swamp milkweed)
Aster novae-angliae—now known as *Symphyotrichum novae-angliae*	(New England aster)
A. puniceus—now known as *Symphyotrichum puniceum*	(Swamp aster)
Carex crinita	(Fringed sedge)—also grows in shade.
C. lacustris	(Lake sedge)—also grows in shade. Rhizomatous, aggressive.
Chelone glabra	(Turtlehead)
Eupatorium perfoliatum	(Common boneset)
Filipendula rubra	(Queen-of-the-prairie) (**T**)
Helenium autumnale	(Sneezeweed)
*Hibiscus moscheutos	(Swamp rose-mallow)—needs full sun.
Liatris spicata	(Marsh blazing star)
*Lobelia cardinalis	(Cardinal flower)—"conserves" its hard-to-reach nectar for hummingbirds, which are thus its principal pollinators.
L. siphilitica	(Great blue lobelia)
Rosa palustris	(Swamp rose)—shrub; sometimes taller, especially in partial shade. Tolerates dryness.
*Scirpus atrovirens	(Dark green bulrush)
*S. cyperinus	(Wool grass)
Spiraea alba	(Meadowsweet)—shrub.
Solidago patula	(Swamp goldenrod)—may reach 6 ft.
S. riddellii	(Riddell's goldenrod)
Verbena hastata	(Blue vervain)

Tall Plants (5 ft. and over)

Aster umbellatus—now also known
    as *Doellingeria umbellata*   (Flat-topped aster)

Eupatorium maculatum—now also
    known as *Eutrochium maculatum*   (Joe Pye weed)

Lilium michiganense   (Michigan lily)

Spartina pectinata   (Prairie cordgrass)—deep-rooted,
    with lovely, delicate flowers.

Vernonia missurica   (Ironweed)

Very Tall Plants (6 ft. and over)

Angelica atropurpurea   (Angelica)

Helianthus giganteus   (Tall sunflower)—needs full sun.
    Aggressive.

Rudbeckia laciniata   (Green-headed coneflower; Wild
    golden glow)—rhizomatous.

Silphium perfoliatum   (Cup plant) (**T**)

Showy Plants for the Sunny Edge of a Natural (or Would-Be Natural) Pond or Lake

*Acorus calamus   (Sweet-flag)—at very edge or in the water.

*Alisma plantago-aquatica   (Water-plantain)—at very edge or in
    the water.

Aster puniceus—now also known
    as *Symphyotrichum puniceum*   (Swamp aster)

Angelica atropurpurea   (Angelica)

Asclepias incarnata   (Swamp milkweed)

Carex   (Sedge)—species listed earlier.

Cephalanthus occidentalis   (Buttonbush)—shrub.

Chelone glabra   (Turtlehead)

Eupatorium maculatum   (Joe Pye weed)

E. perfoliatum   (Common boneset)

Filipendula rubra   (Queen of the prairie)

*Hibiscus moscheutos   (Swamp rose-mallow)

Juncus effusus   (Soft-stemmed rush)

Iris versicolor   (Wild iris)

I. virginica   (Southern blue iris)

Liatris spicata   (Marsh blazing star)

*Lobelia cardinalis   (Cardinal flower)

*Mimulus ringens   (Monkey flower)

*Peltandra virginica   (Arrow-arum)—at very edge or in the water.

*Pondetaria cordata   (Pickerel weed)—in the water.

Potentilla fruticosa   (Shrubby cinquefoil)—shrub.

*Sagittaria latifolia   (Common arrowhead)—at very edge or
    in the water.

Saururus cernuus (Lizard tail)—at very edge or in the water.
Scirpus atrovirens (Dark green bulrush)
S. cyperinus (Woolgrass)
Solidago patula (Swamp goldenrod)
S. riddellii (Riddell's goldenrod)
Spartina pectinata (Prairie cordgrass)—aggressive.
  Excellent for bank stabilization.

Spiraea alba (Meadowsweet)—shrub; aggressive.
S. tomentosa (Steeplebush)—shrub.
Verbena hastata (Blue vervain)
Vernonia missurica (Ironweed)

11

Oak, Dogwood, or Redbud?

What Shrubs and Trees
are most Helpful to Wildlife?

Except during the nine months before
he draws his first breath, no man manages
his affairs as well as a tree does.
—George Bernard Shaw

When we gardeners and homeowners see something we admire on someone else's property, our first response is usually wonderment: "What is *that*?" Then our second thought is often rather envious: "Oh, I'd like one of those for our yard!" Why is it we're immediately attracted to certain trees and shrubs rather than others? And what, exactly, should be our third thought?

Our own half-acre yard, when we began natural landscaping 15 years ago, was already heavily wooded, with well over 30 trees ranging from mature natives to ornamental nonnatives and cultivars. (We had only one sunny corner of the yard for a prairie garden.) Gradually, we've added new natives, but much of the original tree cover remains.

One such nonnative remnant always attracts attention. It blooms spectacularly, in swirling layers, about when we hold our annual spring plant exchange, and some of our fellow native-plant enthusiasts admire it and want to know what it is. Unfortunately, it's an East Asian dogwood (*Cornus kousa*), variously called Chinese, Oriental, or Japanese flowering dogwood. Its dozens of cultivars testify to its popularity with landscapers. We confess to admiring it ourselves every spring. Its fruits, however, grow to be too large for birds;

nor have we ever observed any insect predation. It blooms about a month later than native flowering dogwood (*Cornus florida*) and therefore has little value to early native bees and insects. We're told that the fruits are a favorite food for monkeys, but it appears to be virtually valueless for our own native wildlife. Nonetheless, we see it more and more often in our neighborhood.

Even more often, now, we see Bradford pear (*Pyrus calleryana* 'Bradford') ornamenting the neighborhood, with dense masses of white blossoms in late spring. Another East Asian species, it seems to have many suburban virtues: fast, compact growth; limited height; and inconspicuous fruits that don't leave any mess. It is conspicuous, however, for more than its pretty blossoms; they smell like rotten fish, making us wonder whether its owners get outdoors much. It's brittle and short-lived, and its rigid, sculpted look usually pyramidal—make it "appear out-of-place in most situations." Its uniformity and overuse lead to "monotony and boredom" (www.hort.uconn.edu/plants). Its small, hard fruits attract only the European starling, probably not the most sought-after of your guests.

What leads gardeners and landscapers to plant such out-of-place species? Clearly, they're attractive to the eye—the human eye. They're tidy. They appeal to a widespread cultural preference for artificiality. They're popular, easily available, some-

thing of a fad. Supremely, they are for *us*, and for *right now*—with very little if any attention to the future or to species other than our own.

Why not other relatively compact species, with lovely early blooms, native to our own region? Why not, for instance, Eastern redbud (*Cercis canadensis*)? Its branching strands of lovely, reddish-purple blossoms come earlier than those of Bradford pear or Japanese dogwood, early enough to make them valuable to the always early native bees. It grows to understory-tree height in shade but remains a tall shrub in sun. So why not?

LOOK BEYOND THE NEEDS OF THE GARDENER

The answer, not an easy one, depends in large part on how much space you have and how many species you can accommodate. It depends on how fully you recognize and are prepared to act upon Douglas Tallamy's declaration that "for the first time in its history, gardening has taken on a role that transcends the needs of the gardener" and his warning that "unless we modify the places we live, work, and play to meet not only our own needs but the needs of other species as well, nearly all species of wildlife native to the United States will disappear forever" (pp. 11, 36).

So, given a limit to the diversity your yard or rural property can accommodate and the presence of mature trees you don't want to part with, how do you choose the relatively few species that will be *most* helpful to our stressed and disappearing wild-

life? Is it possible to achieve an objective, ranked list of the most important species for wildlife?

Again, there are complexities. But Tallamy himself, in his book and on his website, offers us one such list, limited in its scope but of utmost importance in helping us to make intelligent choices.

Until recently, most books dealing with plants' value to wildlife rated trees and shrubs for their value to vertebrates (like us) and sometimes to pollinators but not for their value to herbivorous insects such as caterpillars. Caterpillars were—and still are—more likely to be seen as pests to be exterminated, rather than as an indispensable strand of the food web. Only garden flowers, wildflowers, and a few grasses were viewed as valuable—or even possible—nectar plants for Lepidoptera (butterflies and moths) or host plants for their larvae.

> Let me desire and wish well the life
> these trees may live when I
> no longer rise in the mornings
> to be pleased by the green of them
> shining, and their shadows on the ground,
> and the sound of the wind in them.
>
> —Wendell Berry, "Planting Trees"

CONSIDER THE LIFE CYCLE

Now Tallamy provides two vital corrections to such limited views. First, he demonstrates that the importance of Lepidoptera and other herbivorous insects for the entire food web cannot be overestimated. In transferring the sun's energy from plants to animals, they provide indispensable food for other insects and myriad other creatures, including birds, reptiles, and amphibians—and mammals. For example, caterpillars, together with spiders (arthropods that feed on insects), are the essential, protein-rich diet of almost all terrestrial species of baby birds, whatever the mature parents themselves normally eat. Moreover, over 50 percent of plant-eating, or herbivorous, insects are thought to be members of the Order Lepidoptera, not only vital in caterpillar form to the nestlings of *96 percent* of North American terrestrial bird species but also serving, in their adult form of butterflies and moths, as important pollinators and thus regenerators of the plant world.

Crucially important to us gardeners for wildlife, Tallamy and his research assistant Kimberly Shropshire also demonstrate that herbivorous insects such as the caterpillars of butterflies and moths receive far greater support from native than from nonnative plants, and more (measurably more) from some native plants than from others. Thus he provides us with one crucially important basis for choice.

What has this to do with the trees and shrubs you choose for your yard? **Woody plants are the most important hosts—in many cases the only host plants**—for countless species of Lepidoptera. Without a careful selection of trees and shrubs, no "butterfly garden," no "pollinator garden," no "birdscape," no "wildlife garden" can provide full life-cycle support for the species it purports to benefit.

CONSIDER OPTIONS CAREFULLY

So what about that redbud? Is it a good choice? Well, it's not all bad: it will provide early nectar for native bees, and it's a host plant for 19 species of butterflies and moths. Are there better choices, if your options are limited? You bet there are.

What about an oak? The very word invokes power, majesty, strength, endurance, and a wonderfully gnarled old age. Long associated with nobility, celebrated for both its long life and the amount of life it sustains, it is nonetheless *not* the choice that first comes to most people's minds as "just the right tree for the front yard."

> Generations pass while some tree stands, and old families last not three oaks.
>
> —Sir Thomas Browne

Our yard already had three red oaks, and a few years ago we added two bur oaks (to become replacements for expiring nonnatives) and a dwarf chinkapin oak; but until we read Tallamy's book we did not realize that oaks head the list of woody plants valuable to wildlife—yet another reason for regarding these life-sustaining trees as noble. They serve as host plants for over 500 species of native butterflies and moths. The total number of insect foragers on oaks is well over one thousand (Eastman, p. 140). And insect foragers are food for foraging birds. Then there's the obvious benefit to vertebrate wildlife: the acorns, or "mast," rich in fat and protein. Gary Hightshoe, evaluating trees and shrubs in their benefits for wildlife, primarily for vertebrates, gives every common oak species his highest rating, "very high."

Daunted by the vision of bugs, insect predation on your tree's leaves, and messy acorns in the fall? Those are certainly reasons why we don't often see oaks as "street trees" planted by the city or as landscaping trees in new developments. But if we are to be truly gardeners for wildlife, then pristine plants, tidy yards and walks, and our own convenience can no longer dominate our considerations. It's way past time to get over the cultural schizophrenia that encourages us to destroy or otherwise avoid hosting the larval forms of native caterpillars and moths whose mature forms we even create gardens for and whose value as pollinators we are beginning to recognize. And we should welcome evidence that "our" gardens and landscapes are providing food for some of the tiniest and most beneficial creatures of the earth.

Ancient oak trees extend gnarled limbs in extravagant gestures.

SO CONSIDER THE NOBLE OAK

Find room for at least one oak, if you don't already have one. Plant it not only for future generations but for yourself and your children—and for the rich biodiversity it will support, starting immediately and with growing richness for hundreds of years. Tuck that redbud in somewhere if you have lots of space, but provide as much space as possible for the 100-year spread of your oak. They are well worth the space they need, even in a small yard. But many other trees, shrubs, and vines are also very worthy of your consideration. So how are you to make your property or landscaping project as valuable to wildlife as you can possibly make it?

> "I repeat," cried the Lorax,
> "I speak for the trees."
>
> —Dr. Seuss, *The Lorax*

Many researchers have wrestled with the problem of which plants are most valuable to wildlife. For the most part, however, they've considered chiefly the products of the plants—seeds, fruits and nuts—as food for the larger predators, birds and mammals, rather than the plants themselves as food for herbivorous insects. Douglas Tallamy's ranked list of woody-plant genera is the first to fully recognize that "a large percentage of the world's fauna depends entirely on insects to access the energy stored in plants" and that therefore the entire food web—"the health of all terrestrial ecosystems" (p. 21)—depends on the *diversity of herbivorous insects*. Because there are so many lepidopterans in North America (over 12,000 species), constituting over 50 percent of all insect herbivores, Tallamy's research focuses on lepidopteran dependence on woody plants as hosts for their larvae, confident that his rankings "should provide a good estimate of host use by all herbivores." His rankings, therefore, are one of the best resources we have for choosing trees, shrubs, and vines that will "make the biggest difference in the shortest time" (p. 146) for herbivorous insects and for virtually all the other wildlife—including birds and mammals—absolutely dependent on them.

PLANT FOR DIVERSITY OF LIFE

Tallamy's rankings, however, should not be our sole consideration. Trees, shrubs, and vines offer much more than the leaves which serve as food and shelter for caterpillars. So, although my lists are in the same ranked order as Tallamy's, I provide additional information about the plant's value to wildlife in general (as opposed to Lepidoptera alone), try to make information relevant for owners of urban homes and small rural properties, and categorize plants according to relative sizes and landscaping value. I exclude a few species which, although native to Tallamy's mid-Atlantic region, are not native to southwest Michigan, such as chestnuts (*Castanea dentata*). I go far deeper into the rankings Tallamy provides on his web site, of over 200 genera of woody plants, both native and nonnative, for their value to the caterpillars of Lepidoptera. (For Tallamy's full list of over 200 ranked species of woody plants, see his web site: http://copland.udel.edu/~dtallamy/host/index.html.)

I draw my supplemental rankings and information from a variety of sources, but especially from Gary L. Hightshoe's *Native Trees, Shrubs, and Vines for Urban and Rural America*. Hightshoe systematically rates every plant he lists according to the number of vertebrates, ranging from birds to hooved browsers, that use it for food. "Very high" indicates 50 wildlife users or more; "high," 25 to 49 users; "intermediate," 15 to 24 users; "low," 5 to 14 users; and "very low," less than 5 users. Hightshoe's limitation is that he doesn't consider the value of woody plants to invertebrates such as insects or to vertebrates such as amphibians and reptiles, nor their value as shelter; so I include some comments on the value of plants as cover, drawn from my own observation and from other sources. I haven't included in my listings plants rated generally quite low, such as American bladdernut (*Staphylea trifolia*), which, despite its attractive seed capsules (the reason we planted it in the days of our pre-Tallamy enthusiasms), not only ranks very far down on Tallamy's list (#142, hosting only two species of Lepidoptera) but also gets a rating from Hightshoe of "low" and the comment "negligible use."

Nonetheless, our bladdernut will remain right where it is. Not only do our own observations suggest some rather positive values, they suggest that my lists, Tallamy's lists, indeed all lists, are subject to amendment from your own careful observations, your reading, and information from your friends. Bladdernut pods are attractive not only to me and Tom, but also to the chickadees and cardinals we've seen shaking open every last one of them and consuming the seeds during a January spell of severe weather. And we've read that moths are particularly attracted to the rather early blossoms (mid-May). If you have a small yard, there are certainly better choices as host plants for Lepidoptera; but if you've got space for it, you'll find that bladdernut has modest wildlife offerings for every season.

PLANT FOR *ALL* SEASONS

Perhaps it's because they are often food for us as well that most of us think first of seeds, fruits, and berries as food for wildlife. But food comes in many forms, and in all seasons.

- In early **spring**, woody plants—well before producing their official yield of fruits and even before their leaves emerge—offer to wildlife a wondrous variety of food: fruits and seeds remaining from the previous season, sap, tender new shoots, flowers and flower buds, early nectar and pollen, leaf buds, green or flowering catkins, and even early winged seeds, favorites of chickadees, nuthatches, and finches. The American elm (*Ulmus americana*) and red maple (*Acer rubrum*), for example, produce their flowers as early as late March or April and winged seeds by May. In my lists I try to suggest the necessity of providing food in *all* seasons and the particular importance of some species when food is scarce or otherwise especially valuable.

- In **summer**, winged-seed and fruit production ascend sharply, with the fruit of red elderberry shrubs (*Sambucus pubens*) and serviceberry trees and shrubs (*Amelanchier* spp.) ripening as early as late June. Soon waves of fruits and berries are rolling in—first raspberries and blueberries, then later berries and fruits such as elderberries, grapes, and the fruits of viburnums and spicebush.

- **Fall** brings dogwood fruits, rich in fat and protein. These fruits will be stripped off by migrants and resident birds very early, probably no later than October; the migrants need to increase their body weight by as much as half, to be burned off during their long, nocturnal flights to more fruitful climes. But for the birds that stay with us, you also need some *low-fat*, persistent fruits—not so much for dieters as for birds and other wildlife that will eat them later, when times are harder and there are fewer choices.

- **Winter** food, to which most gardeners and landscapers give least attention, is vitally important. Trees and shrubs that hold their low-fat berries include Michigan holly, highbush cranberry (*Viburnum trilobum*), roses, chokeberry (*Aronia melanocarpa*), snowberry (*Symphoricarpos albus*), sumacs, crabapples, and hawthorns (*Crataegus nitida* and *C. crusgalli*). Trees that retain cones, catkins, and seedpods through the harsh winter months are cru-

cial for wildlife survival, especially red pine (*Pinus resinosa*), whose cones stay on the tree until summer, and white pine (*Pinus strobus*), whose cones release their seeds gradually during winter and the following spring (Eastman, p. 154).

Virtually all pines, spruces, larches, hemlocks, and white cedars (arborvitaes), as well as alders and birches, retain their seeds and shed them slowly, thereby sustaining wildlife over a long period of time. Squirrels, by grasping and chewing the cone much the same way we deal with an ear of corn, and crossbills by prying out seeds with their scissorlike bills, are among the first to sample the harvest. As they mature, cones and catkins open wider, and woodpeckers, nuthatches, and small finches come to the trees to claim their share. Other birds will be waiting for the seeds that fall to the ground (Dennis, p. 60).

White-winged crossbill: a bill perfectly shaped for opening the scales of pine cones.

As the tree knows not what is outside of its leaves & bark
And yet it drinks the summer joy & fears the winter sorrow.

—William Blake, *The Four Zoas* (1797)

For valuable additional information on choosing woody plants to provide foods for all seasons, consult Hightshoe's very helpful "Phenological Calendars" on the flowering, leafing, and fruiting times for trees (pp. 62–68) and for shrubs and vines (pp. 443–451). Carroll Henderson, in *Landscaping for Wildlife,* also provides some helpful tables that rank tree, shrub, and other species for value to various forms of wildlife and in particular their seasonal value (Appendix A, pp. 72–100). Henderson's lists include some nonnative species and need to be checked against his own lists of undesirable and invasive species.

NOW FOR MY OWN LISTS

There are several reasons why my lists of trees, shrubs, and vines offer much more detailed information than I've given in the preceding lists of non-woody plants:

- Home gardeners and landscapers are only beginning to understand the **crucial** importance of trees, shrubs, and vines for pollinators in particular and wildlife in general;

- Since most suburban and rural properties have space enough for a rich diversity of wildflowers and grasses but limited space for trees and shrubs, it's important to choose carefully for maximum value to wildlife;

- I speak in some detail about the value and beauty of wildflowers in other sections of this book;

- Finally, Douglas Tallamy's research about the value of woody plants as host plants for Lepidoptera is so important that it needs to be summarized and included in virtually every guide to natural landscaping, but also needs to be supplemented with other information about the value of woody plants to wildlife.

I've divided Tallamy's inclusive, ranked list into three sections, to distinguish heights and growth habits of woody plants and to encourage gardeners to plant as many species and "layers" as possible from Tallamy's highest-ranked genera. For example, my list offers, under "Smaller Trees" and under "Shrubs and Vines," smaller forms of highly-ranked genera, e.g., dwarf oaks, willow shrubs, and dwarf hackberry, for yards with limited space and for special spots in larger yards. All three lists are numbered according to their relative rankings in Tallamy's list.

Following my lists, I offer some tips and general principles to follow in choosing, planting, and landscaping with trees and shrubs.

I. LARGE TREES

Trees included in this section consist of species native to southwest Michigan unless otherwise noted and normally reach at least 40 feet in height. Dimensions are given only for the smaller trees listed in this section.

Genera or species on the Tallamy and Shropshire list that aren't included in this section may possibly be in the following sections, "Smaller Trees" or "Shrubs and Vines." Chestnuts (*Castanea* *dentata*), high on Tallamy's list, were omitted because they were never part of western Michigan's original vegetation (Voss, Pt. II, p. 85); spruces were omitted because the only spruce native to our area, black spruce (*Picea mariana*), is "almost entirely restricted to bogs" (Voss, Pt. I, p. 64). For the reasons other notable species were omitted, such as ash, beech, and tuliptree, see "Other Trees" at the end of this section of my list.

The last of the 17 large or moderately large trees I do recommend, *Juniperus virginiana* (eastern red cedar), supports only 37 species of Lepidoptera but is nevertheless valuable to them and to wildlife in general.

1. OAKS (*Quercus* spp.)

The recent discovery that oaks as a genus host over 530 species of Lepidoptera enhances still further oaks' long reputation as noble and even sacred trees. Much of our region (including our yard) was originally mixed-oak savanna, a complex "ecotone" mosaic of oak woodlands, barrens, and tallgrass prairie openings, providing a wondrous diversity of species that development has almost obliterated. For restoration, we can choose among several oak species suited to different conditions.

Bur oak leaves and acorns

Swamp white oak (*Q. bicolor*) is most suited to the wettest conditions, such as a seasonally wet depression or a pond bank; **scarlet oak** (*Q. coccinea*) is most suited to the driest conditions, along with **Hill's** or **northern pin oak** (*Q. ellipsoidalis*), a very similar species ecologically.

Pin oak (*Q. palustris*) and **shingle oak** (*Q. imbricaria*), though more at home in lowland situations, will also grow in upland ones—but they won't thrive in the middle of a front-yard lawn engineered to drain water quickly.

White oak (*Q. alba*) thrives best in open areas, either mesic or dry; **red oak** (*Q. rubra*) in mesic woods, with light shade; **chinquapin** or **yellow chestnut oak** (*Q. muehlenbergii*) in rich woods with alkaline soils.

Black oak (*Q. velutina*), however, was the dominant oak species in black oak barrens, on dry, sandy glacial outwash and ridges across southern Michigan.

Bur oak (*Q. macrocarpa*), which demands sun but tolerates quite wet or dry conditions, is, in my opinion, the most distinctive and beautiful oak of our region. Our two bur oaks, one from a nursery and one a rescue, have struggled a bit because of our shade, but they persist, the small rescue at first growing slowly after deer browsed its leader, but both are now striving slimly and swiftly upwards for the sunlight. Generally, bur oak is one of the fastest-growing oaks, and one of the most resistant to drought, disease, and urban air pollution. It will serve bravely as a pioneer in the lousy, disturbed soil of a new subdivision. According to Edward Voss, "this was the scattered tree of the savannas called 'oak openings' in the early days of settlement in southern Michigan" (II, 81). Together, **we can bring them back**.

Oak species generally prefer a certain amount of moisture in the soil and will tolerate some shade while young. Many experts maintain that given a little care, oaks will grow as fast as many other trees. It is impossible to overstate the value of oaks to wildlife. John Eastman puts the number of their insect foragers (the caterpillars of Lepidoptera plus

Tiny cynipid wasps lay their eggs on oaks; the oak forms a gall which protects both the tree and the insect's larva. Here we see both a club gall and bullet galls on white oak. At least a thousand insect species depend on oaks, and at least 200 species use oak trees to form galls of some kind, without essentially harming the tree; they're all members of the community. Enjoy the diversity.

other herbivorous insects) easily as high as 1000 (p. 140). The acorns are extremely valuable food for birds, mammals large and small, and hoofed browsers. Cavities in older oaks provide homes for many birds and mammals.

Throughout Michigan, oak trees are subject to oak wilt disease. Members of the red oak family are particularly vulnerable, including red, scarlet, black, and pin oaks; once infected, red oaks usually die within a few weeks. White oaks, including white, swamp white, and bur oaks, are less susceptible and, if infected, take much longer to die. According to Michigan State University Extension, the disease is "potentially as serious as Dutch Elm Disease on American Elm."

The best remedy is prevention. The fungi which cause the disease, and the insects which spread it, are opportunists, taking advantage of open wounds or weakened trees. Avoid pruning oak trees except when they're dormant. If your oak tree is damaged anytime from April to October, painting the wound with a clear acrylic sealer may be helpful. There is an injected fungicide that may help to prevent infection, but it's expensive and not always effective.

My advice: choose a white oak (another point in favor of bur oaks), avoid *all* pruning except when the tree is fully dormant, hope for the best, and enjoy your oak tree.

2. WILLOWS (*Salix* spp.)

Willows run a close second to oaks as host plants for Lepidoptera species—over 450 of them. Our largest native willow, capable of reaching 40–50 ft. (or more), is **black willow** (*S. nigra*). Like all willows, it is dioecious, meaning that staminate and pistillate flowers are borne on separate plants; thus male and female plants are required for the female to bear fruit. Like most willows, it tolerates flooding but not shade. The overall wildlife value of this and other native willows is very high: in addition to serving as host plants for so many Lepidoptera—including the beautiful red-spotted purple, eastern tiger swallowtail, and viceroy butterflies

Black willow (*Salix nigra*)

and the polyphemus, cecropia, and io moths—they offer winter food in the form of buds for squirrels and birds, sap released by the drilling of yellow-bellied sapsuckers, and bark and shoots for deer, rabbits, porcupines, and muskrats. Willow bears an inconspicuous flower, nonetheless rich in sugary nectar and high-protein pollen for early native bees.

The usefulness of willows to humans lies in their capacity to hold and stabilize banks and shores; they also provide beautiful, soft foliage for landscaping purposes. How much more natural a pond looks when lined with willow trees and shrubs than with mowed grass and stones. However, they should be planted far enough away from underground pipes that their extensive root systems don't become a problem.

There are many species of willows native to Michigan, including another large species, **peachleaf willow** (*S. amygdaloides*), but most of them are not easily available commercially. Don't ask at your nursery for a weeping willow; it will be a Eurasian species native to the mountains of China on the upper reaches of the Yangtze River, or a hybrid naturalized here. Enjoy this exotic species in antique Chinese drawings and paintings, but plant natives.

The unmistakable bark of wild black cherry (Prunus serotina) looks like burnt potato chips. Black cherry provides fruits for over 70 species of birds and delectable leaves for a host of mites and insects, including over 400 species of Lepidoptera.

3. CHERRIES and PLUMS (*Prunus* spp.)

The largest native species of these generally small trees is **black wild cherry** (*P. serotina*), considered a forest tree and potentially 50-85 ft. tall. Its fruits are extremely valuable to birds and small mammals, and its leaves to hundreds of Lepidoptera species, including one of our favorites, the beautiful tiger swallowtail. (See the Smaller Trees section for the small trees in this genus native here.)

4. BIRCHES (*Betula* spp.)

Yellow birch (*B. alleghaniensis*) is among our largest deciduous trees and may reach 100 ft. in height, though 60-80 ft. is more usual. In our part of the state, it usually grows in moist lowlands but does not do well in open fields (Smith, p. 54).

The other native birches of our region include the familiar **paper, white,** or **canoe birch** (*B. papyrifera*), which normally reaches 40-60 ft. but may grow taller, and the **bog** or **dwarf birch** (*B. pumila*),

a shrub of 5–10 feet (see under Shrubs). White birch, which grows fast but is often short-lived, is now uncommon in southern Michigan. It prefers north slopes and light soil, where competition from other, longer-lived trees is minimal.

Birches provide excellent food for wildlife, from early spring when the catkins first appear, on through to autumn and winter, when they provide valuable seeds for winter foragers such as goldfinches and common red polls. In winter, twigs and buds are important food for hoofed browsers. In spring, birds use loose papery bark for nest construction.

River birch (*B. nigra*), beloved of landscapers for its ruffled bark, isn't native here.

5. POPLARS, ASPENS, COTTONWOODS (*Populus* spp.)

Poplars and aspens native to Michigan include **largetooth** or **bigtooth aspen** (*P. grandidentata*) and **quaking, smalltooth aspen** (*P. tremuloides*), along with the much larger **cottonwood** (*P. deltoides*). Their bark, twigs, and foliage are valuable as winter food to a number of creatures, and the thickets in which they often grow serve as winter cover for deer.

Tallamy points out that similarities in leaf chemistry among willows, some birches, and poplars, aspens, and cottonwoods make these trees host plants for many of the same Lepidoptera species (p. 164).

Cottonwoods (*P. deltoides*) are much the largest of the three and may, in fact, be prohibited by some cities for fear that their strong, shallow roots will destroy pipes and sidewalks.

Despite their value to wildlife, the short-lived (perhaps 100 years), brittle-limbed, at least partly clonal trees of the Populus species are probably not the best choices for your yard unless you need to stabilize soil or restore degraded land. But if you have the space, plant a cottonwood; it has a noble history as the creekbank tree providing shade and firewood out on the prairies. It was the Romans who gave the genus its name: *arbor populi*, the "people's tree." Tom is fond of aspens because they were the dominant deciduous tree of the Rocky Mountain front range, and he carried a lot of aspen firewood when he was a boy.

6. MAPLES (*Acer* spp.)

Sugar maples (*A. saccharum*) are certainly among our favorite trees for shade and brilliant fall color, but all maples are extremely valuable to Lepidoptera for their leaves as well as to other kinds of wildlife for their winged seeds, which provide food for birds, mammals, and hoofed browsers. **Red** and **silver maples** (*A. rubrum* and *A. saccharinum*) produce seeds early, in late April, and the seeds of **box elder** (*A. negundo*) ripen in late summer and persist on the tree all year long. Every part of a maple tree seems to be used by wildlife: the sap by birds, insects, and red squirrels, the bark by deer and small mammals, the leaves and buds by porcupines, the branches and cavities for birds' nests.

Silver maple grows fast, but its brittle branches break easily from wind or ice. Red maple's pri-

mary habitat is moist lowlands; it spreads aggressively in drier upland sites. Box elder, a fast-growing, brittle-limbed tree, also spreads aggressively in disturbed ground.

7. HICKORIES (*Carya* spp.)

Hickories are host plants for many beautiful Lepidoptera. In the spring, they provide wildlife with sap, birds with their flowering catkins; in the fall, nuts for wild turkeys and many different mammals. **Shellbark hickory** (*C. laciniosa*) requires more moisture than either **pignut hickory** (*C. glabra*) or **shagbark hickory** (*C. ovata*), both of

Shagbark hickory lives up to its name

which are well adapted to droughty, upland soils. **Bitternut hickory** (*C. cordiformis*), like shellbark, prefers moist lowlands. All the hickories grow slowly, perhaps persisting for years as saplings,

White-breasted nuthatch with hickory nut wedged into hickory bark. Easy pickings.

waiting for an opening to reach upwards to the canopy. Shagbark is the fastest growing and has the most picturesque "shaggy" bark of the genus. Hickories don't transplant well because of their long taproot.

8. ELMS (*Ulmus americanus*)

According to Tallamy, varieties of this beloved tree resistant to Dutch Elm Disease are now available. The value of its seed to wildlife is only moderate, but its buds are an early food source for some songbirds and for squirrels. Don't be in a hurry to get rid of an old dead elm; John Eastman points out that dead elms which have lost their bark are no longer a threat to healthy plants and are often used as homes by red-headed woodpeckers and as trellises for vines of high wildlife value such as grapevines and Virginia creeper (p. 80).

9. PINES (*Pinus* spp.)

White pines (*Pinus strobus*) are magnificent trees (70–90 ft.), extremely valuable to wildlife in general as well as to Lepidoptera. They prefer loamy well-drained soils but can tolerate sandy, and prefer sun but tolerate light shade, actually preferring it when young. Their cones open in September, and the seeds, favored by jays, nuthatches, crossbills, goldfinches, and woodpeckers, feed at least 48 species of birds as well as small mammals in fall and

An opened cone of white pine (Pinus strobus)

winter. Pines support 201 species of butterflies and moths. Deer browse on them in winter. Many birds nest in large trees, from bald eagles, hawks, and owls to warblers; like many evergreens, white pines provide excellent cover for many creatures. They also serve very well as windbreaks—for us.

Red pines (*P. resinosa*), when planted in monoculture plantations, are virtual "biological deserts" (Eastman, p. 160); even as single trees, their wildlife value is less than that of other pines because of less frequent seed production--only once in every four to seven years (Smith, p. 9). In central and northern Michigan, **Jack pines** (*P. banksiana*) are used by ground-nesting birds such as the Kirtland's warbler, common nighthawk, and vesper sparrow. An interesting tree, with cones that may persist for 20 years until they're opened by fire, it's not a good choice unless you have dry, sandy or rocky soil and open space.

10. BASSWOODS, LINDENS (*Tilia americana*)

Basswoods or lindens are valuable to herbivorous insects, but also to other types of wildlife. The nectar of their flowers strongly appeals to pollinators, and the trees hold their nutlets into midwinter, a help to overwintering birds. They provide dens for animals and wild honey bees. Their twigs and bark are eaten by rabbits, porcupines, and deer.

11. WALNUTS, BUTTERNUTS (*Juglans* spp.)

Walnuts and butternuts are extremely valuable to herbivorous insects for their foliage and to squirrels for their nuts. **Butternuts** (*J. cinerea*) are smaller, shorter-lived, and more disease-prone than **black walnuts** (*J. nigra*), but they produce less of the juglone which inhibits the growth of many plants. While all parts of the plants are toxic to some degree, the length of the lateral roots—"usually one to two times the crown radius"—certainly contributes to the problem (Eastman, p. 201). There are many lists, not always in complete agreement, of plants tolerant and intolerant of juglone. Two good ones: University of Wisconsin Extension (wihort.uwex.edu/landscape/juglone.htm); Michi-

A beautiful, distinctive tree, tamarack (Larix larisina) *is the only northern conifer that sheds all its needles in the fall*

gan State University Extension (web1.msue.msu.edu/msue/iac/greentip/blackwal.htm). Definitely avoid planting black walnuts near vegetable gardens, and vice versa. Black walnut is host to the beautiful luna moth (*Actias luna*).

12. LARCHES or TAMARACKS (*Larix laricina*)

A deciduous needled tree of bog or boreal forest, **tamarack** is a good choice if you have a sunny, fairly open spot with moist, somewhat acid soil. It will sometimes adapt to drier areas if there's not much competition (Barnes and Wagner, p. 68). If you have the right spot, go for it. Larches are host plants for over 100 Lepidoptera species; they are lovely in all seasons, with wonderful fall color; and the cones, which persist for a year or more, provide good food for birds and other wildlife. Now relatively uncommon, tamaracks were, historically, probably the most common conifer species in southern Michigan.

13. HEMLOCKS (*Tsuga canadensis*)

Shade tolerant and graceful, rising to 60–80 feet, hemlocks provide sap, seeds, shelter and nesting areas for birds, and food and shelter for deer and many other creatures. Because of their dense shade and moisture requirement, it's difficult to establish other plants under mature hemlocks. Surprisingly, perhaps, hemlocks are host plants for about 90 Lepidoptera species.

14. HONEY LOCUSTS (*Gleditsia triacanthos*)

Even though its inconspicuous flowers in May and June provide rich nectar for bees, its seeds are

eaten by squirrels, and it's a host plant for more than 40 species of Lepidoptera, Hightshoe rates the wildlife value of this tree as "very low" (p. 214). The one next to our house, however, is *very* attractive to woodpeckers and nuthatches, who apparently find lots of insects tucked in under its long, loose strips of bark.

15. SYCAMORES (*Platanus occidentalis*)

Although I wasn't surprised to read that sycamore seeds aren't popular with wildlife—we have a tree in our yard and I've never seen anything eat its attractive spherical seeds—I was indeed surprised to learn from John Eastman that both leaves and seeds of **American sycamore** produce an allelopathic herbicide that leaches into the soil and "inhibits competition from grasses and other plants beneath the tree" (p. 189). This I hadn't suspected, because a wide variety of native shrubs and forbs thrive beneath our sycamore. Sycamores are beautiful and interesting trees that provide cavities and hollows for wildlife and support 42 species of Lepidoptera. Our tree also provides lofty mating-call stages for the red-winged blackbirds when they first return in late winter.

16. HACKBERRIES (*Celtis occidentalis*)

A majestic (75–100 ft.), very valuable tree for wildlife, its fruits provide winter food for many species of birds. Its preferred habitats range from moist lowlands to dry-mesic uplands; it does favor calcareous soils. If you don't have space, consider the dwarf species (see Smaller Trees).

17. EASTERN RED CEDARS
(Juniperus virginiana)

Common in disturbed ground, **eastern red cedar** poses problems for humans; it's an alternate host for cedar-apple rust, whose spores can spread from this species to apple or crabapple trees one or two miles away. But red cedar (not a cedar at all, by the way) is a boon to wildlife. It serves as host plant for 37 species of Lepidoptera and provides abundant food and shelter to wildlife in general. Cedar "berries" on female trees contain one or two seeds and are available much of the year, including the lean period from fall through March. Over 90 different species of birds eat these blue-green or gray berries on occasion; human beings use them to flavor gin and other, more substantial foods; and mammals feeding on them range from meadow voles to coyotes.

The tree's dense foliage creates excellent cover, shelter, and nesting areas for birds, especially in hedgerows. Slow-growing, often symmetrically pyramidal, oval, or columnar when young but becoming more irregular over time, the tree rarely reaches more than 40–50 feet in Michigan. Since it spreads rapidly and shades out ground-level flora, this may not be a good choice for a small urban yard or a prairie planting.

Possible problems notwithstanding, William Cullina considers "the tree forms of juniper as among the 10 essential plants to include in a bird-friendly landscape" (p. 148).

OTHER TREES

Now, in case you're wondering about a few notable omissions from this list, such as **tuliptree** *(Liriodendron tulipifera)* or **black tupelo**, also known as black gum *(Nyssa salvatica)*, I'll explain. Both of these are beautiful native trees, tolerant of a wide range of conditions, with lovely foliage in all seasons, of great ornamental value in urban landscapes. Tuliptree, also known as tulip poplar, grows fast and can reach 100 or more feet in height, with a very broad canopy; tupelo grows slowly and compactly, lives long, and has a rugged, pic-

turesque form. But they both have the same drawbacks as redbud: compared to other species listed above, they host a relatively small number of Lepidoptera species, and their general wildlife value is rated as low. If you have lots of space, and a special spot, by all means plant one of them. It will give you great pleasure. But if you have limited space and your objective is to provide maximum habitat and sustenance for wildlife, give first consideration to trees higher on this list.

LARGE TREES UNDER SEVERE ATTACK AND THEREFORE NOT RECOMMENDED

Ash *(Fraxinus* spp.*)* has been a wonderful tree for wildlife, but it's currently under attack by the emerald ash borer, an invasive insect from Asia. Our ash trees have no immunity to the insect, which has wiped out 30 million ash trees in southeastern Michigan alone and has spread through the East and Midwest. The entire lower peninsula is under Level I quarantine by the Michigan Department of Agriculture, indicating "general presence" of the borer. According to the MDA and the Michigan Department of Natural Resources, the main reason EAB is "having such a devastating impact on Michigan's communities is that ash trees have been overplanted. Following the loss of American elm (another over-planted tree) to Dutch elm disease," ash became the favorite replacement. "This reliance on the ash tree caused many communities to lose sight of diversity" ("Emerald Ash Borer Preparedness Plan," 2007, p. 20). Michigan State University scientists have developed a method of prevention and treatment that involves fertilizers and pesticide, but it depends on early diagnosis.

Beech *(Fagus grandifolia),* a magnificent and beloved tree, is subject to beech bark disease, which has been spreading in Michigan since 2000. Michigan State University Extension predicts that as the disease front moves through Michigan, control and losses will be very serious; "beech scale and beech bark disease will affect beech trees throughout Michigan." Millions of the older beeches will be lost, and younger regenerating trees will be infected by a second round of the disease. The fungal phase of the disease weakens the tree to the point where it's subject to "beech snap," sudden collapse of part or all of the tree, creating a "hazard to people and personal property" in public areas and urban yards. Most managers of public areas simply remove infected trees. While there are possible treatments, the process has to be repeated frequently and carries no guarantee of success. The best news is that one to three percent of beeches seem to be immune to BBD, allowing for possible re-establishment of these venerable trees. For more information, see MSU Extension Bulletin E-2746 (2005).

Reluctantly, I have to recommend against planting beech and ash trees at this time, despite their great value for wildlife. If you already have either one, please keep close watch on it and seek expert advice if you see symptoms of disease. Some lovers of beech trees, in order to make sure the species ultimately prevails, recommend encouraging saplings that come up from old roots, letting them grow until they do become infected.

II. SMALLER TREES

Again, all genera, including smaller species within genera listed earlier, are listed here with the same overall rankings as in Tallamy's complete list.

1. OAKS (*Quercus* spp.)

If you don't have room in your yard for a large oak, maybe you can fit in a smaller one: **dwarf chinquapin** or **chestnut oak** (*Q. prinoides*). Remember that oaks are the most valuable genus for Lepidoptera as well as extremely valuable to other wildlife. This slow-growing dwarf oak forms a shrub or small tree that may reach 25 ft. It's not a good understory tree because it's shade-intolerant. In our yard, deer and insects find it irresistible; but it persists; and it's beautiful.

2. WILLOWS (*Salix* spp.)

If you don't have room in your yard for Michigan's largest willow, black willow (*S. nigra*), which may reach 50 ft., what about a **pussy willow** (*S. discolor*), which probably won't get taller than 25 ft., if that tall, or a **Bebb's** or **beaked willow** (*S. bebbiana*), about the same height? Actually, you'll need at least two plants in each case as these plants are dioecious. See the entry for willows in the previous section, under Large Trees, for a brief account of willows' great usefulness to wildlife. The two listed here have the distinction of blooming early, even for willows, thus providing much-needed nectar and pollen to pollinators at a time when they're scarce. That's especially important to native bees—mason bees and several species of bumble bee—which emerge much earlier than nonnative honey bees and, in many cases, live only a few weeks.

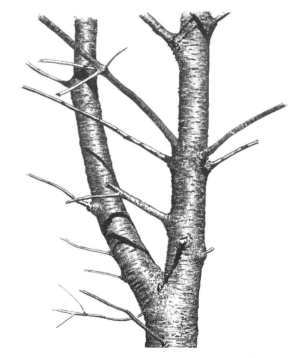

Trunk of pin cherry (Prunus pensylvanica)

3. CHERRIES and PLUMS (*Prunus* spp.)

If you have no space for the valuable black wild cherry (see Large Trees), try to include **American** or **wild plum** (*P. americana*), **chokecherry** (*P. virginiana*), or **pin** or **fire cherry** (*P. pensylvanica*), also called "bird cherry" because its rather sour fruit clusters are nonetheless quite tasty to birds (more common to northern Michigan, it does quite well in our area). These trees, none of them usually taller than about 30 feet and often shorter, reproduce themselves vegetatively as well as by seed, often forming thickets which offer shelter and nesting habitat as well as food. None of the *Prunus* species tolerates much shade, but chokecherry is moderately shade-tolerant.

4. CRABAPPLES (*Malus* spp.)

Tallamy reports that native caterpillars can usually eat the leaves of Old World crabapples, which aren't all that different, chemically, from the leaves of our few native crabapples. The latter have two disadvantages: they are often hard to obtain, and their fruits are comparatively large and remain green even when ripe. Many experts testify to birds' preference for bright red crabapples no more than 1/2 inch in diameter. The fruits of some nonnative trees, if not eaten during the fall migration, remain on the trees well into winter, providing food for winter birds and early migrants (Dennis, p. 59). Particular cultivars Dennis mentions are *Malus zumi calocarpa* [sic] and *M. baccata* 'Bob White.' Other varieties with small fruits that persist through the winter are 'Mary Potter,' 'Donald Wyman,' and 'Prairiefire' (Ross, p. 42).

5. HAWTHORNS (*Crataegus* spp.)

Hawthorns, also known as thornapples, are medium-sized, thorny, sunloving trees and shrubs prone to form thickets. Their leaves are extremely attractive to herbivorous insects and are hosts to over 150 Lepidoptera species. Small, applelike fruits persist until spring. Their formidable thorns make hawthorns extremely valuable shelter and nesting sites for birds. **Cockspur hawthorn** (*C. Crusgalli*) and **dotted hawthorn** (*C. punctata*) are two of the more common species in our area. Many of the commercially available species are not Michigan natives, and you may need to settle for a cultivar (but resist as long as you can!).

6. SERVICEBERRIES (*Amelanchier* spp.)

Serviceberries may be either sizeable understory trees or shrubs, depending on soil and sunlight. For our native species, see under Shrubs.

7. DOGWOODS (*Cornus* spp.)

Dogwoods come in many sizes and forms, and all of the native species are extremely valuable to wildlife, in addition to serving as host plants for over 100 species of Lepidoptera. The most familiar of the small, very shade-tolerant dogwood trees is the **flowering dogwood** (*C. florida*), which provides, like most dogwoods, very high-fat fruits in early fall. Less common is the **pagoda dogwood** (*C. alternifolia*), also a forest understory tree, providing blue-black fruits in August and maroon-red foliage in fall. Its arrangement of branches and leaves to make the best use of limited light give this small, attractive understory tree its "pagoda" appearance. (See also Shrubs.)

Hawthorns provide fruits for food and thorny thickets for secure cover and nesting sites. The female catkins, with tiny winged nuts, often persist through winter.

American hornbeam or muscle-wood (Carpinus caroliniana) *flexes its muscles*

8. HOP HORNBEAMS
(*Ostrya virginiana*)

Also known as ironwood, hop hornbeam provides early catkins, and its later fruits are favorites of cardinals and grosbeaks. Shade tolerant and colorful, it's an excellent understory tree (20–30 feet).

9. AMERICAN HORNBEAMS
(*Carpinus caroliniana*)

Also known as blue beech and ironwood (the latter name more commonly applied to hop hornbeam), hornbeam's hard sinewy trunk accounts for its other familiar name, musclewood. Its curving, serpentine growth pattern gives it a picturesque, bonzai-like appearance. A small tree, very shade tolerant, broadly adaptable, it prefers moist soil but doesn't require it. Deserving of more widespread use in small yards, it provides important fall and winter food (clusters of nuts) for wildlife, as well as playing host to 66 native species of Lepidoptera.

10. SHOWY MOUNTAIN ASH (*Sorbus decora*)

This showy small tree, commonly occurring on lakeshores and woodland edges north of our area, is nonetheless native to Kalamazoo County. Its brilliant fruits mature late and often persist through the winter. The variety common in suburban home landscapes is the nonnative (European) *S. aucuparia* (which can be invasive).

11. DWARF HACKBERRIES (*Celtis tenuifolia*)

Though more concentrated in southeastern than in southwestern Michigan, the dwarf hackberry presumably appeals to the same 41 species of Lepidoptera that its larger version (*C. occidentalis*) does; and its similar fruits should be similarly beloved of birds. The dwarf species may reach about 15 ft. in height.

III. Shrubs and Vines

A diverse shrub layer, as understory to taller trees, as background or anchor to beds of wildflowers, or in biohedges, is essential to providing good habitat for wildlife. This list includes some smaller species of genera listed earlier.

1. WILLOWS (*Salix* spp.)

Willow shrub thickets are common in wet areas, and their wildlife value is extremely high (see Large Trees). Besides their value as host plants, they provide cover and nesting areas for a number of bird species and pollen for early bees. There are several species native to our area, as well as naturalized European species. A typical and common native, **sandbar willow** (*S. exigua*) forms a dense thicket or "living fence" that serves very well to stabilize stream banks. Even botanists have trouble identifying willows, particularly when they are young and partly because they hybridize so easily; so take care, and consult the experts before you make your move. An atypical willow shrub preferring dry to wet ground is **upland** or **prairie willow** (*S. humilis*), an important member of prairie-savanna communities. Whatever size of willow you seek, do your best to obtain a native one.

2. CHERRIES (*Prunus* spp.)

Sand cherry (*P. pumila*), a low shrub (1 to occasionally 3 feet) of sandy and rocky areas, needs sun but tolerates moist to dry soil. Its dark purple fruits (red until ripe) are the largest of our native cherries. Beautiful fall color!

3. BOG or DWARF BIRCHES (*Betula pumila*)

The only dwarf or shrubby species of birch native to our area, the bog birch, common to boggy seeps and northern tundra, has, according to William Cullina, "little to recommend it for use in the landscape" (p. 61). Wildlife, however, might take a quite different view. In our area, the common native is probably *B. pumila,* var. *pumila* (Voss, II, 67).

4. BLUEBERRIES, CRANBERRIES (*Vaccinium* spp.)

These wonderful shrubs are host plants to almost 300 Lepidoptera species, very attractive to native bees, and extremely valuable to wildlife of all kinds. They require strongly to moderately acid soils, but tolerate a wide range of sun and moisture. All of them form dense thickets. **Lowbush blueberry** (*V. angustifolium*), usually not more than 2 ft. tall and spreading, will tolerate shade and dryness.
 Highbush blueberry (*V. corymbosum*), 6–12 ft., is perhaps a little less demanding of acidic soil but requires abundant moisture.
 Cranberry (*V. macrocarpum*) forms low, dense mats. Less attractive to birds and other wildlife and fussier about sun, moisture, and acid soil, it's probably not a good choice for urban gardens and landscapes unless you have some boggy areas.

5. SPECKLED ALDERS (*Alnus rugosa*)

A short understory tree or tall shrub (Voss, II, 64), **speckled** or **hazel alder** forms thickets on stream and pond banks and in open wet areas. Host plants to about 250 species of Lepidoptera, alders are generally valuable to wildlife, providing early nectar for bees and persistent catkins and nutlike seeds for birds and other creatures. Like legumes, alders enrich soil by hosting nitrogen-fixing bacteria in root nodules (Eastman, *Swamp*, p. 1). If you have a confined, wet, sunny area, or need to stabilize streambanks, plant some alders.

Speckled alder seed-cones and fruits

6. BLACKBERRIES, RASPBERRIES (*Rubus* spp.)

I'll limit myself to the three most common species; those more curious or adventurous should consult Voss (II, 340–54). All *Rubus* species are extremely valuable to wildlife, serving as host plants for more than 150 species of Lepidoptera, and providing cover, nesting sites, and summer food for "innumerable" birds, including many of our favorite species (Eastman, p. 35). Other creatures also find excellent cover in the "bramble" (remember Brer Rabbit?), and many relish the berries, including land turtles and *us*. Native bees obtain rich nectar and pollen.
 Common blackberry (*R. allegheniensis*) can form "thickets resembling rolls of barbed wire" (Eastman, p. 34); we sometimes have to fight it in restorations and prairie gardens. It "ranks at top" among *Rubus* species for wildlife food (Hightshoe, p. 680).

Black raspberry (*R. occidentalis*) has all the many virtues of its *Rubus* cousins, and also manages to thrive in the vicinity of black walnut trees.

Wild red raspberry (*R. strigosus*) provides "some of the most important, widely consumed fruit for birds" (Eastman, p. 168).

All the common *Rubus* species tolerate some shade, red raspberry less so; all prefer acidic soil to neutral, with black raspberry the most demanding of acidic soil; all tolerate mesic and dry mesic conditions; all range from 3 to 6 ft. in height.

The one exception to the last characteristic is the **northern dewberry** (*R. flagellaris*), with prostrate or trailing growth habit. Tolerant of quite dry conditions, it's difficult to control in a garden setting. A botanist friend is quite vehement: "it's a *noxious weed!*"

7. ROSES (*Rosa* spp.)

Native roses are beautiful in their simplicity and become still more beautiful as we realize that they are still working members of their respective ecosystems. Unlike highly cultivated roses, with their elaborately arranged petals, native roses allow pollinators easy access to their pollen and nectar. And that's not all. They may also offer dense thickets, protected by thorns, to nesting birds, and small rosehips that persist on the bushes all winter, providing food for nonmigrating birds and small mammals during the winter and even for returning migrants in early spring.

Swamp rose (*R. palustris*), grown in our mesic yard, where it gets less sun and water than it would like, has produced a small impenetrable thicket and still blooms profusely. Our chickadees hang out there constantly, and other birds flicker in and out.

Pasture rose (*R. carolina*) has larger, lighter-colored flowers, but seems to produce a somewhat less dense plant though it manages to cover the lower part of a thicket of other shrubs.

Prairie rose (*R. setigera*), a particularly beautiful climber has, in its search for sunlight, managed to cover much of a small crabapple tree with its fra-grant early summer blooms. So far, it's reached a height of over 15 feet.

In our yard, a thicket of swamp rose is the favorite cover for chickadees and titmice, and a thicket of pasture rose is the favorite for the goldfinches and sparrows. Besides serving as cover, native roses provide food for many species of birds, and numerous species of insects feed on the leaves, stems, and flowers.

8. HAZELNUTS, AMERICAN FILBERTS
(*Corylus americana*)

Hazelnuts or American filberts support a variety of wildlife with their early flowers and catkins and later very nutritious nuts, which often persist into the winter. Commonly found in oak savanna habitat, hazelnut tolerates dry soil and full sun to light shade. It can form a thick hedgerow that provides excellent cover for birds and other creatures.

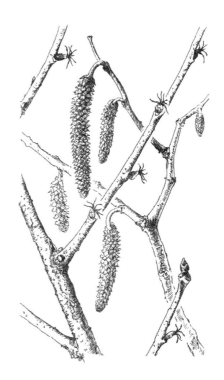

Hazelnut shrubs form thickets which provide food and shelter for all seasons

9. SERVICEBERRIES (*Amelanchier* spp.)

Our natives—known as Juneberry, shadblow, and serviceberry—are *A. arborea*, *A. laevis*, and *A. interior*, all of them small trees and shrubs (30–40 ft.). (*A. canadensis*, a standard nursery species, comes from further east.) Understory trees, they do nonetheless appreciate sun. *A. laevis* likes full sun but will tolerate dry shade; none of the species tolerates wet soil. Blossoming as early as mid-April (especially *A. arborea*—"shadblow"), they provide early nectar for insects and one of the first fruits of early summer, welcome food for 35 species of birds, including rose-breasted grosbeaks, Baltimore orioles. and brown thrashers, as well as for many small mammals. A major food source for early settlers and Indians (as pemmican), they still provide pies and jellies for those of us earlier than the birds. Their gray bark is beautiful.

10. DOGWOODS (*Cornus* spp.)

Like their understory-tree cousins, dogwood shrubs provide late summer or fall high-energy berries for migrating birds and for mammals bulking up for winter. Two whose creamy-white late summer fruits disappear very quickly are **gray dogwood** (*C. racemosa*) and **red osier** (*C. stolonifera*). The dense branching and foliage of gray dogwood make it ideal for nesting and shelter.

Gray dogwood does well in dry to wet-mesic habitats. Red osier and **silky dogwood** (*C, amomum*) both prefer wet habitat and sun but will tolerate light shade. **Roundleaf dogwood** (*C. rugosa*), attractive in all seasons, prefers moist light shade and produces a white-blue fruit for birds and other wildlife in fall. *All* of the shrub dogwoods are aggressive and form thickets.

11. VIBURNUMS (*Viburnum* spp.)

Important for persistent fruits, often lasting through winter, most viburnum species tolerate a wide range of moisture and light. **American (highbush) cranberry** (*V. trilobum*) provides bright red clusters of berries in late summer. Be sure *not* to plant the European highbush cranberry (*V. opulus*), which is invasive and persistent.

Arrowwood viburnum (*V. dentatum*) provides blue berries in late summer and fall. **Nannyberry** (*V. lentago*), one of the first to flower in the spring, is especially important for early native bees, and its dark blue berries ripen late, in September. **Mapleleaf viburnum** (*V. acerifolium*) seems to thrive in deep shade (Billington, 303), and its berries, like those of *V. trilobum*, remain through the winter. Viburnum species vary in height from 10 to 25 feet, with mapleleaf viburnum a short undershrub and nannyberry closing in on tree height.

12. CURRANTS, GOOSEBERRIES (*Ribes* spp.)

Valuable as their foliage is to Lepidoptera, supporting 92 species, and their nectar and fruits to other forms of wildlife as well, *Ribes* species must be planted with care as they are alternate hosts for white pine blister rust and capable of infecting white pines (*Pinus strobus*) a few hundred feet away (Eastman, p. 67).

13. MEADOWSWEET, STEEPLEBUSH (*Spiraea* spp.)

Meadowsweet (*S. alba*), a host plant for many Lepidoptera, needs moist or wet soil and sun. It had lovely fluffy white blooms in our yard for a few years but has lately languished for lack of sun and moisture. Its pink-flowered cousin, **steeplebush** (*S. tomentosa*), has the same virtues and limitations.

14. GRAPES (*Vitis* spp.)

The most common native species, **riverbank grape** (*Vitis riparia*), is a sturdy climber, to as high as 35 feet. It's a favorite food for songbirds and just about all creatures, particularly after frost concentrates the sugar content. It's also a host plant for more than 70 species of Lepidoptera. Quite aggressive, wild grapes can cover and shade out other vegetation; they're quite tolerant of most conditions.

15. WITCH HAZEL (*Hamamelis virginiana*)

Witch hazel, appearing in mesic to dry woods, is distinctive for its yellow, torchlike blooms in late fall to December, after it and other deciduous plants have shed their leaves. At the same time, seedpods from the previous year begin to explode, shooting seeds as far as 20 feet. Wildlife value is low. The "witch" epithet derives from use of forked twigs by water diviners or "well witchers" to locate water (Barnes and Wagner, p. 222).

Witch hazel (Hamamelis virginiana) *is host to over 60 species of Lepidoptera*

16. SUMAC (*Rhus* spp.)

Staghorn sumac (*R. typhina*) provides important food for around 100 species of birds when other food is scarce, as well as nectar-rich flowers for bees and homes for many species of bees and wasps in hollowed-out dead stems. An early successional species in poor soils, staghorn sumac forms extensive clonal thickets. If you have lots of sunny space or an old field, let it grow. **Shining** or **dwarf sumac** (*R. copallina*) is shorter (5–8 ft.) than staghorn (8–18 ft.) and better suited to limited space.

17. NEW JERSEY TEA (*Ceanothus americanus*)

A small shrub of prairies and open savannas, it bears beautiful puffs of white flowers in July, very attractive both to us and to bees and other pollinators. Tolerant of light shade, it prospers in full sun and dry soil. A nitrogen fixer, it promotes growth of other plants in its vicinity. It served as a tea for the colonists who scorned King George's tea tax, and it will serve you and wildlife in many, many ways.

18. HUCKLEBERRIES (*Gaylussacia baccata*)

Black huckleberry needs rather acidic soil but is otherwise fairly tolerant of moist or dry soils and full sun to light shade. Its compact colonies are important as wildlife cover, and it provides fruits for many birds and small mammals as well as nectar for bumble bees and small native bees.

19. COMMON JUNIPER (*Juniperus communis*)

The common juniper, a low spreading shrub, with high wildlife value, wants sun and mesic to dry soil. It's probably most available and useful in its low-growing variant, *J. communis* var. *depressa*. (For its cousin, the eastern red cedar, see Trees, above.) Most creeping and landscape junipers available in nurseries are Asian; some are sterile cultivars and bear no fruit.

20. ELDERBERRIES (*Sambucus* spp.)

Besides hosting 40 native species of Lepidoptera, **Red elderberry** (*S. pubens*) has many virtues: it flowers early for the native bees; it bears early, bright red fruits at about the time its cousin, common elderberry, is just flowering (mid to late June); and it tolerates drier conditions than the common and doesn't form colonies quite so readily. **Common elderberry** (*S. canadensis*) is nonetheless valuable, providing purple-black berries quickly consumed by many species of birds, leaving the bare stem clusters a brilliant red against the shade of August greenery. Not particular about soil, it grows in sun or shade. If cut down to the ground periodically, elder species will provide more fruit. The hollow stems, standing or fallen, provide nesting sites for native bees.

21. NINEBARKS (*Physocarpus opulifolius*)

A very hardy shrub, adaptable to both wet pondbanks and dryish yards, ninebark's wildlife value is "intermediate" (Hightshoe, p. 632); it's a host plant for 40 species of Lepidoptera. Supposedly intolerant of shade, it does well on the shady side of our yard as an understory shrub. In our yard, the fruits are always gone by spring, but only once have we seen anyone actually eating them: on Nov. 21, 2005, I saw shadowy movement in the ninebarks; through the field glasses, the shadows became six cardinals, enjoying the fruits. If cut down periodically to about a foot above the ground, ninebarks will produce more fruit (but I think they're more valuable left alone, for cover and nesting sites).

22. WINTERBERRY HOLLY (*Ilex verticillata*)

Winterberry holly has persistent berries, bright red against the snow; they're eaten in late winter and early spring by many birds, often by returning migrants. In our yard, the berries always last until March; then, quickly, they're gone. Winterberry hosts 34 native species of Lepidoptera. Dioecious, it must have both a male and a female plant.

23. VIRGINIA CREEPER
(*Parthenocissus quinquefolia*)

Virginia creeper, deep-rooted, high-climbing, and wide-spreading, can be a problem in limited spaces. Its dark blue-black berries, however, persist through early winter and provide welcome food for birds and small mammals (but are poisonous to humans). It's a host plant for 32 native species of Lepidoptera.

24. BLACK CHOKEBERRIES
(*Aronia melanocarpa* or *Photinia melanocarpa*).

One of the more tolerant wetland shrubs, black chokeberries prefer sunny and wet but can manage moderate shade and drier areas. Clonal, they form thickets, especially in wet areas. Important for pollinators, they're not a major food source for other wildlife.

Chokeberry (Aronia melanocarpa) *is host for 29 species of Lepidoptera.*

25. CORALBERRY or INDIAN CURRANT and SNOWBERRY
(*Symphoricarpos* spp.)

An attractive, spreading, mounded shrub with multiple arching stems, **coralberry** (*S. orbiculatus*) blooms in late summer with inconspicuous greenish flowers clustered in leaf axils, almost unnoticeable until you see all the bees on them. The coral red berries which follow are said to be food for many birds and small mammals, but they remain through the winter on our shrubs. **Snowberry** (*S. albus*) produces small clusters of white flowers and white berries in late fall. Ours suckers, forming thickets; so it's probably not a good choice unless you have lots of space and need a low, shade-tolerant, dense ground cover (about 2–3 feet). Our small thicket of snowberry, however, seems well worth the trouble: laced and bordered with common milkweed and New England aster, it provides winter cover and food for several species of birds, including goldfinches.

26. BUTTONBUSH (*Cephalanthus occidentalis*)

A wonderful, interesting shrub for shorelines and low areas with some standing water, buttonbush is also known as pin-ball and little snowball for its creamy white ball-like clusters of flowerets with long anthers like pins in a pincushion. The flowers draw butterflies, and the seeds draw birds such as goldfinches. It likes sun and wet ground, but it continues to bloom in our mesic, shady yard.

Black swallowtail butterfly nectaring on buttonbush flowers

27. SPICEBUSH (*Lindera benzoin*)

An early blooming understory shrub, spicebush provides important nectar for native bees and small flies when little else is blooming. Spicebush and another member of the laurel family, **sassafras** (*Sassafras albidum*), are important as host plants for beautiful spicebush swallowtail butterflies (*Papilio troilus*), and spicebush also hosts the showy promethea moth (*Callosamia promethea*). Though perhaps most elegant in early spring, spicebush, with its clusters of minute, yellowish-green flowers set, like lacework, along bare, delicate branches, is a shrub for all seasons. In late summer, the beautiful oval fruits, of brightest red and rich in fat content, are favorite foods for migrating birds. And those delicate, nicely-spaced branches are also elegant in winter.

Spicebush prefers moist soil, but in our yard it tolerates midsummer dryness where it's well protected from mid-day sun under an old sugar maple. It's tolerant of both sun and shade, but seems to draw the line at deep, full shade. Dioecious: must have both male and female plants.

For further information on species:

www.plants.usda.gov. Plant profiles for most species and links to other sources.

www.wildflowersmich.org/plants

For information on Michigan forest communities:

http://web4.msue.msu.edu/mnfi/communities

SOME GENERAL PRINCIPLES ON
LANDSCAPING WITH TREES AND SHRUBS

- Plant for a diversity of food and cover for wildlife, but don't try for one of everything. Pollinators and birds are intelligent creatures and want to save energy by finding as much food as possible without traveling long distances. So, if you have the space, plant several of the same species together in rows or thickets.

- Consider what's already provided by your neighbors or nearby natural areas. "You plant nut trees and I'll plant spruce, you keep a berry thicket and I'll do the tall grass, or the bog, the woodlot, the crowds of fruiting shrubs and beds of wildflowers. But let us weave them together into something big enough to matter by connecting each patch with others at the corners and along the boundaries … This is the ark" (Stein, p. 97).

- Observe, in all seasons, what *works* in your landscape. Get rid of exotic invasives no matter how attractive they seem to be for wildlife; but don't be in a hurry to replace other useful nonnatives until you have a native replacement that serves as well as or better than the nonnative it replaces. For a list of invasive trees, shrubs, and vines you should not only avoid planting but should replace with a native as soon as possible, see Chapter 12.

- Don't plant anything just so you will have one of those. Tempting though it may be (and we've been tempted), you're not primarily amassing an impressive "plant list," or even just satisfying a curiosity. Choose your plantings and experiments for the next seven generations—and beyond.

- **Plant local genotypes**; avoid hybrids and cultivars. Local wildlife has adapted to the blooming, leafing, seed-forming, and fruiting times of local native plants. "Indigenous wildlife are dependent on the native plants with which they have coevolved" (Sauer, p. 178).

- **Plant in layers**: "The natural landscape is typically layered, from the ground to the canopy, rather than reduced to a single layer or two such as turf and shade trees. A forested landscape includes several layers of young trees, shrubs, vines, and herbaceous species, not just specimen plants in mulch or turf" (Sauer, p. 178). See Chapter 9 for lists of shade plants to complete the herbaceous layer in your woodland plantings. Layers, right down to the leaf litter, plant debris, soil, and root systems of varying depth, offer a rich system of mutually supporting plant species and special niches for diverse wildlife. Plant in layers, and chances are better that you'll be planting for the whole food web, not just your own preferences—*and* you'll sequester a lot of carbon.

- A thicket or hedgerow includes all the layers, with food and shelter for all seasons. "A hedgerow typically includes small trees, and vegetation grows so entangled that no individual species can grow to be a specimen. Grasses, ferns, and flowers push into the edges, work their way wherever there is space, forming a ground-filling mulch from which the larger species grow … The growth of a hedgerow is a force of nature" (Sara Stein, "Berrying the Pump Stations," pp. 1, 7).

- Include evergreens: they provide important cover and food, plus winter windbreaks to save you energy (and money you can use for good causes). For basic principles on using trees and shrubs to provide protection from both winter wind and summer heat, try www.pioneerthinking.com/shading.html. For more detailed discussion, try www.state.mn.us.mn/…/ Energy_Saving_Landscapes_110802040030_

Landscaping.pdf. But while saving energy is important, your primary consideration is always preserving native plants and using them effectively to provide habitat and food for wildlife.

- Don't overshade your property: create a mix of shaded areas, "edge" areas bordering and opening onto sunny areas, and open meadows layered with grasses and wildflowers. For habitat, diversity of spaces is just as important as diversity of layers.

- Leave old and gnarled trees and dead standing trees (snags) in place if you safely can. "All ages, and all together growing and dying … That's a natural community, human or other" (Snyder, p. 138).

- **Leave stumps and downed trees and branches** in place if you can. They are essential to renewal of soil and life. As they slowly decompose, they provide food for countless arthropods, worms, fungi, and occasionally salamanders. They also serve as nurseries for new growth, and slowly create small variations in the contours of the land, an important component of a natural landscape. We began with a perfectly flat, boring suburban lot; in 20 years, we have a gently contoured one, partly by relocating what ordinarily passes for waste, partly through just letting it be.

- **Plan for the future**: allow for the future size of the plant and for how long it will live.

- Spend quiet time observing the groupings of plants in local natural areas. You'll not only lift your spirits, you'll gain understanding of what species normally grow together and how they arrange themselves. Insofar as you can, follow the cues provided by natural ecosystems and plant communities to create natural groupings. Provide the appropriate plants, in appropriate groupings, and "appropriate wildlife" will come.

A fallen or cut "nurse log" provides shelter and food for soil organisms, insects, seedlings, birds, and other creatures. Note the mosses, lichens, fungi, and zigzag goldenrod growing from this decaying log, with woodland phlox, sensitive fern, and jack-in-the-pulpit sheltering in its shadow.

- **Allow for change.** Recognize and accept that nature will make choices which may not conform to your plan or preferences but which nonetheless may turn out to be ideal. One of our most used areas is an accidental thicket which began because an ancient crabapple, with sprawling multiple trunks, was subsiding into the ground; so we let the undergrowth grow wild. The birds planted river grape, gray dogwood, and pokeweed; cup plant and common milkweed migrated from nearby; we added *Clematis virginiana*, which climbs on the trellis provided by the dying crabapple, and *Rosa carolina*. The resulting thicket is bordered on one side by a white spruce and a pair of winterberry shrubs; it's now anchored by a wild black cherry we planted in its midst. The whole area, mostly unplanned, is *alive* with birds and other creatures, in all seasons.

- Plant carefully, to give each tree or shrub a good chance for a healthy future. For a tree and shrub planting guide: www.tree-planting. com/tree-planting-4.htm.

- **Remember that your yard is an experiment and a work in progress**, which you are always in the process of upgrading so as to make its plantings more *diverse* and thus more *helpful to wildlife*.

REFERENCES

Barnes, Burton V., and Warren H. Wagner, Jr. *Michigan Trees: A Guide to the Trees of Michigan and the Great Lakes Region.* Ann Arbor: Univ. of Michigan Press, 1981. Clearly illustrated, with helpful notes on habitat and associated species, this guide includes nonnative trees and an abbreviated guide to shrubs and woody vines.

Billington, Cecil. *Shrubs of Michigan.* 2nd edition. Bloomfield Hills, MI: Cranbrook Institute of Science, 1949. Rich in detail and personal observation.

Cullina, William. *Native Trees, Shrubs, and Vines: A Guide to Using, Growing, and Propagating North American Woody Plants.* Boston: Houghton Mifflin, 2002.

Dennis, John V. *The Wildlife Gardener.* New York: Ballantine Books, 1985.

Eastman, John. *The Book of Forest and Thicket.* Harrisburg, PA: Stackpole Books, 1992. *The Book of Swamp and Bog.* Mechanicsburg, PA: Stackpole Books, 1995. *The Book of Field and Roadside.* Harrisburg, PA: Stackpole Books, 2003. Unless otherwise indicated, all references in the text are to *The Book of Forest and Thicket.*

Henderson, Carrol L., Carolyn J. Dindorf, and Fred J. Rozumalski. *Lakescaping for Wildlife and Water Quality.* St. Paul: Minnesota Dept. of Natural Resources, No date.

Hightshoe, Gary L. *Native Trees, Shrubs, and Vines for Urban and Rural America: A Planting Design Manual for Environmental Designers.* New York: John Wiley & Sons, 1988. You should have a copy of Hightshoe's invaluable book: it both illustrates and describes form, branching, foliage, flower, and fruit for each species; it also describes habitat and provides a distribution map for each. At the beginning of each of the two sections of the book, on trees and on shrubs and vines, Hightshoe summarizes, in what he calls "Elimination Keys," virtually all the information for each species, divided into lists, tables and graphs for wildlife value, form, height, spread, coloration (in each season and for each part of the plant), bark character, and—immensely valuable—a graphic phenological calendar showing times for flowering, foliation and leaf retention, and fruit formation and retention. His graphic table of "Plants Suitable for Urban Environments" enables you to make quick comparisons of each plant's sensitivity to urban environment and land use, plus its rooting pattern. These tables are very helpful in choosing appropriate species for your conditions and spaces and in providing year-long food and habitat for wildlife. Be aware, however, that his "wildlife value" ratings are only for vertebrates; that's why Tallamy's rankings are so important, as well as your own careful observations.

Ross, Marty. "Berry Best Plants for Birds," *Nature's Garden*, Fall, 2009.

Sauer, Leslie Jones. *The Once and Future Forest: A Guide to Forest Restoration Strategies.* Washington, D.C.: Island Press, 1998.

Sibley, David Allen. *The Sibley Guide to Trees.* New York: Alfred A. Knopf, 2009. "Beautiful, masterful," says E. O. Wilson. He's right.

Smith, Norman F. *Trees of Michigan and the Upper Great Lakes,* 6th ed. Lansing, MI.: Thunder Bay Press, 1995.

Snyder, Gary. *The Practice of the Wild.* San Francisco: North Point Press, 1990.

Stein, Sara. *Noah's Garden: Restoring the Ecology of Our Own Back Yards.* Boston: Houghton, Mifflin, 1993.

_____. "Berrying the Pump Stations," *Wild Ones Journal*, Nov./Dec., 2005, pp. 1, 6–7.

Tallamy, Douglas. *Bringing Nature Home: How You Can Sustain Wildlife with Native Plants.* Updated and expanded. Portland, OR: Timber Press, 2009.

Voss, Edward G. *Michigan Flora.* Bloomfield Hills: Cranbrook Institute of Science and Univ. of Michigan Herbarium, 1972 (Pt. 1), 1985 (Pt. 2), 1996 (Pt. 3). Now available online in a revised edition: http://michiganflora.net/home.aspx.

For additional useful books on trees, native plants generally, and wildlife, see Chapter 6. For native plants and insects, see Chapter 7.

12

ALIEN PLANT SPECIES WHICH DEGRADE MIDWEST NATURAL AREAS

Three million acres
(an area twice the size of the state of Delaware),
are lost to invasive plants each year.
—Federal Highway Administration, 1996

Many nonnative plants, mostly from Europe or Asia, invade natural areas and destroy them by changing ecosystem processes: e.g., shrinking supplies of surface water; shading out and crowding out native species; and hybridizing with native species and potentially eliminating native genetic strains. Alien invasive species are the second greatest threat, globally, to biodiversity—second only to development.

Such plants are threats in all of our natural or semi-natural areas, including rangelands, grasslands, wetlands, and forests. In national parks and nature preserves, they threaten some of the very species these lands are intended to preserve. These invasive, nonnative plants should not be planted even in yards, for fear that they will escape to, and infest, nearby natural areas.

Characteristic of most of these plants is the production of many small seeds which are dispersed by birds and other wildlife—a process we cannot control except by not planting these dangerous plants ourselves and by discouraging others, including our cities, counties, and states, from doing so. Don't assume, because an invasive plant has not so far spread in your yard, that it hasn't spread to some other area, or won't do so in the future. Also, don't assume that because an invasive species provides food for wildlife

that it should be retained. The fruit of buckthorn (*Rhamnus* spp.), for instance, although gobbled up by birds, is diuretic and causes energy loss in the birds who eat very much of it.

You can best defend against invasive alien plants by maintaining a rich diversity of native plants; the more diverse the ecosystem, the greater its resources for resisting stresses, including invasion by alien species.

When you remove invasive aliens, it's important to replace them with appropriate native species; otherwise, opportunistic weedy species that thrive in disturbed ground will fill the newly opened spaces. Many such species are likely to thrive on climate change, at the expense of native plant communities.

Especially pernicious and widespread species are marked with an asterisk (*).

Alien Trees

Amur maple	*Acer ginnala*
Norway maple	*A. platanoides**
Tree-of-heaven	*Ailanthus altissima*
Black alder, European alder	*Alnus glutinosa*
Paper mulberry	*Broussonetia papyrifera*
White mulberry	*Morus alba*
White poplar, silver poplar	*Populus alba*
Black locust	*Robinia pseudoacacia**
—native to eastern N. A., but not Midwest	
White willow	*Salix alba*
European mountain ash	*Sorbus aucuparia*
Tamarisk—a serious problem	*Tamarix chinensis*
west of Minnesota, but can invade	*T. parviflora*
northern Michigan wetlands	*T. ramosissima*
Chinese elm	*Ulmus chinensis*
Siberian elm	*U. pumila*
Wayfaring tree—a small tree or shrub	*Viburnum lantana*

Alien Shrubs

Barberry	*Berberis* spp.
Peashrub	*Caragana arborescens*
Russian olive—infests 17 western states	*Elaeagnus angustifolia*
Autumn olive	*E. umbellata**
Winged euonymus, burning bush	*Euonymus alatus*
Privet	*Ligustrum vulgare**
Honeysuckle (also see "Vines"):	
Amur honeysuckle	*Lonicera maackii**
Bella honeysuckle	*L. x bella**
Morrow's honeysuckle	*L. morrowii**
Tatarian honeysuckle	*L. tatarica** (and hybrids of these honeysuckle species)
White mulberry	*Morus alba*
Buckthorn:	
Common buckthorn, European buckthorn, Hart's thorn, European waythorn, rhineberry, smooth buckthorn, glossy buckthorn, alder buckthorn, columnar buckthorn, European alder, fen buckthorn, tall hedge	*Rhamnus cathartica** *R. frangula**
Multiflora rose	*Rosa multiflora**
Japanese spirea (pink spirea)	*Spiraea japonica*

Japanese yew—already a problem in Northeast   *Taxus cuspidata*
European cranberry bush, European   *Viburnum opulus* var. *opulus*
   highbush cranberry, Guelder rose

Alien Vines

Porcelain berry   *Ampelopsis brevipedunculata*
Oriental bittersweet, Asiatic bittersweet,   *Celastrus orbiculatus**
   round-leaved bittersweet
Wintercreeper, climbing euonymus   *Euonymus fortunei**
Ground-ivy, gill-over-the-ground,   *Glechoma hederacea*
   creeping Charlie
English ivy   *Hedera helix*
Japanese hops   *Humulus japonicus*
Honeysuckle (also see "Shrubs"):
   Japanese honeysuckle, Hall's honeysuckle   *Lonicera japonica*
Kudzu—has reached Midwest   *Pueraria lobata*
   —including Michigan!
Mile-a-minute—already a problem in   *Tracaulon (Polygonum)*
   Northeast and Wisconsin   *perfoliatum*
Black swallow-wort   *Vincetoxicum (Cynanchum)*
       nigrum or *Cynanchum*
       louiseae*

Periwinkle, myrtle, vinca   *Vinca major* and *V. minor*

Leafy spurge (Euphorbia esula), *carpeting fields and lowlands with a two-foot canopy of yellow-green, has degraded millions of acres of prairies and pastures in the northern Great Plains and is moving ever farther south in Michigan. If you find any trace, remove it* **immediately**. *Large-scale control is very difficult.*

Spotted knapweed (Centaurea maculosa) *takes over in sunny fields. It's allelopathic, i.e. it poisons the ground for other species; and it's mildly carcinogenic—wear gloves if you're pulling lots of it. It pulls fairly easily if the ground is wet; but if you don't get the whole root, it will be back!*

Alien Herbaceous Plants

Goutweed	*Aegopodium podagraria*
Garlic mustard	*Alliaria petiolata**
Cornflower, bachelor's button	*Centaurea cyanus*
Spotted knapweed	*C. maculosa**
Ox-eye daisy	*Chrysanthemum leucanthemum*
Canada thistle	*Cirsium arvense**
Marsh/European swamp thistle	*C. palustre*
Lily-of-the-valley	*Convallaria majalis*
Crown vetch	*Coronilla varia*
Queen Anne's lace	*Daucus carota*
Cut-leaf teasel	*Dipsacus laciniatus*
Teasel	*D. sylvestris*
Water-hyacinth	*Eichornia crassipes*
Leafy spurge	*Euphorbia esula**
Japanese knotweed, Mexican bamboo	*Fallopia (Bilderdykia) japonica*
	or *Polygonum cuspidatum*
Baby's breath	*Gypsophila paniculata*
Orange day-lily	*Hemerocallis fulva*

Garlic mustard (Alliaria petolata) *crowds out most woodland perennials and even prevents new growth of forest trees. It's a biennial, flowering in the second year and then dying. Each garlic mustard plant can produce from hundreds on up to thousands of seeds in slender pods. Seeds remain viable in the soil for five years and more. Density of first-year seedlings can reach thousands per square yard; but less than 5% of those will survive as second-year flowering plants. Pulling up seedlings is very laborious, and thankless. Some report success with raking when the ground is wet, using an edge tool or drag to cut them down, or using a "flame weeder" to wither the seedlings (but not scorch the soil).*

Dame's rocket	*Hesperis matronalis**
Orange hawkweed	*Hieracium aurantiacum*
Common St. John's wort	*Hypericum perforatum*
Yellow flag iris	*Iris pseudacorus*
Butter and eggs	*Linaria vulgaris*
Bird's-foot trefoil, deer vetch	*Lotus corniculatus**
Money plant, Chinese money	*Lunaria annua*
Moneywort, creeping Jenny	*Lysimachia nummularia*
Purple loosestrife	*Lythrum salicaria**
White sweetclover	*Meliotus alba**
Yellow sweetclover	*M. officinalis**
Eurasian water milfoil	*Myriophyllum spicatum**
Wild parsnip	*Pastinaca sativa**
Sulfur cinquefoil	*Potentilla recta*
Bouncing Bet	*Saponaria officinalis*
Bladder campion	*Silene vulgaris*
Narrow-leaved cattail	*Typha angustifolia**
Garden heliotrope	*Valeriana officinalis*

ALIEN GRASSES

Quack grass	*Agropyron repens**
Smooth brome	*Bromus inermis**
Tall fescue, taller fescue, meadow fescue	*Festuca arundinacea (F. elatior)*
Reed canary grass	*Phalaris arundinacea**
Giant reed	*Phragmites australis**
Canada bluegrass	*Poa compressa*
Kentucky bluegrass	*P. pratensis*
Sorghum	*Sorghum bicolor*
Johnsongrass	*S. halepense*

REFERENCES

Bright, Chris. *Life Out of Bounds: Bioinvasion in a Borderless World.* Worldwatch Environmental Alert Series, 1998.

Burrell, C. Colston. *Native Alternatives to Invasive Plants.* Brooklyn Botanic Garden, 2006. Valuable suggestions for plants that provide the same benefits as the invasive species, without destruction of biodiversity. Not all the species Burrell suggests, however, are natives.

Czarapata, Elizabeth. *Invasive Plants of the Upper Midwest. An Illustrated Guide*. Madison: Univ. of Wisconsin, 2005. Indispensable.

Devine, Robert. *Alien Invasion: America's Battle with Non-Native Animals and Plants*. National Geographic Society, 1998.

Gelber, Debra, and William D. Schneider. *Invasive Species Survey*. Ann Arbor: Univ. of Michigan, 1992.

Henderson, Carrol L. "Appendix E: Plant Substitutes for Invasive Non-Native Species," in *Lakescaping for Wildlife and Water Quality*. Minnesota Dept. of Natural Resources, undated.

Howe, Katherine, et al. (eds.). *A Field Guide to Invasive Plants of the Midwest*. Michigan Invasive Plant Network. Online at http://mipn.org.

Marinelli, Janet. *Stalking the Wild Amaranth: Gardening in the Age of Extinction*. New York: Henry Holt, 1998.

Olson, Cassandra, and Anita F. Cholewa. *A Guide to Nonnative Invasive Plants Inventoried in the North by Forest Inventory and Analysis*. U. S. Forest Service, 2009. Good photographs, distribution maps, distinguishing characteristics.

Randall, John M., and Janet Marinelli (eds.). *Invasive Plants: Weeds of the Global Garden*. Brooklyn Botanic Garden, 1996.

Stein, Sara. "The Weeds of Halloween," in *Planting Noah's Garden*, pp. 169–81. Boston, New York: Houghton Mifflin, 1997.

Voss, Edward G. *Michigan Flora*, 3 vols. Ann Arbor, MI: Cranbrook Institute of Science and Univ. of Mich. Herbarium, 1972–1996.

HELPFUL WEBSITES

Brooklyn Botanic Garden—**www.bbg.org/gardening/handbook/native_alternatives**

Center for Invasive Species and Ecosystem Health—**www.invasive.org**. Comprehensive, including lots of links, distribution maps, and lists of native alternatives.

Michigan Invasive Plant Network—**http://mipn.org**

Michigan Natural Features Inventory—**http://web4.msue.msu.edu/mnfi/education/factsheets.cfm**

Wildflower Association of Michigan—**http://wildflowersmich.org/index.php?menu=10**

Wild Ones—Native Plants, Natural Landscapes—**www.wildones.org/download**. Two downloads: Elizabeth Czarapata, "Why We Cannot Ignore Invasive Plants"; Maryann Whitman, "Dealing with Alien Invasives: Know the Enemy."

Wildtype Nursery (Mason, Michigan)—**http://wildtypeplants.com/invasive.html**

Wisconsin Department of Natural Resources—**http://dnr.wi.gov/invasives/plants.asp.** Very good fact sheets and a photo (rogues) gallery.

13

USING NATIVE PLANTS TO IMPROVE YOUR VEGETABLE GARDEN

Would we not better achieve our goal of a pest-free garden
if we employed nature herself to look after things?
—Douglas Tallamy, *Bringing Nature Home*

Replacement of lawn-grass monocultures with vegetable gardens and a few fruit-bearing shrubs and trees is an important step towards health and sustainability. It makes us less dependent on an industrial agriculture that is causing global health problems, climate disruption, and massive loss of biodiversity. But as long as we are using our properties to provide food only for ourselves, we are still part of the problem. Only when we consciously provide food for the soil organisms, for the pollinators of all plants, and for the beneficial insects and other creatures that help to sustain natural systems—only then will we be practicing nature's "law of return," recycling back into the earth as much as we draw out and providing for the creatures who provide for us. Only then will we have fully become part of the growing movement to practice the kind of organic, holistic agriculture and gardening that seeks not to appropriate earth's resources for our own use but to employ nature's own methods to benefit both ourselves and the wondrous diversity of local creatures we depend upon.

> How merrily they creep and
> run and flye
>
> —John Clare, "Insects"

Chapter 7, "Gardens for Pollinators," emphasizes how native plants and native pollinators are dependent on one another. Recent research increasingly demonstrates just how beneficial our native pollinators and other insects are to agricultural crop production and also to home vegetable gardens. We can now clearly realize how important it is that fruit and vegetable gardens include native plants in adjoining or intermingled plantings. Even a small yard and vegetable garden, if it's biologically diverse, can not only provide healthier food right now but also help to restore nature and thus promote healthier ecosystems for future generations.

127

If your space is limited, concentrate on the native plants most attractive to beneficial insects: species of asters, coneflowers, coreopsis, goldenrods, milkweeds, and native sunflowers.

The following sources provide lots of practical information about how to enhance the beneficial relationships between native plants, native insects, and food crops.

Helpful Websites

http://nativeplants.msu.edu
   Includes the pamphlets "Attracting Beneficial Insects with Native Flowering Plants" and "Conserving Native Bees on Farmland," available for download under Publications.

http://www.xerces.org
   Includes fact sheets "Farming with Pollinators," "Upper Midwest Plants for Native Bees," "Nests for Native Bees," and "Farming for Bees."

http://www.xerces.org/2008/07/21/how-to-protect-and-enhance-habitat-for-native-bees/
   "Native Pollinators: How to Protect and Enhance Habitat for Native Bees."

> Let us give nature a chance;
> she knows herself better than we do.
>
> —Michel de Montaigne

http://yolorcd.org/resources/manuals/
Includes the publication "Bring Farm Edges Back to Life!" for download.

http://attra.org/publication.html
Includes the publication "Farmscaping to Enhance Biological Control" for download.

http://plants.usda.gov/pollinators/NRCSdocuments.html
   Includes the publications "Improving Forage for Native Bee Crop Pollinators" and "Native Pollinators" for download.

http://www.ars.usda.gov/Services/docs.htm?docid=12050
   "Gardening for Native Bees in North America." There is also a nice plant list on the site.

http://www.pollinator.org/resources.htm
   Includes the publication "Your Urban Garden is Better with Bees" for download.

http://www.pollinator.org, for North American Pollinator Protection campaign
   A 24-page document to download: "Selecting Plants for Pollinators: A Regional Guide for Farmers, Landmanagers, and Gardeners in the Eastern Broadleaf Forest—Continental Province" (this is us!).

http://www.fsa.usda.gov/mi

A brochure to download from the Farm Service Agency about a new Conservation Reserve Program (CRP). Called CRP-SAFE (SAFE stands for State Acres for Wildlife Enhancement), this program allows people in 22 counties of the western lower peninsula to participate in a program for ENHANCING HABITAT FOR NATIVE POLLINATORS by planting native wildflowers and grasses.

http://www.wildfarmalliance.org

Website of the Wild Farm Alliance, which seeks to promote "a healthy, viable agriculture that helps protect and restore wild Nature." Offers Organic and Biodiversity Guides for farmers and certifiers, extensive summaries of which are downloadable.

http://www.entsoc.org/wildbees.htm

A study published in the Annals of the Entomological Society of America (March, 2009) documents the finding by Michigan researchers of 166 bee species on 15 blueberry farms. The implications of this research, for the production of blueberries and other crops, are enormous. 112 of these bee species were active during the blueberry-blooming period, and many of these species visit more flowers per minute and deposit more pollen per visit than do honey bees (*Apis mellifera L.*). Every blueberry that forms is pollinated by a bee.

AN IMPORTANT BOOK

David Imhoff. *Farming with the Wild: Enhancing Biodiversity*. San Francisco: Sierra Club Books, 2003. This book demonstrates through farmers' own stories that protection of wild areas and creation of wild plantings can not only benefit wild biodiversity but at the same time significantly enhance crop production itself. In 2004, the Independent Publisher Book Awards named it the book "Most Likely to Save the Planet."

… let nature truly take its course—invite a wide variety of these horticultural "good guys" that already live in your area into your garden to gobble up the "bad guys."

—Janet Marinelli,
"A Buffet for Beneficial Insects,"
The Wildlife Gardener's Guide

14

General Guides to Native Plant Gardening For Wildlife

Give me books, fruit, French wine and
fine weather and a little music out of doors.
—John Keats, letter to his sister, 1819

This bibliography includes some books already listed as references and helpful books in earlier chapters, but this is our most comprehensive listing of printed works that are generally helpful to gardeners and restorationists using native plants to create habitat for wildlife. Although these books don't focus specifically on southwest Michigan, they do provide practical information applicable to all areas and, in many cases, valuable information about species and communities natural to our area.

A word of caution. Not every plant mentioned in the books listed below is wild or native to our region or even to North America. For instance, the guides published by the Brooklyn Botanic Garden are too helpful to be excluded even though they include numerous recommendations of nonnative plants or cultivars rather than wild plants. To be sure that a particular plant is native to our area, it's best to consult an authoritative guide, such as Edward G. Voss's *Michigan Flora* or the *Floristic Quality Assessment*. (These two works are described in greater detail in Chapter 6.)

See also Chapters 7, 12, and 13 for helpful websites on special topics. Especially helpful books are marked with an asterisk (*).

Benyus, Janine M. *The Field Guide to Wildlife Habitats of the Eastern United States.* New York: Simon & Shuster, 1989. Organized by habitat, e.g., "Shrub Swamp," this guide lists characteristic plants and animals, describing in detail a few key species.

DeGraaf, Richard M. *Trees, Shrubs, and Vines for Attracting Birds,* 2nd ed. Hanover, NH: Univ. of New England Press, 2002. Detailed.

*Dennis, John V. *The Wildlife Gardener: How to Create a Refuge for Birds and Other Wildlife in Your Own Backyard.* New York: Ballantine Books, 1988. Wonderfully informative.

Dole, Claire Hagen (ed.). *The Butterfly Gardener's Guide.* Brooklyn Botanic Garden All-Region Guides. Brooklyn Botanic Garden, 2003.

Douglas, Matthew M., and Jonathan M. Douglas. *Butterflies of the Great Lakes Region.* Ann Arbor: Univ. of Michigan Press, 2005.

Dramstad, Wenche E., James D. Olson, and Richard T. T. Forman. *Landscape Ecology Principles in Landscape Architecture and Land-Use Planning.* Washington, DC: Island Press, 1996. Suggests the value to wildlife of variously configured natural areas.

*Eastman, John. *The Book of Field and Roadside: Open Country Weeds, Trees, and Wildflowers of Eastern North America.* Harrisburg, PA: Stackpole Books, 2003. Each entry in Eastman's books draws together an amazing amount of information about the plant, its habitat, and the many creatures it supports. *Wonderful.*

*_____. *The Book of Forest and Thicket: Trees, Shrubs, and Wildflowers of Eastern North America.* Harrisburg, PA: Stackpole Books, 1992.

*_____. *The Book of Swamp and Bog: Trees, Shrubs, and Wildflowers of Eastern Freshwater Wetlands.* Mechanicsburg, PA: Stackpole Books, 1995.

Erickson, Laura. *101 Ways to Help Birds.* Mechanicsburg, PA: Stackpole Books, 2006.

Grissell, Eric. *Insects and Gardens: in Pursuit of a Garden Ecology.* Portland, OR: Timber Press, 2001. By appreciating insects and inviting them into our yards, we enrich our yards and lives.

*Henderson, Carrol L. *Landscaping for Wildlife.* Minnesota Dept. of Natural Resources. St. Paul, MN: Minnesota's Bookstore, 1987. Extremely helpful once you master the charts listing plants most useful to wildlife in each season.

Johnson, Lorraine. *Grow Wild! Low-Maintenance, Sure-Success, Distinctive Gardening with Native Plants.* Golden, CO: Fulcrum Publishing, 1998. Lovely photos, lively and eloquent writing.

Kress, Stephen W. *Hummingbird Gardens: Turning Your Yard into Hummingbird Heaven.* 21st-Century Gardening Series. Brooklyn Botanic Garden, 2000.

*Leys, Marilyn and Ron. *Living with Wildlife: Create Wildlife Habitat No Matter Where You Live.* Iola, WI: Krause Publications, 2000. Full of valuable and useful information. Well documented.

Logsdon, Gene. *Wildlife in the Garden: How to Live in Harmony with Deer, Raccoons, Rabbits, Crows, and Other Pesky Creatures.* Bloomington: Indiana Univ. Press: 1983; reprinted 1999. Helpful.

*Marinelli, Janet. *The Wildlife Gardener's Guide.* Brooklyn Botanic Garden All-Region Guides. Brooklyn Botanic Garden, 2008. Extremely helpful, especially on creating habitat for pollinators and other beneficial insects.

Martin, Alexander C., Herbert S. Zim, and Arnold L. Nelson. *American Wildlife and Plants: A Guide to Wildlife Food Habits.* New York: Dover Publications, 1961. Examines various species of birds and mammals for their use of mostly native plants. Then examines various trees, shrubs, weeds and herbs for their usefulness to birds and mammals. A technical classic.

*Nowak, Mariette. *Birdscaping in the Midwest: A Guide to Gardening with Native Plants to Attract Birds,* Blue Mounds, WI: Itchy Cat Press, 2007. Integrates information about birds with information about the native plants that support them in a wonderfully creative and efficient way. Extremely thorough but nevertheless very readable. Nowak's information applies to other wildlife as well as to birds.

Pistorius, Alan. *Everything You Need to Know About Birding and Backyard Bird Attraction.* Boston: Houghton, Mifflin, 1998. Includes specific and well-organized information about birds' use of native and nonnative plants throughout the year.

Redington, Charles B. *Plants in Wetlands.* Dubuque, IA: Kendall/Hunt, 1994. An illuminating book which shows how key plants of various wetland communities are used by wildlife.

Shepherd, Matthew, et al. *Pollinator Conservation Handbook.* For full information about this and other valuable books on providing habitat for pollinators, see Chapter 7.

*Stein, Sara. *Noah's Garden: Restoring the Ecology of Our Own Back Yards.* New York: Houghton Mifflin, 1993. A fabulous classic. I can't recommend it often enough.

*Tallamy, Douglas W. *Bringing Nature Home: How You Can Sustain Wildlife with Native Plants.* Updated and enlarged. Portland, OR: Timber Press, 2009. Tallamy demonstrates the urgency of planting native plants in order to sustain insects and other wildlife and, ultimately, ourselves. Along with Stein, this should be required reading for every homeowner.

Terres, John K. *Songbirds in Your Garden.* Chapel Hill, NC: Algonquin Books, 1994.

*Tylka, Dave. *Native Landscaping for Wildlife and People: How to Use Native Midwestern Plants to Beautify Your Property and Benefit Wildlife.* Jefferson City, MO: Missouri Dept. of Conservation, 2002. Very good on insects' use of wildflowers and grasses.

Part III

Rewards and Joys

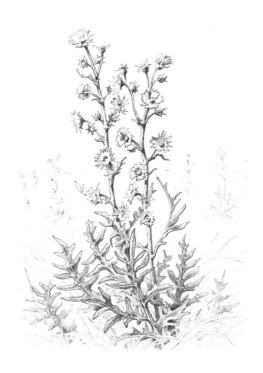

A right relationship with earth
is the state of wonder that we possess as a child.

—Rachel Carson—

When it's over, I want to say: all my life
I was a bride married to amazement.
I was the bridegroom, taking the world into my arms.

—Mary Oliver—
"When Death Comes"

Green dragon (Arisaema dracontium)   Elizabeth Henderson

15

Sightings and Insights

Rewards of Natural Landscaping for Wildlife

… with an eye made quiet by the power
Of harmony, and the deep power of joy,
We see into the life of things.
—William Wordsworth, "Tintern Abbey"

After our Wild Ones chapter began to put out a local newsletter, Tom and I tried more than once to start a column called "Sightings." In order to assure ourselves and other members of the chapter that our native plantings and natural landscaping were making a difference, we asked people to report wildlife seen in their yards and particularly the use by wildlife of native plants. We never got much response, but we ourselves may have gotten more observant. The following recollections and ruminations on the simple delights of *seeing* include many names of friends and associates, as well as names of streets and places, for they are all important to learning where we live and to restoring natural habitat in the city and the suburbs.

Wonderful Surprises

Summer or winter, rarely a day goes by that we aren't richly rewarded for our efforts to turn our yard into better habitat for wildlife by providing food and shelter in the form of native plants. (We also provide water in birdbaths and bowls and seeds and suet for the birds year round.)

Sometimes the reward takes the form of a plant or plants just coming up, for the first time or once again—those you planted and those you're sure you didn't, e.g., the green dragon that came in with rescued Michigan lilies. Or maybe it's a plant coming into bloom, especially for the first time. That was

the case on July 1, 2009, when the purple milkweed (*Asclepias purpurascens*) opened. Instead of being purple, though, it was a strange, beautiful, dark coral red. Closer to purple, actually, was the pinkish-purple flower on the Sullivant's milkweed (*A. sullivantii*), which bloomed this year, apparently for the first time. (Surely we would have noticed if it had bloomed earlier.) It arrived many years ago as a seedling from Chad Hughson and lived in the nursery for several years as an unidentified milkweed, its label lost. A couple of years ago, I planted it in the driest part of the prairie garden, figuring that since it came from Chad, it probably wanted a site as dry as possible. This year I finally did my homework and discovered that it is not a dry but a wet prairie plant, native only in a few counties in eastern Michigan; so we're giving it extra water. But it's worth it: the plant itself—with its narrow, smooth, pointed leaves, held very upright, its strange, grayish-green color—is really elegant and its flower clusters spectacular.

The ever-changing colors of buds, leaves, flowers, even bark, are perpetual delight. "Nature's first green is gold," says Robert Frost, "Her hardest hue to hold." Yes, emerging leafbuds are often a translucent golden-green; but many early buds and leaves are red or dark purple, pink or blue. These pigments soften the light and protect tender buds and leaves while levels of chlorophyll are building. The young leaves of woodland plants like blue cohosh or bloodroot are reddish purple. The early leaves of wild yam (*Dioscorea villosa*) are dark but delicate magenta.

EVERY SPRING A RICHER HARVEST

One April, as I cleared yet another handful of matted vegetation from the prairie garden, spring suddenly revealed itself to me. There, nestled in the bare soil, was something I'd never seen before: a cluster of fat, pointed, deep purple shoots as smooth as polished stone. They turned out to be a clump of blue false indigo (*Baptisia australis*) emerging from the newly warmed earth. A few weeks later, when the plant's graceful stems were lined with tender leaves and flowers of celestial blue, I still saw, in my mind's eye, the vivid purple shoots which spoke so powerfully of spring.

Those tapered purple cones have now joined the sights, sounds, and smells that mean spring to me—a long list headed by the flow of luminous spring ephemerals across a forest floor. But advancing age, increasing intimacy with nature, and—most of all—the generous tutelage of knowledgeable people, keep that list growing. Tom and I are increasingly able to *see* more clearly, to penetrate the less obvious beauties of spring as well as to appreciate the familiar ones more deeply.

All too swiftly, spring's subtle colorations subside into summer's more monotone green. "Leaf," says Frost, "subsides to leaf. So dawn goes down to day." But then come the fresh rewards of myriad flowers and fruits. Every season bears its own unique flowering and plentiful harvest. Always, there are surprises: some newly discovered bounty of delicate flowers and swelling shoots to gather from earth and branch.

There are also the rewards of seeing wildlife, large or small, perhaps only for a few seconds as with butterflies or a few days as with migrating birds, or repeatedly, as with animals that visit on almost a daily basis or actually take up residence, at least temporarily, in the yard.

> We shall see but a little way if we require to understand what we see.
> —Thoreau, *Walden*

Other times, the reward is the sight of wildlife, large or small, perhaps only for a few seconds as with butterflies or a few days as with migrating birds, or repeatedly, as with animals that visit on almost a daily basis or actually take up residence, at least temporarily, in the yard. With most animals, we're never sure just how much our yard is helping them. The toads probably live here. The short-tailed shrew I saw one spring, moving under dead leaves, its lead-colored fur shining in the sun, probably did too. But most of the birds don't, though they (and the squirrels) certainly get through a lot of birdfood. In fact, the only birds we know to have nested in our yard are cardinals, American goldfinches, and Carolina wrens. How delighted we were when the first Carolina wrens started coming around. Perhaps wrongly, we took their appearance to mean that our yard was producing more insects than formerly. However, the wrens are eating at the feeders in winter as well as foraging in the dead leaves next to the house for insects.

The Delights of Seeing Predation

Also extremely gratifying is the ocular proof that wildlife is actually using our native plants. Discovering one snowy November day at twilight that cardinals eat the dry, papery seeds of ninebark was a triumph for me, because at that point I'd never seen anything eat these seeds or come across any reference to their use by wildlife. The same was true of wild spikenard (*Aralia racemosa*) until, I think, a couple of years ago when I saw a squirrel actually eating its (by then quite dry) beautiful fruits—small, wine-colored, and arranged in long, tightly packed clusters. Actually, the fruits are so attractive that I've been tempted to try them myself.

Then there was the January delight of watching a chickadee shaking a dry, papery seedpod (about as large as the bird's head) of the bladdernut shrub (*Staphylea trifolia*) outside the study window. He shook it violently back and forth, he dropped it in the snow, he pecked at it, he picked it up and flew back up on the branch, and he shook it again—and again. Finally, he got it open, held it with his foot, and ate the seeds. By then, a cardinal had joined him, first to observe and then begin some shaking of his own, much more quickly successful. Neither bird seemed to care that the "wildlife value" of bladdernut is rated "low." Perhaps they both enjoyed

Chickadees eat mostly insects and larvae, especially in summer; but they are fond of sunflower seeds. They mingle readily in small flocks and with other species, including human beings. When they find a good source of food, they call to their mates and their flock to come share.

playing with these Japanese-lantern-shaped "rattles," just as Indian children are said to have done with bunches of dried bladdernut seedpods. At any rate, after two very wintry days of vigorous shaking, every single bladdernut pod was gone from the shrub.

Out in the prairie garden, American goldfinches feed eagerly on the seeds of sunflowers and other composites, but mostly we miss seeing other wildlife actually consuming the seeds and fruits provided by our plants. However, we're always watching for evidence that they have, in fact, made use of them—evidence provided by missing fruits on the gray dogwoods, the pokeweeds, the elderberries, and the viburnums (especially the one hanging over a birdbath where the berries disappear as early as December). This evidence is also visible on smaller plants whose fruits disappear: the green dragon, the Solomon's seal, and the wild coffee.

We also welcome evidence of insect predation on leaves, as long as it isn't caused by nonnative invaders such as gypsy moths or Japanese beetles. Besides, there are so many wonderful side effects of insect herbivory. Consider: native plants attract more insects; insect predators produce lots of frass (poop), which is excellent fertilizer; as they die or shed skins or chrysalises, they contribute parts of *themselves* to the nutrient cycle; thus, they both provide and become food for soil organisms, other invertebrates, and the plants they feed on. Not to mention the bountiful poop from the birds that eat them. As long as there's enough diversity in your gardens to achieve a balance of predation and growth, those hungry insects are simply part of a wonderful, provident food web. A plant without some predation is suitable only for a flower show, not for a garden.

There is so little predation by deer, which often polish off remnant bird food and nibble on a few tender shoots as they pass through our yard on their way to happier hunting grounds, or by rabbits or groundhogs, that we're always happy to get glimpses of these animals too. Besides, as often as not, their selective prunings stimulate more branching and flowering; so my laments for a lost or lopped plant don't last long.

In most of our encounters with wildlife in our yard, we are merely observers; in others, however, we are drawn to participate. From all of them, we come away filled with wonder at the strangeness, complexity, and richness of the natural world. Each encounter renews, for us, the insight of Rabbi Abraham Heschel: "The beginning of our happiness lies in the understanding that life without wonder is not worth living. What we lack is not a will to believe but a will to wonder" (p. 37). Each encounter leaves us all the more determined to do as much as we possibly can, little though it may be, to preserve the wondrous diversity of life.

Here, we offer some of our sightings and insights: always, for us, sources of wonderment and promptings to action.

American toad, (Bufo americanus). *We've seen both American and Fowler's toads in our gardens. For whatever reason—perhaps having to do with drastic declines in amphibian populations worldwide—we haven't seen either for three years now. We miss them very much.*

Toads. One summer our yard was filled, front and back, with hundreds of tiny toads, and we did everything we could not to hurt them. We walked on the grass slowly and carefully so that the little toads could get out of the way. We mowed the grass only when we absolutely had to, and before we mowed, we tried to "herd" the toads into the flower-beds at the edges of the lawn. Then we mowed very, very slowly, so they could get out of the way. For years afterwards, our yard had more than its share of toads, many of them living among the damp pots and trays of our little plant nursery; and we think they came from that original deluge. According to Thomas F. Tyning, American toads can live for 5-10 years in the wild and as long as 30 in captivity (p. 25). Another authority reports that "a modest-sized toad might eat an average of 26 insects a day between May and August, or about 3,200 insects in the season" (Harding and Holman, p. 57). Grow native plants to feed insects and you'll also be feeding toads.

Once I saw a toad walking on the edge of the patio on all-fours, instead of hopping, and had to go over and take a good look at it before I realized what it was. From what Tyning says, it was an American toad and had assumed this posture because it was stalking something and was within one or two feet of it. Maybe the toad's concentration on its prey, which I never saw, let me get as close as I did.

> I love you for being a toad,
> for crawling like a Japanese wrestler,
> and for not being frightened.
>
> —Norman MacCaig, "Toad"

Food for Residents and Migrants

Practically every spring, we see robins that seem, at least to us, to have returned too early, reduced to eating the persistent fruits on our shrubs: the roses, the aronia, and the Michigan holly. How glad we are to have these plants that usually keep their fruits through the winter and into the spring. Until we managed to get rid of a little row of Japanese barberry plants (a plant that invades natural areas, particularly on the East Coast), the robins would eat some of these persistent fruits too—and no doubt spread their seeds.

In cold, snowy weather, we've tried to get robins to eat raisins, cranberries, and cut-up apples and pears, but never with much success. The best way of getting the food to them, we've found, is to scatter it on a plank over one side of a heated bird bath, where the robins can't help but see it.

On May 5, 2000, a rose-breasted grosbeak, beautifully marked front and back, ate viburnum trilobum buds (or perhaps insects on them) on the bush above the birdbath in the rock garden and then took a bath.

Woodpeckers. Every year we seem to have more woodpeckers—downies, hairies, and red-bellieds—thanks to the suet we put out and probably to

our old trees, some of them with dead branches. The little woods in the middle of our oddly-shaped suburban block probably helps too. From a picture window looking into the back yard, we often see woodpeckers working tree trunks at the same time others are at the suet feeders. Sometimes, in the summer, adult hairy and red-bellied woodpeckers eat a few bites of suet themselves and then fly off carrying a chunk of suet for someone else. Sometimes, they bring their fledglings and feed them suet or encourage them to eat it. Downies often congregate just outside an upstairs window, on a honey locust tree with long strips of loose bark, under which they find insects and eggs; between searches, a male downy may fly off and return with a piece of suet, pecking it neatly into the beak of a female or a fledgling.

The best thing we ever saw was in the summer of 2008. A red-bellied woodpecker (don't remember its sex) was feeding its fledgling—as large as the parent—chunks of suet while the young bird clung to a nearby tree, looking for insects and apparently finding some. But it eagerly opened its mouth whenever the parent came back with a little piece of suet. At one point the young bird, after swallowing a chunk, seemed to want more and looked as if it was about to peck at the parent's now-empty bill. But the parent was too quick for it and gave the pushy youngster a little peck instead. The fledgling quickly jumped back about a foot and just froze there. Almost at once, the forgiving parent was back again with more suet for it.

This hairy woodpecker's beak, shaped like a chisel, makes very precise holes. The tongue, which circles clear around the skull under the loose skin, can dart out about six inches, with a barbed tip and a bit of stickum, perfect for reaching into holes and spearing a meal. The only woodpecker without barbs is the yellow-bellied sapsucker, with a brushlike tongue, perfect for slurping. The claw, of a red-bellied woodpecker, makes it possible to hang on tight, even upside-down, during all that chiseling and probing. Wondrous creatures, burning bright in the forests—and the cities.

The Bedraggled Hawk

January 11, 2006, a cold, rainy day with no snow on the ground. Coming over to the kitchen sink, I realized that just outside the big window, perched on a branch of the pink dogwood, was a small, bedraggled-looking hawk. (It seemed to be a sharp-shinned, on account of its small size, the shape of its head, and its very delicate legs.) It was looking out into the yard, its back turned toward me. It sat for a long time, looking wet and miserable, spreading out its tail like a fan (trying to dry it?), rummaging under its wings front and back (in search of insects that were biting it?), sometimes turning its head almost all the way around in order—seemingly—to check on my activities. (I was standing perfectly still, trying to give the impression that I wasn't watching it.) All the while, birds and squirrels were moving around further out in the yard, but the hawk appeared totally uninterested. After a while it moved to a nearby branch and continued its toilette.

Then, suddenly, so fast I almost missed the whole thing, it dived past the thicket and through the lowest branches of a big spruce tree about 30 feet away, exiting on the other side with something it had caught. I couldn't see much through the tree's thick vegetation and the prairie grasses on its far side, but the hawk seemed to subdue its prey (a mourning dove—I found the feathers afterward) in the street next to the curb. I was on the front sidewalk by this point, trying to get a better view, but

I didn't want to get too close. The last I saw of the hawk was a glimpse or two of its head and the tips of its upraised wings through the prairie grasses.

I lost track of things at this point because I was trying to head off a woman walking a dog who seemed to be heading in that direction. When I was able to look again, the hawk and its victim had disappeared.

Only once did we ever see a hawk in the yard in summer, and that was during an extremely hot and dry year. We were indoors, but saw it land on a birdbath about 15 feet from the house. It waded a little way into the water and started to lower its head to drink, but was so uneasy that after a few seconds it flew away.

THE NEST WE THOUGHT ABANDONED

On May 17, 2008, working among the pots of plants in the driveway, we saw a pair of Carolina wrens lead their babies out of a nest in the garage—a nest that we thought had been abandoned weeks earlier because it was in such a high-traffic area. Located on a shelf between two plastic spray bottles, the nest lay between a door from the kitchen into the garage (the back door) and a door from the garage to the patio. Our garage, with all its spiders and spiderwebs, must have seemed an ideal location, though.

A couple of times, weeks earlier, as we'd gone out the back door and gotten into the car, we'd obviously disturbed the birds. The first time—I'm not sure we'd even discovered the nest at this point—one of them darted out of the garage so fast and low to the ground that I thought for a moment it was a chipmunk. Another time, as we were getting into the car, one of the birds suddenly flew out of the garage. After that, there was nothing: no sight of the birds in or around the garage, not a peep from the nest.

On the morning of Saturday, May 17, when Eleanore Chadderdon told us that she'd heard little cries from the nest as she came through the garage to the back door, we were amazed and delighted that we hadn't scared off the birds and that there seemed to be babies in the nest. By great good fortune, we were out in the driveway a little later when all of a sudden, driveway, brushpile, and tree branches above the brushpile were full of Carolina wrens moving around very fast. There seemed to be four babies, two of them smaller than the others and grayish rather than brown. I saw them briefly on the driveway, then was never able to distinguish

these two again. (They must have pulled themselves together and looked and acted more like the rest of the family.) Eleanore saw that at least one of them did more hopping than flying.

Things were complicated by wind, the fact that there were three people (Eleanore, Tom, and I) and at least six birds in the driveway, the people trying to see the birds while staying out of their way, the birds flying in and out of the garage—and from brushpile to the tree branches right above it—and trying to avoid us. They were interested, too, in the dirt pile (in front of the brush pile), where Eleanore had been filling some flowerpots and perhaps stirring up insects.

As far as we could tell, the birds never went back to the nest, even though at that time of year the nights were still cold; in fact, they completely disappeared from our yard, and it was weeks before we saw a Carolina wren. Russ Schipper said such

Carolina wren   Thryothorus ludovicianus

behavior was normal and that they had probably moved on because their instinct is to move a new family to a new territory, with a fresh supply of insects after their constant depradations for the nestlings.

We're always delighted to see a pair of Carolina wrens. Once, as Tom was standing at the kitchen sink looking out, he saw a pair flitting back and forth in the shrubbery just outside the window.

Then, they came together on the same branch, snuggled close, tilted their heads together, and for a second were perfectly still, posed, the loving couple. Then, one of them flitted away again. So chubby they seem almost perfectly round, Carolina wrens, as they pick up seeds from the snow or the leaf litter, are as delicate in their movement as the elegantly slender goldfinches.

THE CARE AND FEEDING OF CATERPILLARS

Butterflies and caterpillars. The introduction to this book begins with our most dramatic encounter with a butterfly. Another exciting encounter involved a giant swallowtail, a huge, black-and-yellow butterfly, that I saw lay six eggs on a small hoptree (*Ptelea trifoliata*) still in its container, sitting in the driveway waiting to be planted. Again, it was immediately clear that there wouldn't be enough food for the giant swallowtail's large caterpillars, so Tom put out a request to the Wild Ones e-mail list for food for the caterpillars: either hoptree or prickly ash, also known as wafer ash (*Zanthoxylum americanum*), another of the giant swallowtail's hostplants. Pat Kirklin, of Kirklin Farms, offered us prickly ash, so we went out and gathered several days' supply which we washed and refrigerated. Ilse Gebhard also had prickly ash on her property, and she eventually ended up with the caterpillars, as keeping them supplied with fresh food consumed a lot of both time and travel for us.

The eggs, which the butterfly laid on the tops of the leaves, were clay-colored, but under magnification glowed a deep, translucent orange. The caterpillars' strategy for protecting themselves is to look more like bird poop than like caterpillars.

A less dramatic but nevertheless instructive encounter involved watching a monarch female searching in one of our flowerbeds for a milkweed plant on which to lay an egg or two. First it lighted for a few moments on a common boneset (*Eupatorium perfoliatum*). Since this didn't meet its needs, it then tried another leafy plant of about the same height nearby: New England aster (*Aster novae-*

angliae). After pausing here for a few moments, it flew a short distance to a swamp milkweed, where it laid an egg. As I remember it, none of these plants was in bloom. I thought it was interesting that all three have long, narrow leaves. The olfactory organs by which the butterfly was distinguishing one plant from another were, of course, in its feet.

This year, 2009, we didn't see a monarch butterfly until July 5; it was a large, brilliant male which must have been newly-hatched. But on June 15 we found seven large caterpillars on a stand of common milkweed which has sprung up right along the curb on Argyle Street, the sidestreet where our driveway is. So verdant and lush were the plants that the caterpillars' predation was barely noticeable. On one big leaf, three caterpillars were eating, seriously weighing down the leaf and in danger of coming into contact with one another. We tucked a couple of other leaves underneath the overly crowded one and its stem, which we hoped solved the problem. One caterpillar seemed to have been injured or parasitized: there were a couple of short, shallow slashes on its back. But this early in the season, though the plant was in bud, it was still amazingly free of other insects.

We sent the caterpillars, which seemed to be in their last instar, out to Ilse and Russ's, thinking that it would be easier for the females to find mates and milkweed plants to lay their eggs on in the country than in town. And the more butterflies in this first generation born in our area, the more butterflies—one hopes—migrating to Mexico from this area in the fall. A day or so later we found an eighth caterpillar wandering around on the plants, but during the few minutes it took to go indoors and get a container for it, the caterpillar had made its getaway.

Ilse reported that all seven caterpillars emerged from their chrysalises, even the one that seemed to have been parasitized.

Migrants Taking up Residence

The red-winged blackbirds. Our most reliable, and in many ways most gratifying, wildlife visitors have been a small flock of red-winged blackbirds that first appeared in 1997, the year after we started naturalizing our yard. They were here when we arrived home from the Wildflower Association of Michigan conference, at the beginning of March; and we saw them as a good omen or even more—a sign that we had done the right thing in retiring in the city and trying to turn our yard into better habitat. Little did we know then that these birds almost surely "took up residence" in our yard for lack of a better place to go. Now, over 10 years later, this common species is in decline.

That year, and every summer since, they have used our yard as a place to eat and just hang out but not, as far as we can tell, to breed. We see females quite often and eventually young birds—this year there have been significantly more—but mostly we see males, flashing their gorgeous epaulets at each other or other birds when forced into close contact at a hanging feeder. But the males are never aggressive toward us, wherever we go in the yard, which argues that they have no nests here to protect. We think they must breed at Wood's Lake, the wetland-reconstruction northern end of which is only a block or so away, as the red-wing flies.

We love seeing the red-winged blackbirds—males, females, juveniles—all season long, and we see one or more of them almost every time we look out the window. The arrival of the males (as early as late February) tells us that spring is here, and their raucous clicks, whistles, and chirring sounds gladden our hearts; their departure, usually very late,

Red-winged blackbirds—male and female. Loss of their preferred wetland habitat brings them to urban yards—like ours. We're glad they can adapt and glad to have them—they give us joy; but we worry about the loss that brings them to us.

tells us that winter is closing in. One year around the turn of the century they stayed so late that we asked Roger Taylor, when he ran Wild Birds Unlimited, what to do. He told us not to worry, that their wintering grounds aren't all that far away, perhaps no farther than northern Indiana. In addition to informing us, first, of the arrival of spring and, finally, of the descent of winter, "our" flock of red-winged blackbirds reminds us that the natural world is both fragile and tough.

The mallards. For several years, a pair of mallards arrived in our yard every spring and stayed around for a while, apparently just to eat. The first year was the most exciting as they stayed for almost six weeks and spent a lot of time in the yard, the male standing beside the female as she rested in a small, in-ground birdbath Tom had dug and lined with stones. They ate, usually one at a time, along with other ground-feeding birds under tube feeders, where seeds had fallen to the ground, or at—and even under—the edges of ground feeders. Perhaps they were eating sunflower plants that had just germinated as well as seeds.

That first year, somewhat befuddled by their persistent presence, we tried to make the ducks more comfortable. We bought one of those inflatable plastic pools for kids, surrounded it with brush, and even made a ramp for the ducks with a plank so that they could get into the pool easily (shades of Ibsen and his dark, satiric comedy *The Wild Duck*). But they, not at all befuddled, didn't use it. We were glad when they finally left because our yard is such unsuitable habitat for them.

The pair of them (at least, it looked like the same pair) have come back for years, but never again stayed around so long or spent so much time in the yard.

RESCUING WHAT WE'VE ENDANGERED

The Turtle Society. We've never seen a turtle here, but maybe sometime one will make it up from Wood's Lake or Kleinstuck Preserve to our yard. In the meantime, we try to save all the turtles we can. At the beginning of the summer, Tom saved a snapping turtle that was heading north (toward our yard) across Sheffield Drive on our side of Oakland Drive. He took it to Wood's Lake, which may not have been quite the right thing to do, as it may have been seeking higher ground in order to lay its eggs.

The turtle may have been coming from Kleinstuck Preserve as Tom had already seen two smaller turtles this year that had been crushed by cars on Oakland Drive. Other evidence that we live on or near a turtle route: several years ago, when we were having coffee one morning at Full City Cafe, someone came into the cafe in search of help rescuing a turtle at the intersection of Sheffield and Oakland Drive but on the swamp side of Oakland. We took this first responder back to the corner with us and on the north corner found a huge snapping turtle that had probably come up from Kleinstuck and seemed determined to cross Oakland. So Tom went back to our house and got a box, and the three of us got the turtle into it. Then we took the first responder home—he turned out to live further north on our own street—so he could get his car and take the turtle to the Kalamazoo Nature Center.

The first time I tried to rescue a turtle (in the early '90s), a woman accused me of abandoning a pet. Out walking one morning, I'd found an Eastern box turtle on the curb lawn of Grand Street, near Henderson's Castle—where had it come from? I'd run home for some gloves, a cat carrier—a much smaller container would have been sufficient—and the car. I also got some lettuce for the turtle.

After putting the turtle into the huge cage, I drove to Kleinstuck Preserve and then lugged the carrier into the swamp, trying not to jostle the turtle too much. I turned a corner and suddenly there was a woman coming toward me, looking very grim and saying, "I hope you're not planning to abandon your pet here."

Once I began to explain what I was doing, the woman started laughing and told me that I was now a member, as she was, of The Turtle Society.

No meetings, no dues, the only requirement is that you save a turtle. Well, we can hope that we're saving them, but I wonder. It doesn't seem like turtles determined to get from lower ground to higher ground to lay their eggs or from higher ground to lower ground for the winter are going to be "saved" for long.

A special concern species because of habitat loss, pet collecting, and road kill, the eastern box turtle is rare in southwest Michigan. May apples are a favorite food.

The Determination of Turtles

Tom, also skeptical, recalls to me the incident with the turtle in the opening chapters of John Steinbeck's *The Grapes of Wrath*, where no matter how many times Tom Joad interferes with a turtle he finds trying to cross the road and no matter how far he carries it in his pocket, it always sets off again in exactly the same direction it was headed in originally. That turtle becomes a symbol of the Joad family's determination.

Besides the turtle he rescued from Sheffield Avenue and took to Wood's Lake, Tom moved another, larger snapping turtle from the curb of Crosstown Parkway back down to the banks of Axtell Creek. He rescued still another that was crossing Howard Street toward Maple Street School and moved it back to the little pond next to the Montessori School which it seemed to have come from. A woman coming down the hill on Howard Street saw what we were doing and helped keep traffic stopped. So we had all renewed our memberships in The Turtle Society.

Tom and I worked especially hard to try to save the remnant oak savanna on the Adams Sign Company property after we saw a live eastern box turtle toward the eastern end of the property and after Richard Brewer identified a turtleshell found near the western end of the property as that of a box turtle. We hoped that the presence of a state-listed animal on the property would have more weight than the presence of state-listed plants seemed to have. But we and the many other people who had worked over the years to save this living piece of Kalamazoo's history were defeated by forces more powerful than citizens' wishes or The Turtle Society.

I almost forgot the turtle out at Keka, a piece of their property that Lois and Jim Richmond have donated to the Southwest Michigan Land Conservancy. Knowing that Lois Richmond loves turtles and that she and Emma Pitcher used to mark the shells of turtles they came across, in case they encountered them again, I'm always on the lookout for turtles there. I'm especially watchful as we descend the steep, curving two-track sometimes partly obscured by vegetation, from the main road down into the Keka property. Once my vigilance really paid off: we were able to stop and watch as a box turtle lumbered from one side of the two-track to the other. On another occasion, we saw a small eastern box turtle crossing the road on our way to Keka. We stopped, picked it up and took it to Lois, who carefully marked it and placed it where she knew it would have companions.

WITH INSIGHT COMES WONDERMENT

With all of our sightings have come *insights*, a deeper sense of the wonder, the fragility, and the diversity of the wildlife all around us, persisting among us, often despite our hostility or indifference. Do our insights make a difference? If they lead to a deeper appreciation of all life and greater care to restore and preserve it, at home in the city and suburbs, and in what remains of relatively wild land, then we will have made a difference.

"To open the way, a cultural breakthrough need not involve masses of people but must be done decisively by someone."
—Jim Corbett, founder of the Saguaro Juniper Land Redemption Covenant

REFERENCES

Corbett, Jim. *Goatwalking.* New York: Viking, 1991.

Harding, James H., and J. Alan Holman. *Michigan Frogs, Toads, and Salamanders.* Lansing: Michigan State University Museum, 1999.

Heschel, Abraham Joshua. *Man Is Not Alone: A Philosophy of Religion.* New York: Farrar, Straus & Giroux, 1976.

Tyning, Thomas F. *A Guide to Amphibians and Reptiles.* Stokes Nature Guides. Boston: Little, Brown and Company, 1990.

16

SUMMERTIME

But thy eternal summer shall not fade …
—William Shakespeare

EASTERN OKLAHOMA, CIRCA 2000

The open tall-grass prairie, which used to come as close to us as the very corner of southwest Michigan, extended west through Illinois and Iowa and south through eastern Oklahoma into parts of eastern Texas.

In mid-June, at the Tallgrass Prairie Preserve in northeastern Oklahoma, we waded in a sea of big bluestem that was already thigh-high and flowering with orange milkweed and pale purple coneflowers. Several times our van was halted by small herds of bison—animals whose dark, massive solidity is impossible to convey. They unhurriedly crossed the road, the small red calves never more than a step or two behind their mothers. Bison, unlike cattle, we were told, are always on the move, never overgrazing, even sparing most wildflowers.

We also stopped for plants, butterflies, birds, especially scissor-tailed flycatchers, and turtles, which our tour leader—a herpetologist—was able to spot just as they were about to cross the road. After we'd all had a good look at the turtle, he'd put it back in the grass, heading it away from the road. One evening we all piled out of the van to look at a

Timber Rattlesnake (Crotalus horridus). Beautiful creatures, quite venomous but mild-mannered, timber rattlesnakes are endangered or threatened in 11 states and generally rare, declining in numbers and local populations. Once fairly common in New England and fascinating to the early settlers, the timber rattlesnake became for them a potent symbol, inspiring Benjamin Franklin's "United or Die" woodcut in 1754 and many variations on the "Don't Tread on Me" flag and imagery in the 1770s. At first a generic rattler, the image soon became identifiably a timber rattlesnake.

timber rattlesnake stretched full-length across the gravel road of the preserve. Marveling over what a "beautiful specimen" it was, our leader tried to get it off the road and out of harm's way by prodding it with a dried stalk of pale Indian plantain, the closest thing he could find to a stick. When the snake tried to get away by sliding under the van, our leader suddenly seized it by its tail, dragged it off the road, twirled it over his head, and slung it into the prairie.

This all happened so fast that if you'd blinked you would have missed it.

Once we were back in the van, he allowed as how, "I wouldn't have done that if it'd been a diamondback; they're a lot quicker and meaner than timber rattlers." Later, coyotes sang at the exact moment the sun sank below the horizon (just as our leader said they would), and white evening primroses lining the roadsides glimmered in the twilight.

KALAMAZOO (SAME SUMMER)

At home in Kalamazoo, where we're turning our yard into better habitat for wildlife, we lack both bison and rattlesnakes. But even in the inner suburbs, nature is a source of constant wonder. This summer the cup plants (*Silphium perfoliatum*)—named for the "cups" formed by the leaves where they meet the stalks—bloomed lavishly. One July day, their yellow daisylike flowers were visited by a steady stream of eastern tiger swallowtail butterflies, sometimes many at a time. Another day, on the rosinweed (a fellow silphium, this one *Silphium integrifolium*), we saw a giant swallowtail, black with a diagonal band of yellow spots across each wing—only the second one I've seen in Kalamazoo. This is the largest butterfly in North America.

From the kitchen window every afternoon, we could watch a hummingbird work its way through the bright red cardinal flowers (we watered them every day), and one day in the yard we came across two different species, and several different sizes, of toads. When the bottle gentians bloomed, we watched bumble bees muscle their way past the white fringe of the almost closed, budlike flower and disappear into its blue depths. About a minute later, they would re-appear, one wiggly leg at a time. No other bees are strong enough to enter and exit the bottle gentian flower this way. The New England asters (*Aster novae-angliae*), covered by neon-purple flowers almost two inches across, drew monarch butterflies preparing to fly south, and, one day recently, an orange and brown Milbert's tortoiseshell. Best of all was the flock of red-winged blackbirds

which—for the third year now—has arrived in early March and stayed to raise young.

Our experiences this summer re-emphasized for us the necessity of both saving wild land and restoring degraded land made inhospitable to wildlife. We can help to save wild land by supporting land trusts. Here, virtually in our own backyard, with headquarters in Kalamazoo, the Southwest Michigan Land Conservancy protects land in nine counties of southwest Michigan. Headquartered in Grand Rapids is the Land Conservancy of West Michigan, which protects land in eight other west Michigan counties. But however successful these conservancies become, there will still not be enough protected land to save our area's wildlife. In turning already degraded land into better habitat for birds, butterflies, bees, and toads, we all have to start with our own yards, front yards as well as back. At the same time, we must do all we can to help preserve what remains of relatively wild land.

> If you accrue any kind of wealth, in whatever currency, the wisest thing you can do is convert that wealth into wilderness saved.
>
> —Tom Eisner, Chairman, Endangered Species Coalition

Kalamazoo, 2005

The green dragon (*Arisaema dracontium*) magically appeared in our artificial wetland in 2004. We didn't plant it; in fact, we didn't know what it was when it first came up. It must have arrived, as a seed or tuber, a few years previously with a Michigan lily we rescued from a site near the Kalamazoo River that was going to be paved over. Last year, the berries produced by the green dragon's strange, elegant flower disappeared before they seemed ripe enough to collect—eaten, I suppose, by some animal. This year I was determined to get them for myself and try to germinate them, so I put a little cage around the plant and waited for the berries to turn from green to orange. I pondered. Should I remove the pulp around the seeds, as experts advise, or just scatter the berries in a tray? Would the seeds germinate as easily as those of the closely related jack-in-the-pulpit (*Arisaema triphyllum*), whose cluster of bright red berries, if it falls on bare ground, often gives rise to a clump of baby jacks? No need to wonder. When I went out to collect them, the green dragon's cone of fruits had once again disappeared without a trace.

I did manage to capture some seed from the prairie phlox (*Phlox pilosa*), which bloomed lavishly for much of the summer on the tip of our sunny corner. The original plants came from Chad Hughson, and until now I've never found the right place in our yard for them; but I keep them going by saving seed every year and germinating new plants that I try in different places. While these beautiful plants, with their slender, opposite leaves and clusters of bright pink flowers, are easy to grow from seed, collecting the seeds isn't easy. First, the seeds don't ripen at exactly the same time, for the flowers even in a single cluster don't all bloom at once. Then, the pale brown seed capsule is spherical and, when it's ripe, is likely to roll off the calyx—or your fingers—before you can get it into a container. That is, if it doesn't burst first and send its three tiny black seeds flying in all directions. No wonder Prairie Moon Nursery charges $17.50 for 1/8 of an ounce. The seed of several other plants is even more expensive.

Marvels of Persistence, and Fleeting Beauty

After two years, the American columbo (*Frasera caroliniensis*) seeds gathered by Jason Cherry and distributed to Wild Ones members for germination finally came up, and I transferred about 100 seedlings to large pots to accommodate what I hoped would be their rapid growth. Most of the plants, however, never grew very much; and the plants dug up by squirrels (and replanted by me) hadn't even developed especially long roots. Toward the end of the summer, most of the seedlings went dormant or died. But before winter closed in, I covered the pots with a thick layer of leaves and hoped for the best. Two years later, I sent a few spindly survivors out to the Southwest Michigan Land Conservancy's Chipman Preserve. (I don't know whether they made it—probably not.) But then, thanks to careful directions from Ilse Gebhard and Eleanore Chadderdon, Tom and I got to see a spectacular stand of American columbo in full bloom between a road and the Kal Haven Trail. Even the lush rosettes of the nonblooming plants were beautiful. I'm sure that all our frustrated efforts to cultivate the plant made us appreciate even more the stubborn, wonderful persistence of those wild plants despite human disturbance all around them. How long had they been there? And would they be there much longer?

We also marvel over the toughness, persistence, and beauty of much more common plants. Hoary vervain (*Verbena stricta*), when we first started our prairie garden out on the corner, looked as if it would dominate the whole planting. But within two or three years, as other plants established themselves, the vervain persisted only at the edge of the street. And does it persist! It comes up in the cracks of the asphalt and migrates clear across the street to bloom in the crack between the asphalt and the concrete curbing.

Nor is that the only plant to find its niche in asphalt. Tom tried several times to establish path rush (*Juncus tenuis*) in our yard, where surely it belongs. In our paths! But no—it languished and died. Now, several years later, it comes up in the cracks in our asphalt driveway, and the seed, washed down the gutters, germinates new plants in the street. So plan as carefully as you like; but stand by to be disappointed, or surprised. And delighted!

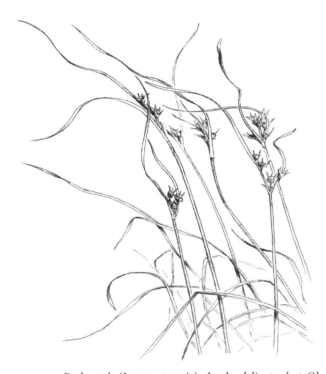

Path rush (Juncus tenuis). *Looks delicate, but Oh, so tough. Some of its other common names, poverty grass and wire grass, are appropriate. Each capsule contains hundreds of tiny seeds, easily carried on shoes, trousers, tires. As John Eastman notes, it's common "wherever people or animals move."*

Much of summer's delight and beauty was too fleeting to be captured, even with a camera: the dark swallowtail butterflies that dashed through our yard too fast to be identified—a hummingbird taking a fluttering bath in the wet leaves of a tall meadow-rue—the spiral dance (seen through the kitchen window) of an eastern tiger swallowtail with a dark-form female—the rustling of unseen birds in the thicket in our front yard as I walked by—the toads I startled whose large size offered evidence that, despite crows and neighbors' cats, the living in our yard is pretty easy. Once in late summer I saw something move in the shade of the overgrown thicket. I bent down and briefly glimpsed a Carolina wren on the ground, prospecting for insects in the greenish gloom.

Our most dramatic rescue involved a green frog that we inadvertently brought home from a workday at Axtell Creek in an empty pot or plant tray that had been tossed into the trunk of the car. When I opened the trunk two days later, the frog made an astonishing leap from the trunk to the driveway and disappeared into the yard. We were afraid it was a goner because our yard isn't wet or even wet mesic. It's truly mesic, with no water except in birdbaths. But we spotted the frog about six weeks later among some wetland plants that were sitting in trays of water, waiting to be planted at the creek. So we were able to catch it and take it back home, where it could sing to us as we worked on the creekbanks.

Green frog (Rana clamitans). *Green frogs used to sing to us as we cleared invasives and replaced them with native wetland plants on the floodplains of Axtell Creek, a degraded urban stream in Kalamazoo. Lately, they are silent.*

PROLONGING SUMMER—WITH ASTERS

In 2000, our New England asters started blooming on August 13th—while summer still lay upon the land—but it wasn't until a month later, as summer was starting to slip away, that they reached their peak. At that point, I counted 104 buds and flowers at the end of one large stem, some of the buds still minute, some of the flowers already spent. Each flower measures as much as two inches across, its yellow center surrounded by as many as 100 ray flowers of light-purple, brilliant stars sprung from the earth (*aster*—Latin and Greek for *star*). A few plants, however, have rich pink flowers. Even the tall leafy plants, which may (at least in partial shade) reach eight feet in height, are attractive: their slender, pointed leaves clasp the stem tightly and then arch gracefully downward. The asters bloom until frost—or almost.

> Bright star, would I were
> steadfast as thou art.
>
> —John Keats, "Bright Star"

The first time I saw New England asters blooming was in the early '90s on the campus of Western Michigan University in a little strip of land that had escaped development. So large, bright, and numerous were the asters' purple and pink flowers, it never occurred to me that they were anything except garden plants. (The cattails growing among them should have given me a clue.) And, indeed, New England aster is important horticulturally as the source of numerous cultivars.

Its tolerance for a wide range of growing conditions amazes me—and sometimes scares me a little—as it makes itself more and more at home in our small suburban yard. But I shouldn't be surprised. The species has an enormous geographical range, extending from southern Canada to Alabama and Mississippi, from the eastern seaboard to Wyoming and North Dakota. It occurs naturally in many Michigan counties, including some in the Upper Peninsula, and though a resident of wet thickets, meadows, and swamps, nevertheless thrives under drier conditions. It has seeded itself, for example, in the driest, sandiest part of our generally mesic yard. In fact, it seems to balk at nothing except deep shade or unrelieved dryness. But the plant's numerous offspring are easy to recognize and pull up—or pot up for friends.

Great spangled fritillary on New England asters. Favorite foods for fritillaries: milkweeds, thistles, many composites (such as asters)

The flowers and foliage of New England asters combine beautifully with other plants. In our yard, which is full of unplanned juxtapositions, they complement especially well the big leaves and yellow flowers of cup plant and prairie dock; the delicate, toothed leaflets and orange hips of *Rosa virginiana* (native east of us); and other, paler asters of prairies and woodlands which they seem to serve as a kind of forerunner or stepping stone.

THE VALUE OF BLOOMING LATE

But it was New England asters, rather than other aster species, that helped make clear to us the dependence of wildlife on native plants, maybe because these asters were closer to the house than our other asters and thus more visible. We were almost forced to notice that different kinds of butterflies and bees nectared on them. When we cut their flowers in the early morning or late fall, we found sluggish bees still sheltering within their folded petals. On windy days in early fall, we saw monarch butterflies clinging to their flowers for support or nectar or both and were thrilled to think that our plants were helping these butterflies on their amazing journey south.

Native Americans used aromatic smoke from the roots of New England asters to attract game. But native asters, as a group, have many more benign and valuable attractions for wildlife. According to Douglas Tallamy, asters rank third among native herbaceous plants as host plants for Lepidoptera, following only native clovers (*Trifolium* species) and goldenrods (*Solidago* species). As a group, native asters support 105 species of native butterflies and moths, even more than sunflowers (*Helianthus* species)—73, and native plantains (*Plantago* species)—63. One of the great values of Tallamy's ranked listing is that it indicates the relative value of woody and nonwoody plants to herbivorous insects—caterpillars—at the base of the food web. It's available at http://copland.udel.edu/~dtallamy/host/index.html.

Among southern Michigan butterflies using asters as a host plant, according to a list on the website of Bill Schneider's Wildtype Nursery near East Lansing (www.wildtypeplants.com/butterflyplants.htm), are the pearl crescent, silvery checkerspot, painted lady, gorgone checkerspot, and northern crescent. Among southern Michigan butterflies using aster species for nectar are the eastern tailed-blue, silver-bordered fritillary, American lady, buckeye, viceroy, and common wood nymph. To this latter list, I can add from personal observation the monarch and Milbert's tortoiseshell. The late-season nectar provided by asters and other flowers is also useful to bumble bee queens, which must not only survive the winter in hibernation but produce a colony the following spring.

Taxonomic correctness now compels us to call New England aster, and many other asters, *Symphyotrichum* (instead of *Aster*). Flat-topped aster will be correctly known as *Doellingeria umbellata* (instead of *Aster umbellatus*), and big leaf aster as *Eurybia macrophylla* (instead of *Aster macrophyllus*). So let's recognize these beautiful, crucial members of our native flora as the bright stars they are while it is still permissible to call them asters.

And thus, without a Wing
Or service of a Keel
our Summer made her light escape
Into the Beautiful.
   —Emily Dickinson

An earlier version of the last section of this essay, "Prolonging Summer—with Asters," was published as "Bright Stars" in the Wildflower Association of Michigan newsletter in 2001.

17

A Yardful of Yellow Flowers

Celebrating the Sun

… full of bees and yellow beads and
perfect flowerlets and orange butterflies.
—Mary Oliver, "Goldenrod"

At every stage of the growing season, it's the yellow flowers that seem to liven up our yard and help reveal the beauty of the other flowers. I used to think these roles were played by white flowers and, indeed, they make a garden more pleasing during the daytime and, at dawn and dusk, ethereal and mysterious. To the mostly pale flowers of spring, yellow flowers bring a kind of substance and zest. In summer, yellow flowers come into their own, blazing away like miniature suns even in patches of shade. In early fall, goldenrod foams up along the highway and in vacant fields. Later on, as the growing season comes to an end, yellow flowers provide the last rays of light in an herbal layer that, despite the bright colors of the leaves overhead, is steadily darkening.

Some of spring's yellow flowers are themselves pale and small, e.g., wood betony or lousewort (*Pedicularis canadensis*), which for some reason we've never succeeded in growing in our yard, and great bellwort (*Uvularia grandiflora*), whose hanging, twisted petals seem not to have opened yet or to be already wilting. However, we have one clump of bellwort (presumably wild) whose petals aren't pale at all but a bright yellow. Also called merrybells and a member of the lily family, *Uvularia grandiflora* is a beautiful plant, with its smooth, thin leaves and neat clumps. In fall these leaves turn a delicate shade of tan. Other spring flowers we've coaxed into at least temporary residence in our yard are bright but very small: yellow violets (*Viola pubescens*) and yellow trout lilies (*Erythronium americanum*), which arise from a bed of such beautiful glossy and spotted leaves that the common name "trout lily" seems the most apt of this plant's common names.

Trout lily   Erythronium americanum

155

There's nothing pale or insubstantial about the vast golden splashes of marsh marigolds (*Caltha palustris*) along wet banks and low-lying areas. In our mesic yard these flowers are represented only by a single clump hanging on in an artificial wetland that isn't wet enough. And neither is there anything shy or understated about the bright silky petals of wood poppies (*Stylophorum diphyllum*), which flower early and freely on plants that look rather like chrysanthemums. After a dozen years, however, the plants are beginning to multiply too quickly in our yard. Never mind, the extra, easy-to-grow plants will be easy to find homes for.

Late Spring

In the prairie garden on our sunny corner, we planted too many golden Alexanders (*Zizia aurea*) to start with and have been struggling with them ever since. Along the way, however, this yellow, and native, version of the familiar Queen Anne's lace, has provided us with a lot of plants to give away and probably hosted a lot of black swallowtail caterpillars. It is one of the last of spring's yellow flowers.

prairie alumroot (*Heuchera richardsonii*), with tall, graceful stalks and delicate greenish flowers.

Wild columbine (Aquilegia canadensis). *This yellow and red columbine is the only Michigan native, and the only Aquilegia species accessible to the only Michigan native hummingbird, the ruby-throated.*

Black swallowtail butterfly on golden Alexander (Zizia aurea), *an early-blooming native host plant for the black swallowtails.*

I can't resist including one of my favorite early flowers, wild columbine (*Aquilegia canadensis*), which combines yellow with red. And please, while we're on early favorites, let me mention at least one of the yellowish-green flowers that I'm very fond of:

Still a spring flower but among the first yellow composites to bloom are the ragworts (*Senecio* or *Packera* spp.). The round-leaved ragwort (*Senecio obovatus*) next to the curb has been crowded out by other plants or killed by salt from the street, and the golden ragwort (*S. aureus*) that grew in the first bed we made from leaves was crowded out long ago by taller plants. For native dandelions—*Krigia* species—our mesic yard isn't dry enough. Nor is it suited to that beautiful plant *Coreopsis lanceolata* (lance-leaf, tickseed, or sand coreopsis). Oh, it will survive for a year or two right next to the curb, in the harshest conditions our yard offers; but then it disappears, as the result of too much moisture, too much salt from the street, too much competition, or some combination of all three. Now I'm trying to grow it in a huge pot full of sandy soil in our only other sunny spot, the driveway.

Composites: The Eye of Day

Coreopsis and other members of the composite family (Compositae) with yellow flowers announce, softly at first and then with increasing intensity, the arrival of full summer. A yellow daisy-like flower—its central disk enclosed by yellow rays—inevitably reminds us of the sun, the source of all life. Some are even called sunflowers. Even the word daisy—as clearly seen from its Middle English spelling "dayeseye" (day's eye)—refers to the sun. Of course, not all members of this family, still referred to as the Aster (star) or Daisy family, bear yellow or even daisy-like flowers. Blazing stars (*Liatris* spp.) and goldenrods (*Solidago* spp.), which are also composites, don't look at all like daisies.

The daisy-like flowers, typical of the Aster or Composite family, are not the simple and straightforward flowers they seem. Each flower is actually a dense head composed of many smaller flowers. Those forming the prominent center are disk flowers; those surrounding the center, their strap-shaped corollas posing as individual petals, are ray flowers. The Asteraceae, or Compositae, in all their variety and elegance, are perhaps the most highly evolved, most efficient family of flowering plants. One of the largest families too, the Compositae boast more than 1100 genera and 19,000 species.

Anticipated in some years by ragwort and lance-leaf coreopsis, the first yellow composites of summer that bloom in our yard are black-eyed Susans (*Rudbeckia hirta*). No longer quite the galaxy in our prairie garden that they used to be, they are still miniature suns among the common milkweed, the white wild indigo, and the pale purple coneflowers. And they bloom all summer long, in the prairie garden and elsewhere in the yard, depending on how much sun they get and whether they're blooming on an old or new plant. Each ray (petal) is sculpted by two longitudinal veins, the mounded center a glowing maroon and smooth as satin—a close look at an individual flower can take your breath away. The yellow composites that follow them are taller and more aggressive, and with them come problems—at least for people like Tom and me, with a small yard, and an even smaller area of sun, who want to grow these plants but also to maintain diversity.

Many Reasons to Love Them

Without these yellow composites in your prairie garden—sunflowers, silphiums, goldenrods—you don't have anything that resembles a prairie. They are as basic to prairie as heat is to summer, and they're beautiful. So you dig them up when they start to take over some of the other plants you can't do without, for example, other composites such as purple coneflowers and blazing star and plants of other families such as prairie phlox, wild indigo, and newly-planted New Jersey tea. You cut them down or dig them up and give them away, especially to people who have more space than you do. You finally learn to put smaller and young plants elsewhere, beyond the reach of your pushy composites, along with those species which are less competitive and perhaps less well-adapted to your site. You learn to take strong measures, like isolating the most aggressive plants on islands where they can fight it out with each other, or sinking very deep edging around a patch of, say, downy sunflowers (*Helianthus mollis*); but you never consider getting rid of them entirely. At least we don't, though we sometimes feel that we are sorely tried. Tom and I complain a lot, but these aggressive plants provide us with surplus for friends and neighbors as well as for restorations around the community.

Downy sunflowers (Helianthus mollis), *a threatened species in the state of Michigan.*

The most important reason, however, is not the sunlike brilliance they bring to our lives but all the nectar and seeds they provide to wildlife, as well as their value as host plants. If these prairie plants

hadn't been so attractive to wildlife, so adaptable and opportunistic, they wouldn't still be around, given the wholesale destruction of their habitat by our forebears, still continued by us. A number of the plants mentioned here are state-listed.

By late July, almost all the yellow, daisy-like composites will be in bloom. Both the genera mentioned earlier, Coreopsis and Rudbeckia, include other species that we now have, or once had, in our yard. Prairie coreopsis (*Coreopsis palmata*), with its palmate leaves, is a lovely plant—about three feet tall and with smaller flowers than lance-leaf coreopsis—but it is one of the few plants permanently banished from our yard. It tried to take over our prairie garden and almost succeeded. Years after the enormous main roots of this rhizomatous plant were removed from our yard, we were still finding and pulling little outcroppings of it. Tall coreopsis (*C. tripteris*) is still taller, reaching about six or seven feet in height, with very slender stalks and delicate flowers; but eventually it too becomes very aggressive. In fall, however, its leaves, which fall into three narrow, downward-pointing leaflets, turn orange and red, making this elegant plant seem an apparition from a Japanese painting.

In addition to black-eyed Susan (*Rudbeckia hirta*), our yard contains another member of this genus named by Linneaus for one of his teachers. This is *Rudbeckia laciniata* (tall or cut-leaf or green-headed coneflower, or wild golden glow). This is another beautiful, aggressive plant, whose disk flowers are greenish at first and its leaves attractively cut—hence the description "laciniata." It's a tall plant, all right, but closer to seven feet than to the 12 feet indicated in one catalog.

CONEFLOWERS AND SUNFLOWERS

Gray-headed coneflower (*Ratibida pinnata*), also has several other common names, yellow coneflower, drooping coneflower, prairie coneflower (also applied to *R. columnifera*), and—best of all—weary Susan, because its petals, unlike those of *Rudbeckia*, the black-eyed Susan, are drooping. (Keeping these yellow composites straight is

powerful incentive for learning botanical names.) Tall, branching stalks and widely-spaced, divided leaves make this a rather airy, graceful plant. The cone or disk of its flower is taller than it is wide, grayish-green at first and later turning brown. The long slender rays are translucent—almost silky or gauzy—and a vivid lemon yellow. The Native

Americans used the plant to make a vivid yellow-orange dye. Stirring slightly on long stalks above the leaves, their delicate rays drooping from the ends of the cones, these flowers are a lovely sight. Gray-headed coneflowers can tolerate considerable shade, and even they can become aggressive.

Notorious for their aggressiveness are sunflowers (*Helianthus* spp.), but who would be without them? We've now, after a decade, lost all our western sunflowers (*Helianthus occidentalis*), which seem to find our yard a little too damp or shaded. The place I've seen them growing best is in the extremely harsh environment of the former raingarden at the Maple Street Magnet School for the Arts, in sand, full sun, and the baking heat of a courtyard enclosed on three sides. What thrives in our prairie garden is downy or ashy sunflower (*H. mollis*), an elegant, gray-green, softly hairy sunflower about five feet tall—a favorite of American goldfinches. We have had to confine it, though, by means of a lot of deep edging. A woodland sunflower (*H. decapitalus*) that lights up a shady recess in the front yard has been allowed to form a monoculture; we just haven't had the energy to downsize it. We do keep pulling up another bright yellow plant that does all too well in shade, jewelweed or touch-me-nots (*Impatiens pallida*), but it graciously ignores our efforts and comes up somewhere else to brighten our lives.

IRRESISTIBLE SILPHIUMS

We're lucky in southwest Michigan to have four Silphium species—all of them at or near the limit of their range—and all but prairie dock (*S. terebinthinaceum*) state-listed. They are coarse, majestic plants that capture our imagination as they did Aldo Leopold's: "What a thousand acres of Silphiums looked like when they tickled the bellies of the buffalo is a question never again to be answered, and perhaps not even asked" (July, "Prairie Birthday," *A Sand County Almanac*). It is probably prideful and self-indulgent to plant them in a small yard (and then to plant more than one or two of each), but they are irresistible (when they're not trying to take over your garden).

Least remarkable in appearance is rosinweed (*S. integrifolium*), which forms clumps about five feet tall and seeds itself abundantly; but once, in the late '90s, we were thrilled to see a giant swallowtail—not all that common here—nectaring on its flowers in the prairie garden.

Compass plant (*S. laciniatum*) is the most dramatic—and our current favorite. Though we planted our first one in 1996, and it was at least a year old then, it didn't bloom until 2000. But then it was spectacular: starting at the top of a tall, bare stalk, the bright yellow flowers bloomed in pairs, each flower five inches across. But only after we got

Compass plant (Silphium laciniatum). *Also a threatened species in Michigan, compass plant is strikingly beautiful. Its woody roots reach down 10 to 12 feet into prairie soil, and its strong, hairy stems raise bright yellow flowers 8 to 10 feet above the ground.*

rid of two shrubs that were casting a fair amount of shade onto the prairie garden did the compass plant really come into its own. The next year, 2008, it sent up not one but seven flowerstalks, slightly shorter than usual, admittedly, and with slightly smaller flowers. The sight of it was positively riveting! Compass plant is not aggressive, nor is it as tolerant of shade as the other three silphiums. We've heard that, in the absence of convenient shrubs, bobolinks use the compass plant's sturdy dried flowerstalks as perches.

Its leaves, like those of prairie dock and cup plant, are striking. Held upright at the base of the plant, they are "slashed" almost to the leaf's central vein into a series of narrow ribbons. The still-larger leaves of prairie dock, in contrast, are toothed but undivided. A leaf on one of our prairie docks measures over 19 inches long, and that doesn't include the lobes that extend below the blade of the leaf and make the leaf somewhat heart-shaped. In order to protect themselves from drying out, both compass plant and prairie dock tend to hold their leaves so that only the edges are presented to the midday sun. As a result, the leaves are always surprisingly cool to the touch. The more or less north-south orientation of their leaves supposedly provided a "compass" in past centuries to prairie travelers on cloudy days. Prairie dock doesn't bloom in our yard until early September, and its comparatively smaller flowers are also spectacular, borne as they are in abundant but airy clusters at the tops of bare, slender, extremely tall stalks—stalks sometimes nine or ten feet high, stiffly holding their flowers up to the sun. The main root of prairie dock grows rather quickly to great depth and can reach impressive girth (up to football-size diameter, we're told); transplanting or uprooting an established prairie dock plant is difficult—in fact, after repeated tries, we usually give it up as impossible.

Those lovely, tall stems of compass plant and prairie dock persist during fall and winter, providing perches and seeds for the birds, and harboring more insects both in the stems and in fallen litter than almost any other plant.

Silphium is a Greek word signifying "resinous juice." The upper stems of Silphiums do, when the plant is in bloom, exude a gummy juice that was used by American Indian and early pioneer children as chewing gum.

STILL MORE SILPHIUMS AND SUNFLOWERS

Cup plant may be even more distinctive than the other silphiums, first for the oddity of its leaves, which clasp the plant's big square stalk so as to form a cup with a rounded lip able to hold rainwater. Birds drink from these cups and perhaps find insects in them. Some leaves reach a great size: one leaf in our oldest clump measures, from tip to the bottom of the cup, over 15 inches. Clumps themselves, if left alone, seem only to get larger and larger, crowding out or shading out everything in the vicinity. In fact, they look (and act) almost tropical. A clump containing only a few cup plants is as big and dense as a shrub though clumps not sheltered by walls or braced by other tall plants are vulnerable to storms.

When in bloom, its big sprays of yellow flowers held on high, the plant is at least eight feet tall. Its large, many-rayed flowers are gorgeous and smell of summer itself. Eastern tiger swallowtail butterflies, among others, are attracted to their nectar.

Eastern tiger swallowtails on cup plant (Silphium perfoliatum)

One summer day several years ago, around the largest clump of cup plants in our yard, these butterflies were swarming, seeming almost as numerous as the flowers themselves.

Blooming as late as prairie dock is still another composite, Maximillian's sunflower (*Helianthus maximilliani*), which is almost as tall. The flowers of these two yellow composites wave over New England asters and goldenrod, both composites themselves.

Variations on Sunlight

Many yellow flowers that bloom in summer aren't composites, and they too are beautiful. We've had a couple of primrose species in our yard, Missouri evening primrose (*Oenothera macrocarpa* or *missouriensis*), whose flowers were huge, but now this low-growing plant, native southwest of here, has been crowded out. We've also had common evening primrose (*Oenothera biennis*) which is native, but was too aggressive—and not showy enough—to put up with in a small yard.

For a while we had a couple of prickly-pear plants (*Opuntia humifusa*), whose yellow flowers are beautiful; but our yard really isn't dry or sunny enough for this plant, the only hardy cactus in our region.

Other yellow sunloving flowers which aren't composites that we currently enjoy are shrubby cinquefoil (*Potentilla fruticosa*), whose flowers are dazzlingly bright against its dark green foliage, wild senna (*Cassia hebecarpa*), and Indian grass (*Sorghastrum nutans*), with its gracefully curving, brownish-gold inflorescence. Wild senna is a striking plant—tall, with pinnate leaves and large clusters of pea-like, almost golden flowers. Our sunny prairie garden may actually be a little too dry for it, but one plant persists and gradually spreads.

Prickly pear cactus (Opuntia humifusa). *Tough and very adaptable, there are Opuntia species in just about every continental American state, in Mexico, and on south to Chile and Argentina. Easy to grow, if you have a location that's sunny and dry, with poor soil. Gorgeous yellow flowers.*

As in the case of Indian grass, some plants have small, delicate flowers that need a close look if you're to appreciate their beauty—there are several native grasses, for instance, with lovely, short-lived yellow or bronzish flowers. Or they have other virtues besides their flowers; such a one is small-flowered leafcup (*Polymnia canadensis*), partial to moist shade, with an inconspicuous yellow flower but with large, heavily lobed, wonderful leaves. They have a strange, slightly ominous look to them.

And while we're on impressive plants, here's one more of my green-flowered favorites: spikenard (*Aralia racemosa*), which achieves shrub-like proportions, with long, branching clusters of greenish umbels, turning in fall to scrumptious-looking red-purple berries.

LATE COMPOSITES—AND MORE

Goldenrod, upon casual inspection, doesn't seem to have much in common with the daisy-like composites discussed above, but under magnification, its florets can be seen as quite similar in structure. That goldenrod causes hayfever is of course a myth—the real culprit is ragweed, which blooms at the same time and has inconspicuous green flowers—but the aggressiveness of goldenrod in cultivation is no myth at all. Even shade-loving goldenrod species, supposed to be less aggressive than the sun-loving species, are aggressive. We have zig-zag goldenrod (*Solidago flexicaulis*) and blue-stemmed goldenrod (*Solidago caesia*) in the shade, and stiff goldenrod and showy goldenrod in the sun, all of them vigorous. All of them "full of bees and yellow beads and perfect flowerlets" (Mary Oliver, "Goldenrod"). I don't know how the all too vigorous Canada goldenrod, or perhaps it is tall goldenrod, got into the yard—we didn't plant it—but I pull it every time I see it. The ideal time to pull it is of course after a rain, when a few more inches of its rhizomatous roots are likely to come up.

Why tolerate this genus in your yard? For the same reason you tolerate other aggressive plants: the flowers are beautiful, especially in combination with asters, and extremely valuable to wildlife. On Tallamy's ranked list of native herbaceous plants, goldenrods as a group rank second in importance, after native clovers, as a host plant for the caterpillars of many butterflies and moths (115 species, to be more precise). Asters, which are also composites, rank third, playing host to 109 Lepidoptera species. Goldenrods are also extremely important as a source of late nectar for pollinators, including monarch butterfies on their way to Mexico and queen bumble bees, preparing to hibernate over the winter.

Another source of late nectar, and the very last yellow flower to bloom in our yard, is brown-eyed Susan (*Rudbeckia triloba*), which starts blooming in August and continues till frost. This plant will tolerate a great deal of shade, in which it grows tall and lanky, though nevertheless covered with flowers from ground level to head-high. Though not rhizomatous, it seems to produce enormous amounts of seed, which germinates with great ease. If we didn't pull up a lot of it, we'd have a problem. But Tom enjoys shouldering his way through its lush growth to refill the bird feeder.

THE SUN'S BLESSINGS ENDURE

When, as winter approaches and the last yellow composites burn out, we're not by any means left comfortless and desolate. They have blessed us with a rich harvest of seeds which will help support birds and small mammals through the winter. Indeed, one of the joys of late summer is observing the goldfinches, still in their summer yellow-and-black plumage, already feeding on ripe seeds, bright against pale yellows of the last tall coreopsis or rudbeckias. The roots of some composites will also provide food, while dead stalks and leaves will offer cover to many creatures, including insects in various stages. But there are other, less obvious benefits that flow from these plants whose flowers resemble miniature suns. Some, with their rhizomes, will help hold the soil in place. Others, the Silphiums in particular, continually enrich the soil as their large and powerful roots penetrate its depths. (The roots of a compass plant, for example, may reach down 15 feet.) Year after year, such plants silently produce wealth beneath our feet. And when Spring comes round again, it brings a crop of new plants springing up from the seeds and rhizomes of their parents. Truly, these plants with yellow flowers are not just for summer and fair weather but for all seasons.

A much shorter version of this essay appeared in the Wildflower Association of Michigan newsletter in 2001. Inspiration for the essay came from Emma Bickham Pitcher's beautiful meditation on purple flowers, "The Purple Time," in *Of Woods and Other Things* (Kalamazoo: Beech Leaf Press, 1996).

PART IV

RESTORING COMMUNITY

In a certain sense, everything is everywhere at all times

—Alfred North Whitehead—
Science and the Modern World

The truth is that everything causes everything else.

—John Cage—
A Year from Monday

And the world cannot be discovered by a journey of miles, no matter how long, but only by a spiritual journey, a journey of one inch, very arduous and humbling and joyful, by which we arrive at the ground at our feet, and learn to be at home.

—Wendell Berry—

Holding Turtle Island   Relief print with collage   Nancy Stroupe

18

GATHERING THE LIGHT

BY NANCY AND TOM SMALL

Still life is dancing life.
The dancing life of light.
—Jeanette Winterson, *Sexing the Cherry*

The theme was "Gathering the Light." In the first week of July, in 1995, about 1600 Quakers met here in Kalamazoo, for the annual gathering of Friends General Conference, with workshops, discussions, field trips, and worship. Ever since then, the two of us have continued to contemplate what it means to "gather the light." What light have we managed to gather, what have we added to our store?

Every morning during the week, we participated in a workshop on "Achieving the Ecological Economy." Our leader, Tony McQuail, an organic farmer from Ontario, Canada, who farmed exclusively with oxen and horses, got us started by talking about how plants sustain themselves through periods with little or no light. They *store* the light within cell structures—tiny, dynamic storehouses of energy. They then draw on this "gathered" light to survive through the darkness or drive new growth as light and warmth return in the spring.

We environmentalists seek, so we say, to *restore* the earth. Since we can't possibly return the earth to its previous condition, we must mean something else: perhaps "to give back; make restitution." To restore, then, would be to replenish earth's store of light, so that what is in reserve, in store, will sustain those dynamic structures we depend on through all the days and nights—all the summers and winters—of our lives.

RESTORING LAND-BASED COMMUNITY

All week the image of "storing" and "restoring" kept recurring. On Monday afternoon, Maynard Kaufman, from Michigan Organic Food and Farm Association, spoke on "Eating to Build Community and Heal the Earth." By raising some of our own food, he said, buying local produce, and participating in community-supported agriculture (buying a share in the produce of a local farm), we can begin to rebuild the vanishing land-based community of our own area, encourage rebuilding

167

of the soil, and greatly reduce the profligate waste of energy (stored light) required to bring our food to the table.

Given the total process by which food gets to us, we're not giving back even a fraction of the gathered light we're using up. Since our food travels an average of 1500 miles to arrive on our dinner table, we're expending not just current sunlight but an immense quantity of the ancient sunlight stored in the earth as fossil fuel. In pre-industrial times, we learned in our workshop, it took only one calorie of stored energy (mainly human and animal power—energy stored in muscles) to produce from five to 50 calories. Now, in our post-industrial age, we have reversed that ratio. We obtain only one calorie of energy from every ten calories of input, which we burn up in fuel, labor, chemicals, equipment, storage, processing, transport, and industrial infrastructure.

What, then, is *in store* for us? Inevitably, a growing deficit—continuing loss, as into an energy sinkhole. Then, a gathering darkness without enough gathered light to carry us through.

RESTORING OUR OWN PLOT OF LAND

At the end of the week, some of us took a field trip to the Kalamazoo Nature Center, where we toured a prairie restoration project. Steve Keto, a local grower of native plants, showed us, first-hand, the marvelous system by which a tallgrass prairie (a pre-settlement ecosystem) progresses through the season of light, from tiny, delicate spring blooms to the towering grasses and showy flowers of late summer, each succession of plants taking its moment and place in the sun and then giving way to the next, all together gathering and storing, as a *system*, the maximum possible amount of light.

> I take it into me and grow
> Say the trees
> Leaves above
> Roots below
>
>   —Gary Snyder,
>   "The Uses of Light"

We began our week of "Gathering the Light" with a vision of renewed community based on the land; we ended with living proof that an ancient biotic community, one that evolved over millennia on that same land, *can* be restored—at least to some extent. So how shall we, in our daily lives, begin to re-store?

We can, first of all, restore our own plot of urban or suburban land. We can establish, in our gardens, a generous diversity of the native plants that 200 years of settlement have almost extirpated; and thus we can welcome to our yards the native creatures that are displaced because the plants that provided their habitat and food are lost.

A VISION OF HOW TO LIVE

The two of us, in July 1995, were just about to marry, and we were seeking a vision of how to live. Steve Keto showed us a way. Sara Stein's book, *Noah's Garden*, inspired us. For a whole day of the "Ecological Economy" workshop, Tony Mc-Quail and our fellow workshop participants brainstormed with us on how to transform our little plot of land and our household into a restoration project not just for ourselves but for the neighborhood *and* for the broader community of creatures that share the earth with us, all of us seeking the restorative powers of the light. Thus we can begin to give back what we have taken. And now our own book—which you hold in your hands—is itself a gathering, a way of passing along and giving back.

We can also give back by using less, not just of that cumbersome monster, the automobile, that gorges itself on stored sunlight, but also of the little things. They matter also. For instance, we can carry a kit with us wherever we go: a few reusable plastic bags for produce, a travel cup for beverages and table utensils for food so we never use disposable ones, a string or cloth bag for purchases, a cloth napkin/towel so we never use paper ones. A throwaway, even a recyclable, uses up light. How are we to make restitution, or at least reduce the deficit, if we throw away so much? Is our land a sink and a landfill for us rather than a storehouse, an Earth House Hold, to use Gary Snyder's phrase?

We can give back by building and enlarging community, also a process of storing and sharing light. Consider, for instance, the communal traditions of barnraising and "harvest home." Folks come together from far and near, as a community, to share in raising a storehouse, or to celebrate the gathering and storing of the harvest. Another of our field trips during that memorable week in July 1995 was to Tillers International, which preserves, cherishes, restores, and teaches these communal traditions. We have seldom seen anyone so absorbed and appreciative as Tony McQuail when he took over driving a team of Tillers oxen.

True Economy of the Circling Year

We can give back by nourishing neighborhood, a community of goods, a restored *commons*. Instead of gathering as much light unto ourselves as we can, let us begin to share and exchange plants, goods, tools, food, ideas, and labor. We can make of our own Earth House Hold a true meeting place, a gathering together as *ecos*, a true *economy*, for mutual aid, for symbiosis, where everything circulates and returns, instead of vanishing away, all used up.

Finally, we can *celebrate* the seasons of our lives: the solstices when the sun stands still before turning back; equinoxes when light and dark are in balance; crossquarter days midway between, such as May Day, celebrating youth and flowering; Lammas Day (August 1), when light and care bring forth the first loaf of bread from the grain; or All Saints Day, when, the harvest now fully stored, we begin a fallow period of rest, and we honor all those elders, the living and the dead, who gathered light and who are now the "store" on which we must draw; and then that in some ways most wonderful of days, Imbolc or Candlemas Day (Feb. 2), when we celebrate the *return* of the light.

> The resistant stuff we are,
> blood and bone,
> is not the opposite of light
> but light's incarnation.
>
> —Scott Russell Sanders,
> *Staying Put*

A version of this essay appeared in *Leadings* (August 1995, vol. 2, no. 2), by Nancy and Tom Small, a bimonthly publication of Quaker Earthcare Witness.

Rising to Light

A leaf is a small miracle, for through it a transubstantiation occurs—of a lifeless gas into a solid, living being. It's a sort of resurrection of CO_2, the gas given off with death and decay, the gas that enshrouds dead planets. Yet from it plants forge beauteous forms that support all the hosts of earthly life, ourselves included.

—Tim Flannery, *Here on Earth*

19

Sharing the Garden with the Whole Community

By Nancy and Tom Small

Membership in a place
includes membership in a community.
—Gary Snyder, *The Practice of the Wild*

In the mid '90s, we made a big decision, not to retire to the country but to stay put, and turn our half-acre yard near downtown Kalamazoo, Michigan, into "some kind of nature preserve." The next spring, galvanized by Sara Stein's *Noah's Garden: Restoring the Ecology of Our Own Back Yards* and guided by a local nurseryman/friend, we started a prairie garden on our front corner—the only place we have full sun. We removed the sod, improved the soil, and put in plugs and larger plants.

By summer, when our little prairie began to bloom—attracting birds, butterflies, and many insects new to the yard—we knew we'd made the right decision. Four years later, we extended the prairie garden for the third time and created a wetland garden in the middle of the front yard. The driveway became a temporary nursery for plants waiting to be planted or given away.

Before long, we realized that our half-acre is too small and isolated to preserve nature (as university professors, we taught literature, not biology); nonetheless, we rejoice in the number and variety of plants and animals it appears to help support. Every year, we see more bees, birds, "bugs," toads and butterflies, including great spangled fritillaries (*Speyeria cybele*) and several kinds of swallowtails (*Papilio* spp.). For many years now, a small flock of red-winged blackbirds has arrived in late February to bring joy to the yard and has stayed to raise young—or at least bring them back to us from nests in nearby wetlands.

Sharing with Wildlife is Not Enough

We've also realized that sharing our yard with wildlife is not enough. We must share it with people, too, in order to convey the *urgency* of saving wild land and of turning conventional, sterile yards into refuges, stopovers and corridors for wildlife. Located on a corner without sidewalks, our prairie garden goes right up to the curb on both streets. People riding bicycles, running, walking dogs and pushing strollers can't miss it, and cars sometimes slow down (or even stop) for a look.

When we're outdoors, we greet passersby. If they seem at all interested in the garden, we explain what we're doing and offer to give them a tour and seeds or plants. Often, they accept.

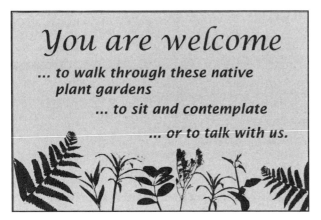

This sign out by the street, colorful but unobtrusive, lures passersby onto a shady, branching path, first to the arbor, with a comfortable seat, and then on into the yard.
Design by Pamela Rups.

In a more subtle effort to lure passersby into our yard, we tried to blur the boundaries of the "private property" temporarily under our care. We installed a "Welcome" sign near the street. In several places, stepping stones lead from the curb into the prairie garden. Major paths and openings are wide enough for at least two people to walk side by side. Laminated cards on stakes identify plants, and give information on the plant's natural and cultural history. Not far from the street, one path bends around an arbor with a wide seat, suggesting a resting place for passersby and for people viewing the garden. There are other garden chairs and seats farther into the yard.

At every opportunity we not only sing the virtues of native plants, but do our best to get them into people's yards and onto the grounds of parks, schools, churches and commercial establishments. Our yard provides us with quantities of certain plants. Others we started growing under lights over the winter; but we soon realized we could germinate and grow them outdoors with less effort. We distribute surplus plants—our own and other people's—through a plant exchange every spring, and usually another in the fall as well. We press plants into the hands of friends, neighbors, repair and delivery people, folks we encounter at stores, offices and meetings; and, of course, passersby. We take native-flower bouquets to friends and to businesses we patronize.

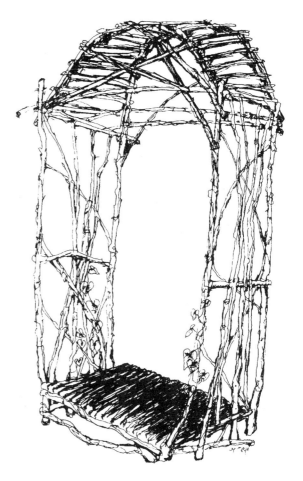

The Arbor   Jana Pyle

Artist, departmental secretary, dear friend, Jana Pyle drew this illustration of our first, newly acquired arbor for our article in The Prairie Reader, *a lovely journal now, alas, defunct.*

Teaching, and Learning

Our hope is that people who tend a few native plants, or are at least regularly exposed to them, will feel a proprietary interest in them and the animal life they support, notice these plants along roadsides and in natural areas, and realize the importance of preserving wild land and wild species in a time when they are under great stress.

Kalamazoo officials, once hostile to urban "prairies," have—after some strenuous effort on our part—aided in our consciousness-raising efforts; they allowed us to help rewrite the city's weed ordinance and then to write the city's new handbook on natural landscaping, illustrated with photos of our yard, and still available on the city's web site.

When we began, we had no idea that our "nature preserve" would also function as a nursery for native plants, a demonstration plot for natural landscaping, and an outdoor classroom for ourselves and others. Nor did we realize that we were signing up for one last course, the most challenging and all-consuming that we've ever taught or taken—and also the most rewarding.

> Enjoy the land,
> but own it not.
>
> —Thoreau, *Walden*

In the spring of 2010, following Nancy's death, my friends and I renewed the paths into the garden, some of which had been overgrown, had a new arbor-seat built of willow and sassafras to replace the original which had been destroyed by vandals, and installed a new sign, which reads, "YOU ARE WELCOME to walk through these native-plant gardens, to sit and contemplate, and to talk with us."

This essay was adapted from our article in *The Prairie Reader,* Fall, 1999 (vol. 4, no. 2), p. 8.

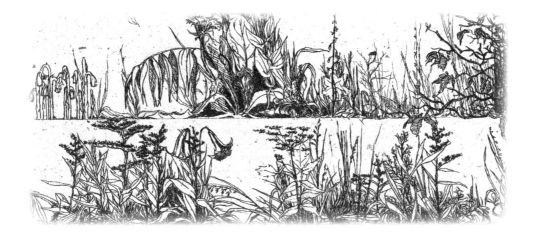

20

GIVE IT TO THE WIND

BY NANCY AND TOM SMALL

The wind bloweth where it listeth, and thou hearest
the sound thereof, but canst not tell whence it cometh, and
whither it goeth; so is every one that is born of the Spirit. (*John* 3:8)

Some years ago, a Malaysian student who did some work for me referred to our house and yard as "your compound." The image this brought to mind—a colonial enclosure, wrested from an encroaching wilderness and native population—was unsettling. It suggested something *exclusive*.

The more I thought about it, the more fitting the term became. Throughout our suburban neighborhood, each front yard—whether hedged and fenced or not—is itself a barrier. Not much human activity takes place in these front yards, except for "yard work." They constitute a collective No Man's Land, briefly occupied by one neighbor's maintenance squad or patrolled by another neighbor on his riding mower.

The life of the household goes on behind the closed front door, or in summer behind the house itself, in the back yard with its patio and gas grill, where temporary disorder is permissible. Furtively, we sneak into our houses through the garage or through the side entrance off the driveway. People at the front door are suspect—surely they *want* something.

THE DREAM OF PERFECTING NATURE

The intention of nineteenth-century designers who invented this idea of a yard was to make towns into great parks, with tree-lined lanes and continuous lawns, a pastoral Arcadia—the grass close-cropped, as if by sheep. Not only would we fashion a democratic equivalent to the vast estates of the landed gentry, we would recover Nature itself, regularized and idealized by human management.

The invention of the lawnmower in 1830 made it all possible.

The result is a vast, sterile, industrialized monoculture (more than 45 million acres of lawn nationwide) that robs the soil of nutrients, robs the streams of water, robs many of the region's creatures of habitat, and robs the neighborhood of community. In establishing our neatly subdivided

175

"compounds," we are colonists, and not much bet-ter than thieves. Most of us make the payments on time, but even so, when it comes to our *practice*, Proudhon, back in 1840, was right: "Property is theft."

Maybe that's too harsh a term. We're not thieves—merely consumers. We use up a resource without giving back. We squander our inheritance, impoverishing ourselves and our heirs.

What then are we to do?

Giving it all back to the expropriated Native Americans is not really an option. Nor can we give it back to the wild nature that our treefelling, sodbusting ancestors labored to conquer and domesticate. But we can still make some suburban restitution.

RECOVERING THE SPIRIT OF THE LAND

The nineteenth-century landscape vision of a united society within an ordered, green world, was admirable; but the project failed. Instead, we've separated ourselves—from each other and from the land. Now we must learn to cooperate more fully with the spirit of the land itself, the spirit of our particular place—not the spirit of an eighteenth-century aristocracy driven by pastoral nostalgia and colonial ambition.

To free ourselves from a vision that lays waste our land, we must begin to loosen our grasp and allow the spirit of place to *move us*. We must listen to the wind as it "bloweth where it listeth," heedless of our antiquated weed ordinances and arbitrary property lines.

The cloud is free only to go with the wind.

—Wendell Berry

Common milkweed (Asclepias syriaca)—*ripe seedpods, open to the winds.*

Here, then, is how the movement begins, the change that our changing times require:

- On our "compounds," here in southwest Michigan, let us **restore** something like the plant communities that evolved over millennia to thrive in this region: the plants of tall-grass prairie, oak savanna, wetlands—a beautiful seasonal succession of flowers and grasses, providing cover and nourishment throughout the year for a rich variety of creatures, requiring no petrochemicals, no poisons, and little water other than rain.

> Front yards are not made to walk in but, at most, through, and you could go in the back way.
>
> —Thoreau, "Walking"

- Let us **open out** our lands towards the street and the neighborhood, with resting-places for passersby, a *front-yard* porch or patio, paths with signs and invitations to share and learn about the living history and cooperative intelligence of a prairie or savanna ecosystem, perhaps the most powerful soil-building and life-supporting process in nature.

- Let us **persuade** our neighbors to help us make new connections, create lanes and corridors—not for automobiles but for creatures (including ourselves). Nearby our half acre is a degraded but still intact wetland habitat, Kleinstuck Preserve. A little farther, in the opposite direction, is Asylum Lake, with remnants of wetland, prairie, and savanna. Wildlife needs corridors and stepping stones connecting such patches of natural habitat. A few urban "compounds," transformed into habitat and integrated as corridors, will give back some land and freedom of movement to the creatures, to the rain, to the wind.

As Pulitzer Prize winning playwright Susan Glaspell wrote in 1920, in her play Inheritors, "The world is all a moving field … To keep it, you must give it away—give it to the wind."

A version of this essay was published in our column, "Leadings," in *BeFriending Creation*, May–June, 1996, p. 5.

21

SEEING THE TREES

BY NANCY AND TOM SMALL

A fool sees not the same tree as a wise man sees.
—William Blake, *The Marriage of Heaven and Hell*

We're always much involved with trees: planting trees; topping a dead tree in our yard, to leave a snag for birds, insects, fungi; digging and potting up seedlings and saplings for our twice-yearly plant exchanges; gathering downed branches and discarded stumps from the neighborhood to use as borders, seats, pedestals, or harbors for wildlife. As we work, or pause to observe, our trees hold out to us certain truths: how much life an old tree—or a dead one—supports; how firmly rooted even a very small tree can be. But one tree in particular grasps our imaginations.

For an old, unprepossessing crabapple tree in our front yard, we've come to feel a reverence perhaps not unlike what ancient peoples felt for trees. When Tom first moved here 35 years ago, the tree, though it produced clouds of deep pink blossoms every spring, was already well past its prime. Its four gnarled trunks sagged and sprawled. Then a neighbor's child, playing horsy, broke one of them.

Long ago we gave up mowing beneath the tree, but for a while nothing grew there except violets and myrtle. Gradually, as the three remaining trunks gently reclined into a shoulder-high island of greenery, mostly planted by wind and birds—wild roses, asters, gray dogwood, grapevine, pokeweed, cup plant—the resulting thicket became a haven for wildlife. Summer and winter, finches, chickadees, sparrows, cardinals, red and gray squirrels, chipmunks, rabbits, voles, toads, and downy woodpeckers find food and shelter there. At all seasons, the thicket is alive with the flickering shadows and sounds of birds.

Aging apple trees become venerable as their trunks sprawl and limbs gesticulate wildly to the earth and the sky. Each tree hosts and embraces an ecosystem.

179

Fairy Ring   Ladislav Hanka

There are about 60 species which can grow in a fairy ring pattern. The best known is the edible scotch bonnet (Marasmius oreades), *commonly known as the fairy ring champignon. It loves grassy areas: lawns, meadows, roadsides. We're fond of the French name: Nymphe des montagnes.*

DEATH AND BIRTH INTERWOVEN

A few years ago, another trunk collapsed, subsiding to become a trellis for grape vines and Virgin's bower. The spring bloom, still lovely, became sparser. Then, after a rainy fall, the crabapple began to produce an abundant and strangely luminous crop of large white mushrooms. One rainy evening at twilight, with the mushrooms gleaming palely against wet vegetation, we realized that they formed a magical pattern—a fairy ring. Starting from a spore, feeding on decaying wood below the surface, criss-crossing and circling outwards in all directions to form a complex web of invisible threads or hyphae, our underground mycelium had surfaced at the outer limit of its circle, to manifest itself and reproduce, sending out new spores to the wind and rain. Here, then, in the fairy ring—new growth encircling decay—were death and new birth interwoven, the sign of a hidden presence, visitation, and ghostly dance—a revenant.

This past winter, another trunk broke. We left it untouched because it was still connected to the earth by a substantial splinter; and it bloomed this spring—for the last time. Now it too is a trellis. Only one trunk still lives. But the thicket thrives that rises through the tree's remains.

Though Michigan's ancient tall-grass prairies, savannas, and forests are gone, we can still recover something of ancient wonder, a vision of trees as sacred, oracular, participating in the mysterious process that is eternity. Our dark, gnarled, dying crabapple, leaning on the earth, speaks with the same message

The affinities of all the beings of the same class have sometimes been represented by a great tree ... As buds give rise by growth to fresh buds, and these if vigorous, branch out and overtop on all sides many a feebler branch, so by generation I believe it has been with the great Tree of Life, which fills with its dead and broken branches the crust of the earth, and covers the surface with its ever branching and beautiful ramifications.

—Charles Darwin, 1859

that Gary Snyder offers: "The human community, when healthy, is like an ancient forest. The little ones are in the shade and shelter of the big ones, even rooted in their lost old bodies. All ages, and all together growing and dying." And all species too, both visible and invisible. Both original and revenant.

We Intervene to Restore

These days the two of us struggle to mediate between the need to leave things alone, allowing natural cycles to happen as they will, and the need to intervene, to restore whatever we can of what has been lost. So we work to keep the thicket as diverse as possible; and we plant new bur oaks, once an essential part of the mixed-oak savanna that was our neighborhood's pre-settlement ecosystem—now commemorated dimly in local names: Oakland Drive, one block from us; the Oakwood neighborhood, just down the road; Burr Oak Court, towards downtown. We support our friend's native-plant nursery, Mary Ann's Michigan Trees and Shrubs.

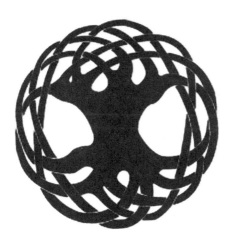

In the ancient Celtic symbol of the World Tree, all things are connected in endless spirals and circles, and—as the Greek philosopher Heraclitus stated 25 centuries ago—"The way up and the way down are one and the same." This symbol was the logo for the World Tree Multicultural Center for Peace, Justice, and Mother Earth.

We celebrate renewals. And as we grow older, we mourn losses. We mourn the loss of The World Tree, a Multicultural Center for Peace, Justice, and the Earth, established by young people in a store front on the downtown mall. It lapsed after a few years, painfully giving way to a radical theatre group that shared its space and now is also gone; and yet both are survived by a thriving counterculture that they helped to spawn and support.

In all our actions, even in our sense of loss, we conspire to recreate the "community of communities" represented by and embodied in a tree. In our urban landscapes, we work to revive a dream of ancient savanna—trees, thickets, and prairie openings restored where once they grew, new life springing from ancestral bones.

Our inspiration is a gift from ancient forest to all of us: a sacred ring interweaving past and future, age and youth, death and life, self and community. Through our aging crab, and a visionary World Tree, we may yet learn the ancient reverence and wisdom spoken by Black Elk, holy man of the Oglala Sioux:

> *And*
> *I saw the sacred*
> *hoop of my people was*
> *one of the many hoops*
> *that made one circle, wide as*
> *daylight and as starlight, and*
> *in the centre grew one mighty*
> *flowering tree to shelter all the*
> *children of one mother and*
> *one father. And I saw*
> *that it was holy.*

REFERENCES

Blake, William. *The Marriage of Heaven and Hell* (1790–93).

Neihardt, John G. *Black Elk Speaks: Being the Life Story of a Holy Man of the Oglala Sioux*. New York: William Morrow & Co., 1932.

Snyder, Gary. *The Practice of the Wild*. San Francisco: North Point Press, 1990.

A version of this essay, titled "Two Trees," appeared in our column, "Leadings," in *BeFriending Creation* (Nov./Dec., 1996, pp. 4–5), the newsletter of Quaker Earthcare Witness.

Chickadees—Getting Together   Elizabeth Henderson

22

Look Up to See What's Always Been There

By Nancy and Tom Small

Therefore all seasons shall be sweet to thee …
—Samuel Taylor Coleridge, "Frost at Midnight"

A book that we consulted before taking a trip to Costa Rica warned us that, at first sight, a tropical rain forest may seem virtually uninhabited by animals. You'll see much more, the book advised, if you can persuade some of the people who live in these places to guide you. Your cost, we were warned, is likely to be more than monetary and include serious damage to any pride you might have had in your powers of observation. Indeed, the warning concluded, you may have difficulty persuading the native people of the rain forest that they have to point out to you what is so obvious to them.

Actually, we're already feeling quite humble enough, right here in Kalamazoo. After decades of merely enduring Michigan's gloomy winter, we're seeing what we've never really noticed before. What happened this year, to let us see more clearly, more vividly, as if we now, all of a sudden, had become native to this place?

Many trees still had their leaves—some trees hadn't even turned—when the snow came and stayed; and perhaps it was this strange and abrupt beginning to winter that seized our attention. Suddenly, as we drove around town or walked in the neighborhood, we were looking up. And we saw not just whether trees had kept their leaves and how they bore up under their mantles of snow, but how they branched and whether they contained nests.

Silhouettes and Flickering Shadows

The more we looked up, the more we saw: crows stiffly upright on the topmost twigs of trees—pigeons in tight rows on telephone wires—Canada geese in ragged formations—starlings noisily congregating at night in a row of evergreen trees next to a many-windowed (and no doubt heat-leaking) building downtown—the papery globe of a wasp's nest suspended high in a tree—motionless hawks, silhouetted on light poles high above a busy boulevard—the tops of soaring fir trees so thick with cones that they arch downward under the weight.

Red-tailed hawk, watching from a power pole. With vision five to ten times sharper than yours, imagine looking down from up there.

Even in our own yard, we find much to embarrass us for not having noticed it earlier. Looking up through the branches of two fir trees near our back door, we discover two large nests (squirrels?). Then, looking down from our kitchen window into snow-laden yew bushes, we see, for the first time, flickering shadows of juncos sheltering from the wind—

and perhaps from the Cooper's hawk that watches from the fir tree. A streak of darkness flashes across the path to the feeder—a vole dashing across the interruption to its tunnel in the snow. Red-breasted nuthatches at the feeder, intent on their food, ignore our slow approach; and for the first time we see how much smaller they are than their white-breasted cousins.

If we look up yet again, and look closely, we see into the future, already here in the tightly furled, sharp-pointed buds of the beech trees and the rounded, tightly clustered terminal buds of the bur oaks, ready and waiting for the spring that is to come.

> And the end of all our exploring
> Will be to arrive where we started
> And know the place for the
> first time.
>
> —T. S. Eliot, "Little Gidding"

ON THE CONFINES OF ANOTHER WORLD

What do we learn—or recognize—from all this?

Even in winter—even in the city and inner suburbs, where our species has done its best to control or eliminate all others—even when we're totally unaware of it, nature is vividly present; and we are in and of it. We wonder at it, as Thoreau did a century and a half ago in his lovely essay, "Walking": "For my part, I feel that with regard to Nature I live a sort of border life, on the confines of a world into which I make occasional and transient forays … The walker on the familiar fields which stretch around my native town sometimes finds himself in another land than is described in their owners' deeds."

Nature and the wild persist; we have only to look up. And within. But it takes the sudden

strangeness of an event outside our ordinary routine to make us see what is obvious to those who, like the people of the rain forest, dwell beyond our narrow confines.

Fortunately, the extraordinary wildness just beyond the brims of our hats conspires to preserve itself despite us, and to preserve us as well—by startling us from our torpor, by "awakening the mind's attention from the lethargy of custom," as Coleridge puts it, providing "sudden charm" to a "known and familiar landscape." The coppery winter leaves of the beech tree, caught in a ray of sunlight; the deer mouse popping up from its leaf-lined hole for a quick look around; the hawk swooping across the window as the indignant bluejays scatter and screech. In these sudden illuminations, we sense anew—and strangely—the intimacy of our connection to the natural world. Nature itself kindly arouses our flagging determination to live more simply, and breathes new life into our efforts to live in harmony with other members of creation and recognize, as if for the first time, *where* we live.

To paraphrase William Blake: when you see this hawk and his perch, dark against the gray winter sky, you see a portion of eternity:

"Lift up thy head!"

Fence row   Ladislav Hanka

"The walker on the familiar fields which stretch around my native town sometimes finds himself in another land than is described in their owners' deeds." —Henry David Thoreau, "Walking."

REFERENCES

Blake, William. *The Marriage of Heaven and Hell* (1790–93).
Coleridge, Samuel Taylor. *Biographia Literaria* (1817).
Snyder, Gary. *The Practice of the Wild*. San Francisco: North Point Press, 1990.
Henry David Thoreau, "Walking" (1861).

A version of this essay appeared in 1995 in our column, "Leadings," in *BeFriending Creation*, the newsletter of Quaker Earthcare Witness.

23

THE HEAVEN UNDER OUR FEET

BY TOM SMALL

Heaven is under our feet as well as over our heads.
—Henry David Thoreau, *Walden* (1854)

Though, as a species, we may have journeyed through immense reaches of time and space, we remain close to our origins, to Eden, and to wilderness. They are within us and right beneath our feet. Literally.

Scripture tells us God formed us "of dust from the ground" (*Gen* 2:7); created us "from dust, then from a drop of seed" (*Koran*, Surah XXII.5). Our progenitor, Adam, is *adama*—soil, or clay. We *Homo sapiens* are capable of wisdom, perhaps, but most assuredly *Homo* (from *humus*, of soil or earth).

Astrophysicists inform us that the very elements of our being are stardust, exploded matter of unimaginably remote stars, our ancient progenitors. Agronomists note that all life receives its nourishment from rocks ground down to dust by ice and water, then spread by the winds of time.

Wendell Berry marvels over the formation of organic humus as "the chief work of the world," an immemorial process that all creatures live by and die into. For soil scientist Francis Hole, the human creature—with all other creatures—is an "extension of soil," a temporary articulation of dust and humus.

No less than ourselves, the soil—the very basis of our being—is alive. About 80% of the earth's biomass is beneath the surface. A handful of good soil contains more living creatures than there are human beings on the earth. We know names and relationships for perhaps 5% of them—no matter whether they live in Costa Rican cloudforest or a Michigan backyard.

> The soil thawing outside my window contains humus from generations of decay, silt from glaciers which last visited these parts ten thousand years ago, clay from the decomposition of three-hundred-million-year-old limestone, and the debris from supernovas that exploded before the birth of our sun. A handful of that soil may contain a billion organisms, each one burning with life.
>
> —Scott Russell Sanders, *Staying Put*

The most numerous of these creatures are the bacteria. Take a pinch of good soil: you hold about a billion of them, of perhaps five thousand different types, communicating and evolving so swiftly that they outwit our antibiotic strategies. They invented recycling, photosynthesis, and genetic engineering. As Stephen Jay Gould cheerfully admits, they "rule the earth."

THE WEB THAT HOLDS IT ALL TOGETHER

Your same pinch of soil may also contain thousands of wispy root hairs and miles and miles of mycorrhizae—networks of fungus threads interdependent with the roots of plants, drawing energy from them and in turn enabling them to absorb phosphorus, nitrogen, other nutrients, and water. All terrestrial ecosystems depend on this underground "web that holds it all together" (Snyder, p. 129). Without mycorrhizae, which extend a plant's root system by 1000% or more, most plants could not have emerged from the water, to thrive on dry land. Phosphorus fertilizers and rototillers are both lethal to mycorrhizae. Either by themselves or combined with algae as lichens, fungi are indispensable to the creation of soil and the evolution of life.

We are equally dependent on the lowly roundworm, which endlessly ingests, turns over, and fertilizes virtually every crumb of soil on earth. Nematode worms account for four out of every five animals on earth. In a square meter of soil, there may be as many as ten million of them. In that same space, we might find a billion protozoa, hundreds of thousands of springtails and mites, and thousands of arthropods—insects with jointed legs—some of them so tiny that 20 or 30 might dance within the period at the end of this word.

Almost all these creatures are beneficent, even from our limited human point of view. Indeed, they may all be indispensable. At the very least, they serve to demonstrate how the humble (*humus* again) sustain the great. Such humble ones inherit the earth, despite our relentless decimation of them with monocultures and chemical aids to agriculture and to better homes and gardens.

Hidden, too, beneath our feet is the *radical* life of plants, the basic and only essential part of our food chain. Their roots support them—and us. Prairie grasses foraged far beneath the surface to form the deep, rich "America's breadbasket" soil on which we depend for grains and legumes. A single mature clump of big bluestem grass (*Andropogon gerardii*) may have a dense system of 15 million roots with a total length of 3000 miles and a total surface area of several thousand square feet. Such native grasses, unlike our exotic lawns, are independent of chemical aids and sprinkling systems.

Cartoon from Punch, *the British humor magazine, December, 1881, depicting Charles Darwin benignly observing man's evolution from Chaos to worm to monkey to English perfect gentleman. Darwin's last book, published in 1881, was* The Formation of Vegetable Mould, from the Action of Worms, *the result of years of observation of earthworms, as well as many other of the "little things" essential to life.*

We discount the intelligence of plants, worms, fungi, or bacteria at our peril. If, as Gary Snyder says, "the information passed through the system is intelligence" (Snyder, p. 19), then Lynn Margulis is right to suggest that human intelligence, despite its ingenuity, is very limited:

> As tiny parts of a huge biosphere whose essence is basically bacterial, we—with other life forms—must add up to a sort of symbiotic brain which it is beyond our capacity to comprehend or truly represent (Margulis and Sagan, p. 152).

Albert Einstein felt it was enough for him "to try humbly to comprehend even an infinitesimal part of the intelligence manifested in nature."

In our bodies, as in the soil-body of the earth, remnants of the most ancient life forms are virtually immortal: bacteria, mitochondria, and other tiny organisms, subsumed by our cells and our selves. Together, they constitute as much as half of our dry weight; and their DNA is other than human. The arrangement is symbiotic: one of mutual aid. But from the long view, it appears that *we* are the ones subsumed, colonized, co-opted—and *con*sumed as well—by a bodily organism greater than ourselves (call it Gaia if you will). Our very bodies are not owned by us; they are community property and habitat. Nor do we comprehend the intelligence of the soil's body—we are *of* its intelligence, just as we are of its body—temporary, upstart extensions of both.

Will we achieve—by design or default—mastery of the universe? Or are we something like a *synchytrium*, a form of pond scum that spreads over the available surface and parasitizes other forms of life? Science offers no prediction—comforting or otherwise—in answer to such vexing questions. But if we think of *fungus* in the popular connotation of the word, as an unpleasant, expendable, morbid outgrowth that's out of place—in human terms a *creep*—then the word might sometimes better apply to our species than to the millions of fungal species that cleanse the world's dirt and bring forth life from decay.

> Am I not partly leaves and vegetable mold myself?
>
> —Henry David Thoreau, *Walden*

Certainly we grossly abuse the soil's body—and therefore our own. Each year, for instance, soil erosion in the U.S. exceeds soil formation by a factor of at least ten; and as soil degrades it contributes carbon dioxide to global warming. The topsoil of the Mississippi watershed spews into the Gulf of Mexico at the rate of 15 tons every second. Each year up to half the nitrogen we pour onto our farms, golf courses, and lawns leaches into ground and surface water as nitrate—toxic in high levels to humans and countless other organisms—or leaks into the air as nitrous oxide, a greenhouse gas hundreds of times more potent than CO_2 and a contributor to acid rain. Each year acid rain kills not only trees but also soil organisms, including the life-giving

What Is Man?   Woodcut   William Blake (1793)

mycorrhizae. After a clearcut on the Olympic Pen insula, 90% of the fungi vanished from the soil in the first year; with them went the primal memory of how to sustain an ecosystem. We can project an extinction rate for birds, or plants (up to 25% of species in the next 25 years, according to UN pro-

jection0). We don't know enough about soil organisms to make any projection.

We begin to grasp, however, that whatever fouls the soil also fouls the human body. We are animated dust; and whatever befalls the dust …

LISTEN FOR "EARTH'S SENTIENT SYMPHONY"

But despite all the losses, "There lives the dearest freshness deep down things" (Gerard Manley Hopkins, "God's Grandeur"). The wilderness we seek, the secret to the restoration of Eden, is alive and breathing just beneath our feet.

What then are we to do?

The first precept: do no harm; preserve as much as possible of what remains. Tom Eisner, a world-renowned expert on tiny invertebrates, puts it this way:

> Organisms are linked by their interdependencies. In principle therefore, if you are preserving land with one group of organisms in mind,

you are also creating shelter for others … I would say that one should simply try to save as much land as possible … The future is in wilderness preservation. It's as simple as that (Seidl, p. 9).

Wilderness, fortunately, is close at hand—or at foot—not just in precious land trusts and wildlife refuges but also in small patches of earth, accessible within seconds, harboring an astonishing remnant of wilderness. "Untrammeled nature exists in the dirt and rotting vegetation beneath our shoes," says world-renowned entomologist Edward O. Wilson (Gorman, p. D1).

Beneath the Surface   Etching with drypoint   Ladislav Hanka

*" … beneath the surface, eddies and currents of the inner eye swarm with
insects, roots and predators … " —Lad Hanka*

If you keep your ear to the ground, you may yet hear what Lynn Margulis calls "earth's sentient symphony" and Lewis Thomas "the music of *this* sphere." By harmonizing with the *music* of the soil, by partaking in the *intelligence* of the soil, we may yet become wiser and restore our souls. Eden, the unfallen world, endures and is continually renewed in the very dust of the native soil we repeatedly seek to shake from our restless feet. Take a stand wherever you are.

Practice mindfulness and do no harm. Then, seek to restore. Begin with your yard. Continue with the grounds of the school and the church, a garden in the park, your neighborhood. "Maintaining biodiversity among the little creatures," says Edward O. Wilson, "shockingly rich in unexplored behavior and biochemistry, can be done on the cheap, in relatively tiny patches" (Gorman, p. D4).

Learn the flowers and grasses that evolved in the place where you stand. Bring them back, and the creatures that evolved with them will be fostered and revived—yourself as well. The spirit will be manifest. In this faith, in this work of hands, the world is "all alive" and "every particle of dust breathes forth its joy" (William Blake, *Europe*, 1794).

REFERENCES

Baskin, Yvonne. *Under Ground: How Creatures of Mud and Dirt Shape Our World*. Washington, D.C.: Island Press, 2005.

Gorman, James. "A Wild, Fearsome World Under Each Fallen Leaf," *The New York Times*, Sept. 24, 2002, pp. D1, D4.

Harding, Stephan. *Animate Earth: Science, Intuition and Gaia*. White River Junction, VT: Chelsea Green Publishing, 2006.

Logan, William Bryant. *Dirt: The Ecstatic Skin of the Earth*. New York: Riverhead Books, 1995.

Margulis, Lynn, and Dorion Sagan. *Microcosmos: Four Billion Years of Microbial Evolution*. Berkeley, CA: Univ. of California Press, 1997.

Nardi, James B. *Life in the Soil: A Guide for Naturalists and Gardeners*. Chicago: Univ. of Chicago Press, 2007.

Shiva, Vandana. *Soil Not Oil: Environmental Justice in an Age of Climate Crisis*. Cambridge, MA: South End Press, 2008.

Seidl, Amy. "Little Things: An Interview with Tom Eisner," *Wild Earth*, Fall 2000, pp. 7–11.

Snyder, Gary. *The Practice of the Wild*. San Francisco: Northpoint Press, 1990.

Thomas, Lewis. *The Lives of a Cell: Notes of a Biology Watcher*. New York: Penguin, 1995.

Wolfe, David W. *Tales from the Underground: A Natural History of Subterranean Life*. Boulder, CO: Perseus Publishing, 2002.

This essay was originally published in Louis Cox, et al. (eds.), *Earthcare for Friends: A Study Guide for Individuals and Faith Communities* (Burlington, VT: Quaker Earthcare Witness, 2004), pp. 104–107.

24

"Do Everything You Can"

A Review of Terry Glavin, *The Sixth Extinction: Journeys among the Lost and Left Behind*. St. Martin's Press, 2006.

By Tom Small

What rises from the wreck will depend on what evolution has left to work with.
—Anthony D. Barnosky, *Heatstroke*

Terry Glavin's *The Sixth Extinction* is a love story. Written by a lover of stories and of all creatures—whether they fly, swim, slither, creep, or walk; a lover of all the different ways of life embodied and stratified in memory, languages, and cultures. A lover of apples, cougars, spinach, scarlet macaws, whales, petroglyphs, of all things lost or saved.

It's a paean to all other lovers who, against the odds, save whatever they can of all that is vanishing, or left behind—the ghosts, the living dead, surviving forlornly in zoos, parks, and remnants.

It's a book truly about diversity—all kinds of diversity. It treats, lovingly, angrily, the full range of ongoing losses in this, our era, the time of the Sixth Great Extinction, the most catastrophic in 64 million years.

It's a celebration. An elegy. A jeremiad. A call to action.

A Plague of Sameness

Its author, a journalist and a professor at the University of British Columbia, would agree with the microbiologist Lynn Margulis, that "the essence of living is a sort of memory, the physical preservation of the past in the present" (p. 66). He would agree with the phenomenologist Maurice Merleau-Ponty that "Nature is the memory of the world" (p. 120). He bears witness to the degradation of that essence, our collective memory, "the bleeding away of differences in the living world," the "plague of sameness" descending on the plants and the cultures of the world. The squandering of our legacy—from the past, and for the future.

The statistics are disheartening. By 2040, 70% to 95% of forest in Africa will be gone; in Southeast Asia, 75%. In the oceans, as many as half of fish species are threatened with extinction. In the U.S., 29% of plant species are in danger of extinction—even without taking climate change into consideration.

Among food crops, 90% of vegetable varieties are already gone; another goes extinct every six hours. All around us, a global pandemic spares nothing, objectifying, commodifying, wiping out the differences: over half the shrinking global seed reservoir is controlled by only ten companies. We know the names: Monsanto, Dow, Novartis, Cargill, Dupont, Pioneer. The harvest has been stolen, and we are in the hands of a kleptocracy.

As globalization flattens the world, entire cultures vanish; another spoken language dies every two weeks. It's like, says Glavin, "libraries going up in flames." In our struggle for power, we are forfeiting "the right of people to live sustainably on the natural resources around them." Perhaps Richard Manning will yet be proved right: the green revolution, which brought us globalized industrial agriculture, is "the worst thing that ever happened to the planet" (*Harper's*, p. 41).

> Since each microbe, animal, and plant possesses some innate portion of the know-how that makes the whole earth work, the loss of any species erases some portion of the organic intelligence and leaves the land more stupid.
>
> —Sara Stein

LOVE AND PATIENCE OFFER HOPE

Na Pali alula   Brighamia insignis

But always, amid the lamentation, Glavin offers us hope. Conservation did not, he argues, begin with Rachel Carson. He cites the battle, in the late 1870s, in the Petoskey forests of Michigan, to save the passenger pigeon from extinction. He tells a compelling story of the Hawaiian botanists who lower themselves down a Kauai cliff face every year to pollinate by hand the surviving wild remnant of Na Pali alulas, because their only natural pollinator, a tiny moth, is now extinct.

He lauds the World Conservation Society, working to protect the last tracts of habitat for endangered species, patiently saving one creature, one species, one ecosystem, at a time. He admires the Seed Savers, seeking out old heirloom seeds forgotten in attics, lost species surviving in abandoned orchards and fields.

In Costa Rica, he celebrates "efforts to maintain the diversity of living things that the rest of the world was losing," made possible because "a constitutional prohibition on maintaining a standing

Less than 20 plants remain in the wild, on the Na Pali coast of Kauai. The stout, fleshy stem may rise from the earth as much as 15 feet before producing the single rosette of leaves and a few fragrant flowers. The Latin insignis means "remarkable" or "distinguished." Since more of these remarkable plants are being bred in conservatories, would it matter if there were no wild alulas left? Since wildness is the preservation of the world, **yes***, it matters.*

army immunized Costa Rica from the U.S. government's usual method of bullying, corrupting, and brutalizing Central American societies."

It is there, in Costa Rica, after a long vigil, that he finally sees what love and painstaking patience had made possible: the sight of "two impossibly beautiful scarlet macaws," saved from the holocaust.

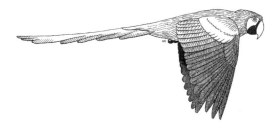

A pair of scarlet macaws (Ara macao)   Nancy Halliday

Tom and I traveled into Costa Rican rainforest with naturalists who had worked for years to restore these long-lived, beautiful birds to their native habitats. We and the naturalists were very quiet, partly in order not to disturb the ones we saw, partly out of respect and wonder.

WE STILL HAVE CHOICES

Glavin's litany of loss is also an index to growing recognition that our privileged view of the world has been much too narrow. Slowly, environmentalists recognize that there can be no hard-and-fast distinctions among human communities, domesticated species, and "the wild." Slowly, we expand our notion of rights to include creatures other than ourselves. Slowly, we recognize that our notions of survival, of freedom, of intelligence, of culture, of diversity—all that we supposedly value—are anthropomorphic and elitist. Too slowly? Time will tell—not much time. Finally, painfully, we begin to comprehend (or rediscover) that all action and all suffering are related and have consequences.

We live, says Glavin, among ghosts, in a "night of the living dead," doomed creatures and cultures and intelligences passing among us and around us, almost unnoticed. For Glavin, Jeremiah said it best: "The summer is past, the harvest is over, and we are not saved" (8:20).

But even if we are not to be saved, we can still be saviors. We still have choices. Choices, to be sure, that narrow every day, choices "every bit as stark and momentous as the choices we faced in the darkest moments of the twentieth century."

> It is no use saying, 'We are doing our best.' You have got to succeed in doing what is *necessary*.
>
> —Winston Churchill

"Serious decisions require that we believe in things, and believe deeply." Glavin is a true believer. If I may paraphrase an ancient Zen saying, to believe, and not to do, is not to believe at all. "You join the epic battle," Glavin adjures, "with the demons that are devouring the world, and you do what you can. It's all anyone can expect of you. You do everything you can."

REFERENCES

Barnosky, Anthony D. *Heatstroke: Nature in an Age of Global Warming.* Washington, D.C.: Island Press, 2009

Coetzee, J. M. *The Lives of Animals.* Princeton, NJ: Princeton Univ. Press, 1999.

Leakey, Richard, and Roger Lewin, *The Sixth Extinction: Patterns of Life and the Future of Humankind.* New York: Doubleday, 1995.

Manning, Richard. *Against the Grain: How Agriculture Has Hijacked Civilization.* New York: North Point Press, 2004.

_____, "The Oil We Eat," *Harper's Magazine,* Feb., 2004, pp. 37–45.

Margulis, Lynn, and Dorion Sagan. *Microcosmos: Four Billion Years of Evolution from our Microbial Ancestors.* Berkeley, CA: Univ. of California Press, 1986.

Merleau-Ponty, Maurice. *Nature: Course Notes from the Collège de France.* Evanston, IL: Northwestern Univ. Press, 2003.

Shiva, Vandana. *Stolen Harvest: The Hijacking of the Global Food Supply.* Cambridge, MA: South End Press, 2000.

Snyder, Gary. *The Practice of the Wild.* San Francisco: North Point Press, 1990.

Survival and Extinction   Ladislav Hanka

A survivor—the pileated woodpecker (Dryocopus pileatus)—and various skeletal Campephilids, all of them among the world's largest woodpeckers, stare at one another across the eternity of extinction. The one in full-feathered glory is the ivory-billed woodpecker (Campephilus principalis), lately reported but with no conclusive evidence of its continued existence. About 20 inches in length and 30 inches in wingspan, the ivory-billed shares its glorious size and power with Michigan's pileated and its probable extinction with the Cuban ivory-billed and the imperial of Sonoran Mexico, and with Campephilus dalquesti, known only from Late Pleistocene fossils in Texas. The eleven species of Campephilids, both extinct and extant, all native to the Americas, are all shadowed by the gathering darkness of extinction.

25

FREEING OURSELVES FROM OUR POSSESSIONS

BY TOM AND NANCY SMALL

We are close to waking up when we dream that we are dreaming.
—Novalis (1798)

When the following essay appeared as one of our columns in BeFriending Creation *(1994), we could list both of us as co-authors; but when it was republished as a separate leaflet it had to appear as my work alone, since it was written in first person and is apparently based on my experience. But it is also based on a comment by Nancy's psychiatrist, about images and relics we retain of selves we have lost, left behind, or failed ever to realize. Moreover, the essay emerged from the life Nancy and I tried to live, and we wrote it together. So I have restored it to joint authorship.*

It expresses our belief that restoration and reform of the outer world—whatever portion of the earth we human beings belong to and that, in some sense, belongs to us—depends on reforming and simplifying our innermost images of ourselves and our households—above all, a radical reformation of our ingrained habits of accumulation, our practices as consumers.

Of course, Nancy and I did not truly "free ourselves of possessions" or every false dream, any more than we expelled from our yard every last nonnative plant—every last reminder of the disastrous dream of a disciplined, parklike, and sterilized nature. There are still icons of past dreams on our walls and shelves, as there are still nonnative, horticultural remnants of former gardens in our yard. Some remnants I still value. But where they mostly just take up space—physical, mental, and spiritual—that could better serve us and the community of life, I continue to clear them away, for the sake of clarity, light, and new life. —Tom Small

For some time now, my house has been becoming more transparent. I can see across it, sometimes almost through it. There's a little more clarity. More space.

Every few days I walk through it, very slowly. It's a kind of spiritual exercise. I try to see more clearly a few of the things that are in it, without the veil of custom that ordinarily obscures them. I ask them a few nosy questions: What are you? What do you mean? Who do you belong to? Perhaps I move something away, into some other space; then I check a few days later to see how much of a shadow it left behind. Or perhaps the space it occupied has now become clear, transparent.

I am discovering that many objects in my house have become accidental. They no longer belong here or to me (perhaps they never did). They are images of a self that I dreamed, a self that never fully emerged from the shadows. Once I know this, I'm free to give the image away, as a gift for the person it really belongs to: my stepdaughter; my neighbor; the poor person on the street. Or I can exchange it for something I need.

"SUCH STUFF AS DREAMS"

We dream many selves during our lives. We accumulate objects, images which make these dream-selves visible; thereby we gain status, a kind of false identity. It's difficult, then, to part with the image, even if the self for which it stands has always been only a dream. "We are such stuff as dreams are made on," says Shakespeare's Prospero; and our "stuff" is made from dreams. When the dream, however, becomes only an object filling space, then it stands in our way.

Gifts, too, are embodiments of dream—somebody else's dream of who we are. Perhaps we keep the gift in recognition of the giver and her dream. But the ancients were wiser. For the receiver of a gift to retain it for his own aggrandizement is to invite misfortune. The gift is in the giving, the action, not the thing itself, which must move. Or else lose its identity as gift. A *gifted* person must pass the gift on to others.

An object is static; a relationship grows. Not to change is to falsify and atrophy. And yet the images that we dream or that dream us are so potent that we are charmed by them, transfixed. We are addicted. "All change is a miracle to contemplate," says Thoreau; "but it is a miracle which is taking place every instant." How shall we participate in this miracle? How shall we escape our addictions? Possibly the same way that I stopped smoking some years ago: I changed my image of myself and so changed my behavior. Can we *re-imagine* our status, our identity, as depending not on things but on space, open to action and possibility?

What then shall we do with our surplus of images?

> And the gift must move. What is given must be passed on. In the end, nothing can be held or possessed—a truth grasped by every culture that approaches what we've come to call sustainability.
>
> —David W. Orr, *Down to the Wire* (2009)

THE ART OF TRANSPARENCY

- Try a spiritual journey through your home, just for the exercise. Meditate on your space as an ecosystem, a complex entity that consists entirely in relationships and endures by changing.

- Look past the shadows. Try to see through the object, into the space it displaces. Possibly the walls will seem farther away, clearer, even transparent. Perhaps you will breathe more easily. Perhaps you will be free to act. Simplicity is not a noun; it's an active verb.

- Discover where these things that stand in your way really belong. The extra coat that rarely leaves the closet: it belongs to the poor. The antique too precious to use: that's for the museum, for everyone. The boxes you never unpacked: straight to the fund-raising rummage sale.

> Have nothing in your houses that you do not know to be useful, or believe to be beautiful.
>
> —William Morris,
> *Hopes and Fears for Art* (1882)

- Or hold your own fundraiser, the way a friend of ours does. Bring out that stored-away surplus of nice things you'll never use, and have a benefit sale. Don't bother pricing everything; let your friends and neighbors make voluntary *contributions* to your favorite environmental organization in exchange for each item. You'll do well; the buyers will be doubly pleased; the land and its creatures will benefit.

It's not as easy as it sounds, though, is it—this changing of our ways? It takes a *shock* to make us see. A dozen years ago a visiting Episcopalian abbot, admiring my house, commented on how many "icons" I possessed. Startled to hear them so described, I worried, for a long time, over what he meant. It was a much greater shock when, a few years ago, I returned from travel in Africa to find that my ex-wife had moved out half the contents of the house. I was stunned. I made up lists of things I *had* to have back. Three weeks later I tore up all the lists—I realized I didn't need *any* of those things.

Such shocks seem extraordinary, but I think they come to us often: an unexpected word; a sudden change, loss, or separation; a flash of insight. If we open ourselves to its ministry, the shock releases energy, a new possibility. Suddenly we see things in a new light.

In the Preface to *No Nature: New and Selected Poems*, Gary Snyder asks for "An open space to move in, with the whole body, the whole mind." In the final poem of the volume, "Ripples on the Surface," he invokes "The little house in the wild, the wild in the house." The little house, the vast wild—both of them are ecosystems. They are what we live in, the habitation of both body and mind; and they live *in us*. But they are, Snyder warns, "Both forgotten." We strive to control and enclose them. Only in remembering that they are both of them, together, our true home—only in that recognition will we find wholeness, restoration, the sudden freedom of "an open space to move in."

This little house in the wild—our home. Awakened, we must remember that we do not possess it. It is a gift. Long before we die, we are called on to pass it along to our heirs—even to the seventh generation.

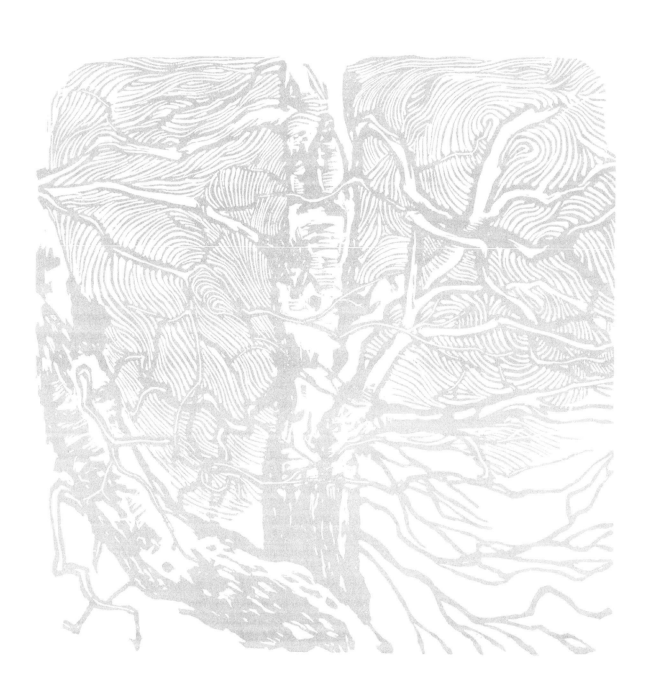

26

LEARNING FROM CROWS

BY TOM SMALL

What a delicious sound!
It is not merely crow calling to crow, for it speaks to me too.
—Henry David Thoreau

As I break up their bread into the battered aluminum pie tin, the crows caw from a nearby tree. I feel exhilarated. I wonder how I ever found their calls intrusive, irritating.

Many years ago, on a day of persistent cawing, I suddenly made a decision. The crows would not go away or change. It was up to me to change—from a person annoyed by noisy crows to a person who welcomed their dark, vivid presence and their raucous music.

I figured it should be easy. After all, hadn't I stopped smoking by changing my image of myself? No longer would I be a smoker; I would imagine myself as a non-smoker, a man who finds the smell of cigarettes obnoxious. It worked. Surely, then, I could succeed in a much easier transformation, into an admirer of crows, a connoisseur of crow music.

I began to listen more carefully, distinguishing all the nuances of their calls, trying to appreciate their extensive vocabulary, which can include up to 250 different calls. I imitated them feebly, cawing back to them. They seemed to listen, briefly silent. I watched as they hopped and flapped about, sometimes intently turning over leaves and searching the ground, sometimes quite casual, out for a little stretch, a passegiata, sidestepping squirrels and enjoying encounters with one another.

> I love the sooty crow nor would provoke
> Its march day exercises of croaking joy
> I love to see it sailing to and fro
> While feelds, and woods and waters spread below
>
> —John Clare, "The Crow" (1820)

We began setting out our stale bread for them every day. If I'm late or forgetful, they let me hear about it. If the bread is too stale and hard, a crow carefully gathers up several pieces in his beak, flies to the birdbath, and drops them in, to soak. First, he tests a piece for softness. Not ready. Back it goes, for another dunk. Then, finally, just right. The crow gobbles two pieces, gathers up the rest in his beak, and flaps away, dribbling a bit, to a nearby tree.

When the bread is gone, one crow seizes the rim of the pie plate in his beak and flips it over, perhaps hoping for more bread underneath. Disappointed, or playful, he picks up the plate again and flings it away. Then he runs after it, and flips it again—a solo game of frisbie. Sometimes, to retrieve their toys, I have to search the area.

> One to rot and one to grow,
> One for the pigeon, one for the crow
>
> —Old English planting rhyme

Enlarging Our Images

We have learned a little bit of crow language, both physical and vocal. The crows entertain and inform us. With a little outreach from us, they have enriched and enlarged our images of ourselves and our community.

What if all of us were to decide, one day, to change our images of who we are in a more radical way? Could we?

Well, to be honest, it wasn't quite that easy to break a 30-year addiction and become a non-smoker. The moment of decision and conversion seemed to come as a sudden shock—a powerful realization of too many painful coughing fits and obvious damage to my whole system. Then came the withdrawal symptoms—more pain. For several days I needed constant reminders of the humiliations and stinks and stains and stresses of the ad-

diction. Finally, there came a wonderful realization that I now lived in a newly recreated world, of keener tastes, clearer vision, freer breath, where everything I did mattered more because I was no longer killing myself, no longer the victim of an insidious, lying industrial conspiracy to keep me addicted to my "pleasures."

What kind of shock will it take to break us of other, even more damaging addictions—to oil, to accumulation of stuff, to an illusion of security, to the manicured, sterilized suburban landscapes sold to us by another insidious, lying industrial conspiracy to keep us hooked on what is poisoning the whole system of nature? What shock would open us to a realization, first, of the destructive power of our addiction and then to the possibility of a newly recreated world?

The Possibility of a Blessing

You know why we traditionally bless people when they sneeze, don't you? It's not because the sneeze indicates some physical disorder that requires a blessing; it's because the sneeze is a momentary powerful interruption to normal routine and opens both body and spirit to the possibility of a blessing.

What breakthrough can overcome our deadly routines and allow the possibility of a blessing, a radical change, a re-creation?

For the two of us, the moment came when, after a struggle to discover where and how we would live out our retirement, we encountered a new image of the self and the spirit in Sarah Stein's *Noah's*

Garden, a powerful vision of how traditional landscaping is degrading habitat and contributing to mass extinction of species. Could we, Tom and Nancy, learn to do the work of Noah, saving species from the flood of overpopulation, overproduction, and overdevelopment?

Instead of people who want to avoid, control, or even eliminate what seems disorderly, disruptive, and annoying, could we imagine ourselves as people who welcome the visitations of a more wild world? Could we learn to accept wild creatures and the native plants they depend upon into our lives and our landscapes, participate in their intense life, their vividness, their strange intelligence? Could we learn to be part of *their* community?

The shocking evidence of our cultural addictions and their consequences comes to us every day, from many messengers—from the crows, from the frogs, from the bees, from a book, from the imagi-

nation. It is, however, necessary to be ready, to be open, and then to *learn* from the messengers. Can we open ourselves to the shock of recognition, a sudden revelation or blessing, a new mission—that of Noah—despite our doubts and the indifference or scorn of the neighbors? Do we dare bear witness—in the way we live—to the awful and wonderful truth?

Yes? And what then?

> What is now proved was once only imagin'd.
>
> —William Blake,
> *The Marriage of Heaven and Hell (1793)*

REFERENCES
(More Messages from the Crows)

There are wonderful books about crows and other corvids—their intelligence, their complex behaviors, their significance for us human beings. Here are four that we've found especially wonderful.

Haupt, Lyanda Lynn. *Crow Planet: Essential Wisdom from the Urban Wilderness.* New York: Little, Brown, 2009. A gracious tribute to crows, a meditation on their successful adaptation to urban life, and an urgent invitation to inhabit "our home ecosystems with some semblance of knowledge and grace."

Heinrich, Bernd. *Mind of the Raven: Investigations and Adventures with the Wolf-Birds.* New York: Harper-Collins, 1999. Well-written observation and reflection by a sociobiologist on the intelligence and complex interactions of ravens.

Reid, Bill, and Robert Bringhurst. *The Raven Steals the Light,* 2nd ed. Seattle, WA: Univ. of Washington Press, 1996. Raven is the trickster creature and the bringer of light for the Haida First Nation, of the Queen Charlotte Islands, British Columbia. The stories of his tricks and his downfalls are humorous, wise, and also sad, because he is one of the "old ghosts" who "continue to haunt the land until new spirits can be born" (p. 109).

Savage, Candace. *Bird Brains: The Intelligence of Crows, Ravens, Magpies, and Jays* San Francisco, CA: Sierra Club Books, 1997. Wondrous photographs. Informative, delightful text, providing ample support for the Norse god Odin's trust in two ravens, named Thought and Memory, to keep him informed about what's going on in the world.

Crow Spirit   Charcoal drawing   Elizabeth Henderson

27

LEARNING FROM EXPERIENCE

BY NANCY SMALL

My heart is moved by all I cannot save:
So much has been destroyed.
I have to cast my lot with those
who age after age, perversely,
with no extraordinary power,
reconstitute the world.
 —Adrienne Rich, "Natural Resources"

We usually have called them "work days," but that's never seemed right. We tried to say "stewardship days" instead, in those early days when we planned and worked with the Southwest Michigan Land Conservancy's Stewardship Committee, newly formed to tend the growing number of SWMLC preserves. To be sure, we volunteers did work hard: we inventoried plants and animals, put up signs, maintained trails, hauled water for our nurseries of native plants, and fought invasive exotic plants.

Being a steward, however, implies a lot more than work: watchfulness, care, service, responsibility for a gathering place, a household, a community. Stewardship also carries some more shadowy connotations of respect and reverence. In using the word, we recognize that as we work together in grasslands, wetlands, and woodlands, we strengthen our ties to the natural world, to the land in our care, and to one another. Sometimes, now, in organizing the work on Wild Ones native-plant gardens and restorations, we refer to "community work days." For Tom and me, though, those early days with SWMLC were always, most satisfyingly, "learning days."

> To learn and then put it in practice—isn't that a delight?
>
> —Confucius (6th cent. BCE)

My first outing with the Stewardship Committee, however, was a disaster: neither a work day nor a stewardship day; and the only learning was painful. It was a cold spring day in 1997, and the first official work day of the new Stewardship Committee. Walking with a small group along the edge of Jeptha Lake, I stepped into a hole and was suddenly waist deep in icy water. Frank Ballo and my husband Tom quickly hauled me out; Frank Behie rushed me in his pickup to the entrance of the preserve; Jennifer Hansen gave me her extra pair of socks, and Stan Rajnak sped us back to Kalamazoo with the heat in his van turned up as far as it would go. I wasn't cold, however, but burning with embarrassment and determination never to stray off a clearly-marked trail. Maybe never off a well-groomed garden path.

To Find the Way, Get Off the Path

That resolve didn't last long. Tom and I kept going to work days at the preserves, and that icy encounter with nature was followed by a wealth of happier ones. On another occasion at Jeptha Lake Fen, while considering how to lay out trails, Becky Csia, Stan Rajnak, Tom and I came across an eastern hognose snake so beautifully marked in rose and dark gray that even I moved closer for a better look. It didn't flee but coiled its thick body in loose knots and hissed at us. As we didn't disturb it except by our admiring presence, it didn't proceed to more dramatic display in which—according to one authority—it fakes convulsions, smears itself with feces, and turns belly up, pretending to be dead.

Once, at Topinabee Lake Preserve, while down on my hands and knees near the edge of the lake pulling up invasive garlic mustard, I surprised a great blue heron (and myself). It suddenly, and noisily, took flight; and as it rose over my head, I seemed to see its every feather, and the beating of its wings rang in my ears. A few minutes later, the brightness of a yellow warbler in a patch of sunlight almost hurt my eyes.

When we helped to form the Stewardship Committee in 1997, Tom and I—married for only two years—were just beginning to explore our dedication to saving whatever we could of the threatened biodiversity of the earth. How much the two of us learned about the natural world, and especially about plants, from those early years of working on the preserves! We've been lucky enough to see Jeptha Lake Fen ablaze with spikes of reddish-purple liatris, and in the wet field nearby, eastern tiger swallowtail butterflies feeding on ironweed's purple flowers.

Great blue heron, foraging, intent.

> The relentless complexity of the world is off to the side of the trail.
>
> —Gary Snyder

Appreciating the "Insignificant"

But we've also come to appreciate more subtle beauties: the small tufts of yellow-green flowers on the bare branches of a spicebush; a lobelia whose pale blue flower is as small as a child's fingernail; the delicate flowers of prairie grasses and spiky seedheads of sedges. Once, at the Paw Paw River Preserve with Ken Kirton, we came across a Michigan lily so long past its prime that we almost didn't recognize the flower. But the three of us were nonetheless delighted to see it and know that it was safe there. We felt the same way about the eastern box turtle—its shell caked with mud—which crawled across the path a few minutes later. Both Tom and I increasingly appreciated the beauty and importance of small, unspectacular, "insignificant"

> Small is beautiful.
>
> —E. F. Schumacher

plants and animals—thanks largely to the work of stewardship, which gets us out to grasslands, woodlands, and flood plains in all seasons, in the company of people such as Stan and Ken, and Becky, and Richard Brewer who can tell us where to look, and how to see more and more of what's there.

Our work with the Stewardship Committee also helped us see that native plant and animal communities must be protected not only from development but also from aggressive, nonnative plants. Such plants, brought to the continent accidentally or deliberately, invade our natural areas at the rate of *4,600 acres a day*. Until the Stewardship Committee got going, Tom and I knew about these plants only in theory. Now we have gone *mano a mano* with some of them—garlic mustard at Tower Hill and Topinabee, spotted knapweed and buckthorn at Consumers Power Prairie—and have seen for ourselves their tenacity and dreadful power to disrupt and even destroy ecosystems.

Applying Field-Learning at Home

What we learn from work on SWMLC preserves, we try hard to apply at home, in our half-acre suburban yard. There we attempt to restore, to the extent that this is possible, the wild community which has been destroyed by development and over half a century of conventional gardening

> Caretaking is the utmost spiritual and physical responsibility of our time, and perhaps that stewardship is finally our place in the web of life, our work, and solution to the mystery of what we are.
>
> —Linda Hogan, *Dwellings*

and lawn care in our suburb. Step by step, we rid the yard of dame's rocket, barberry, myrtle, honeysuckle and lawn grass—all of them invasive exotic plants—and replace them with native shrubs and perennials.

The evidence is all around us that, like communities of native plants and animals, human communities are also threatened by fragmentation and weakening of the links which hold them together. So it's very gratifying to know that as SWMLC works to preserve and restore wild communities on the land in its care, it is also creating and fostering community among its members, especially among its active volunteers. We all come together for a single purpose; and as we try to achieve it, we become a real community. We carpool, visit each other, exchange seeds and plants and books, share information about the natural world ("Are the warblers back?" "The cardinal flower is blooming at

Jeptha!"). All this, in addition to the satisfaction of protecting land that's relatively undisturbed and learning how to restore the degraded monocultures of our own suburban yards!

You can make a difference, however small; and you can *see* the difference that you make. If you're not yet a member of a community of volunteer stewards of the land, we urge you to join one now. You'll be warmly welcomed, and your life will be enriched.

A version of this essay appeared as "Reflections of a Charter Member of the Stewardship Committee" in the newsletter of the Southwest Michigan Land Conservancy, Spring/Summer 2000, pp. 1–2.

28

THE GRACE OF SUMMER

BY NANCY AND TOM SMALL

And so the seasons went rolling on into summer,
as one rambles into higher and higher grass.
—Henry David Thoreau, *Walden*

"*Summertime, an' the livin' is easy ...*" Easier, at any rate, than it is in winter—easier, certainly, for people to walk more gently on the earth. We can turn off some of our machines ... let the sun and wind dry our hair and clothes, use the bicycles for all but long trips and heavy loads, turn off the heat in our homes and cars and not turn on the cooling unless we're fainting.

Instead of buying fruits and vegetables from distant lands at the supermarket, we can get them from farmers' markets or buy a share of a local farmer's yield. In addition to supporting local agriculture, we can use summer's variety and abundance of fruit and vegetables to reduce consumption of meat and fish or even eliminate them from our diet. Who knows? By fall, if we're in the habit, we could eliminate them for good.

The greatest blessing of summer, however, is that the richness and diversity of creation are now supremely accessible—not merely to the senses and appetites but also to the mind and spirit. Nature in flower and leaf—and later, fruit—can't be resisted. Summer's grace not only refreshes and re-inspires us but makes easier our task of communicating our love of the creation and extending the *community* of those who cherish it.

WHAT CAN WE GIVE?

We can't give our own children and their friends quite the same images and experiences of nature that we had as children. The world now contains fewer toads and frogs and monarch butterflies, fewer nearby fields and neighborhood vacant lots. Nor can we pass on our still vivid images

and memories as effortlessly as we eventually hand down the family treasures.

Rather, we must insure that these children, from an early age, experience nature often and deeply enough to gain real appreciation of what it is and of our true place in it. We must make sure their knowledge is intimate and detailed enough that they won't be fooled or satisfied by the ersatz nature of theme parks and malls or the neatly trimmed lawns and shrubs of suburbia. We can't even depend on the exotic images of television nature programs to lead children to appreciate their own local heritage. Let us, therefore, while nature is at its most accessible in summer, immerse our

> The child is father of the man.
>
> —William Wordsworth

children in its sights and sounds, as these are revealed in our yards and parks and, more fully, in fields and woods and swamps.

What, in practical terms, can individuals do to accomplish this? We can keep ourselves and our neighbors informed about local opportunities for introducing children (and adults) to the beauty and strangeness of the natural world, and see that the children (at least) take advantage of them. By providing ideas, expertise, materials, transportation, or perhaps nothing more than another adult presence, we can encourage teachers in our children's schools to organize activities which involve children with nature.

WHAT IS THE ULTIMATE VALUE OF A GIFT?

If we don't have children of our own, we can make a point of taking young people with us when we go nature-watching. We can give the children of our friends and neighbors gifts of books, both fiction and non-fiction, which deal with nature. Or native plants for the child to begin a garden all his or her own. Don't hesitate if the parents and the child don't already have an interest in such things.

> I sit now and watch
> my children watching me,
> To their lives, there must
> be a new beginning,
> a new place to learn
> that has no boundaries
> of time or profit.
> I must teach my children
> to set out again
> until they discover their place
> to begin.
>
> —Michael Robinson
> (Cree Nation, Canada),
> "The Freedom of Silence"

As teachers for many years, we recognize that we can't know what might ultimately be the truly life-changing gift to a pupil, or a child, whom one barely knows and who quickly passes on, out of our lives.

Like the richness and variety of creation, the people in our neighborhoods are also more accessible in summer as they work in their yards, or run, walk, and bicycle—often with their children—in the neighborhood. It's easy to strike up, or renew, acquaintance with them. Often, they make the first move, commenting or questioning about the native prairie garden on our sunny corner, or all the sounds of birds and insects they hear in our yard. If nothing else offers, it's easy to move from the indispensable opening, "the weather," to other aspects of nature.

As the two of us grow older, we become gradually more forceful with both friends and strangers about our mission and its crucial importance. While it might not be advisable to leap at once from the weather to climate change and species extinction (unless you want to send your audience running), there are many smooth and less alarming transitions to the importance of native plants for wildlife and native pollinators and healthy soil. Sooner or later, one might even venture a comment about why it's essential to reduce the size and upkeep of lawns.

The World Tree, or Indra's Web   Charcoal and pencil   Elizabeth Henderson

The Gift Beyond Measure

The diminished but nonetheless wondrous wildlife all around us is a particularly rich though delicate topic which allows us—if we can summon appropriate courage and tact—to remind people that we suburbanites are now occupying—and degrading—land which was once habitat for plants and animals, and that it's cruel, unfair, and ultimately self-destructive, to try to exclude them from it.

In other words, we must use summer, when they're more accessible than in any other season, to make common cause with those neighbors who, like us, are concerned to protect and heal the earth, and to proselytize among those who aren't. We can lure both groups into our yards (as we lure birds and animals) by offering gifts—plants and seeds and fruits, the gracious gifts of summer. The greatest gift is summer itself, an opportunity to enjoy, to converse, to share, to restore—ourselves and the wondrous creation all around us.

A version of this essay appeared in our column, "Leadings," in *BeFriending Creation* (July–Aug., 1996, pp. 4–5), the newsletter of Quaker Earthcare Witness.

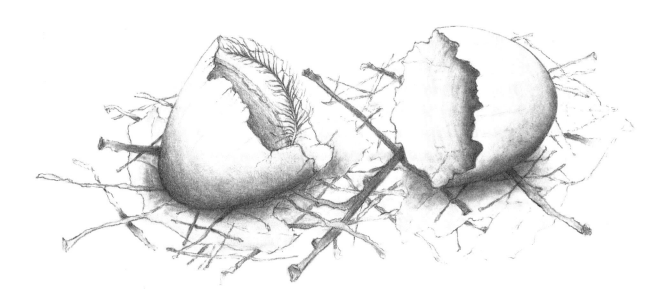

29

WHO ARE WE?
WHERE ARE WE GOING?

BY TOM SMALL

Talk of mysteries! … *Who* are we? *Where* are we?
—Henry David Thoreau, *The Maine Woods*

A few years ago, as I bicycled through Mashonaland, the eastern highlands of Zimbabwe, day after day children ran across the fields and the bush, waving and shouting as they came: "Who are you? Where are you going?" I would wave and shout back: "Rusape"; or "Masvingo"; or "Birchenough Bridge." Sometimes, I would stop to talk.

Once, when two of us were lagging behind our group and it was getting dark, a whole band of youngsters—boys and girls, ages maybe 6 to 11 or 12—ran alongside us, barefoot, mile after mile, the older ones testing out their English, curious to know what two white people, on shiny mountain bikes, were doing on this little traveled road. At every long hillclimb, we were sure they would fall behind and drop off. No. They kept up their steady, even strides, never out of breath. These children ran five miles to school every morning.

Then one little girl fell down hard, on the rough road; and we all stopped. We squatted down beside the wailing child and gave her little presents, to comfort her; when we left, all the children were gathered around, examining her treasures.

TEACHING IN THE DARK

Altogether, there were seven of us bicycling around Mashonaland: three Canadians, one Haitian, myself, our American leader, and his Zimbabwean assistant. We stayed in school dormitories, on farms, in schoolteachers' homes, even in a motel (once). We visited a lot of schools, talking with teachers and students. We visited a dark cement-block classroom where uniformed students studied Business, without textbooks, basic supplies, or electricity.

At one school, near Rusape, the headmaster came to greet us with apologies for his old clothes and dirty hands—he had come from tending vegetables in the school's garden. His teachers showed us, proudly, the artwork and writing exercises of their students. We left some maps, for the geography class. Asked what he most wanted, the headmaster said, books—a *library*.

When we returned to Harare, I went to a bookstore, bought as many books as I could afford, and sent them to the school at Rusape. Back in the U.S., I collected picture books, old readers, paperback novels, and shipped them to the two schools that seemed most in need. To the headmaster at Rusape, I included packets of seeds for the school garden. Always, at first, the responses were swift and very grateful. Once, the headmaster included a thick packet of carefully spelled thank-you letters from students, and a photograph of himself opening the cartons of books, with dozens of children eagerly looking on.

The school at Rusape was the best rural school we visited in Zimbabwe. The teachers cared very deeply about their students; everyone showed us great courtesy. The following year I received many letters from boys and girls, from both third graders and seventh graders, all of them beginning with the same formula, but then adding special details, and all of them very touching.

LOSING TOUCH

Then, as the political and economic situation in Zimbabwe deteriorated, there was no longer any response to my shipments. I had to assume they were not getting through, or there was no one to receive them. Sadly, I stopped trying.

I still wonder what has happened, amid the economic shambles and the violence endemic in Zimbabwe, to the teachers, the headmasters, the students, to all the children so curious to know where I was going, and why. I wonder also what has happened to the hospitable tobacco farmer at whose spacious colonial home we stayed one night. He feared his farm would soon be unprofitable, probably expropriated. Nonetheless, he had started to gather a menagerie of wild animals—giraffes, a lion, some duikers—hoping to establish a nature preserve, make a living from tourists. His wife provided sanctuary and medicine for wounded

East African bush duiker   Sylvicapra grimmia

About 24 inches tall at maturity, the bush duiker is one of the smallest of African antelopes. Principal predators include lions, leopards, eagles, humans.

Serval cat   Leptailurus serval

Only about two feet tall, servals resemble small cheetahs, with very long legs, short tails, and big, lovely ears.

or motherless wild animals, brought to her from all over the area. A wild serval cat, recently added to her household, circulated among us, curious, fearless. Her greatest difficulty, she confided, was persuading it not to chase the chickens.

"Old Rhodies," unreconstructed racists who had fought on the white government side in the civil war, they both lamented the loss of wildlife during the war and under the Mugabe government. Full of fierce energy, they vowed that if the "Blacks" continued to destroy the wild creatures of the Zambezi, the two of them would come back after death and "*haunt Them!*"

"COLLATERAL DAMAGE"

I thought of Doris Lessing's impassioned lament for vanished wildlife in her book *African Laughter*, the journals of her return to Zimbabwe at the end of the civil war, after 25 years of political exile as a communist troublemaker. The bush was no longer wild, and full of life, as it had been in her youth. Human violence and hunger, the needs and depredations of guerrilla warriors and colonial armies, living off the bush, had almost destroyed the wildlife: "the animals had gone, the birds and the insects ... myriads of small balances, hundreds in every small patch of bush, necessary for water, soil, foliage, climate, had been disturbed" (p. 80).

We all lament the loss of innocent life, "collateral damage." Ordinarily, it's the civilian casualties killed in the crossfire or bomb blast that we lament. But what about the innocent wild creatures? I remember standing on the border between Zimbabwe and Mozambique, marked every 50 yards or so by rusting signs, "DANGER LANDMINES," with skull and crossbones. "No danger," said my Zimbabwean guide. "Many months, we heard mines go off, mostly at night—set off by baboons maybe, anything heavy enough to explode them. Silent now. All gone."

The landmines may be gone, but now it's the snares and traps that leave remnant wildlife limping along on three legs. In an impoverished nation, collateral damage accelerates: more than 90 percent of animals on Zimbabwe's private ranches and national parks have been lost to commercial and subsistence poaching since 2000 (as much as 10 tons a day of bushmeat ends up in the London market); some 60 percent of the nation's total wildlife has been slaughtered in response to Zimbabwean economic collapse; woodland and

On the Border   Nancy Halliday

savanna habitats have been sacrificed for fuel. The Zimbabwean Conservation Task Force estimated in 2008 that at the present rate of loss, there will be no wildlife left by 2013 (Hammond, pp. 46–49).

This is not something happening far away; it impoverishes the whole earth and future generations—our own children, and theirs. "We don't have to go anywhere: it comes to us," observes John Cage (p. 223). Collateral damage, driven by conflict, poverty, economic pressures, climate change, is everywhere around us. And within us as well, whether we are conscious of it or not. Better that we should be conscious of it; otherwise, there is no remedy.

Will the remnant baboons and elephants escape to a safer place? Is there such a place? Who will care for the motherless serval cats? Will the bush itself, with all its decimated but still wondrous life, survive us? What, I ponder, has become of those barefoot children, who want only to know who we are and where we are going?

Indeed, where *are* we going? How shall we cope with painful awareness of all the collateral damage of civilization itself, waging relentless war on nature, living off conquered and colonized cultures and lands? Are we all of us, like my racist hosts, caught between our desire to save whatever we can of vanishing wild creatures and our complicity in the violence and subjugation that afflict them, and all of us? By what ghosts of the lost and left behind will we *all* be haunted?

REFERENCES

Cage, John, "Where Are We Going? and What Are We Doing?" in *Silence*, Middletown, CT: Wesleyan University Press, 1973, pp. 194–259.

Hammond, Robin, "Game Over?" *The Ecologist* (June, 2008), pp. 45–49.

Lessing, Doris. *African Laughter: Four Visits to Zimbabwe*. New York: HarperCollins, 1992.

A few details in this essay appeared in the original issue of *Leadings* (July 1994, vol. 1, no. 1), a bi-monthly publication of what was then Friends Committee on Unity with Nature, now Quaker Earthcare Witness.

30

What Does It Cost to "Bear Witness"?

By Tom Small

A garden … is a solution that leads to other solutions.
—Wendell Berry, *The Gift of Good Land*

Wild Ones—Native Plants, Natural Landscapes is a national organization devoted to environmental education, advocacy for native plants, and the preservation and restoration of native-plant communities. www.wildones.org

It's discomforting to be called to a mission, to feel that one *must* bear witness to some fundamental truth. In early 2007, Joe Powelka, at that time national President of Wild Ones, called on all 3000 members of the organization to "set examples," especially in dealing with climate change: more persuasion of the unconvinced; "more native plants" and "larger natural gardens" (p. 2).

As a native-plant restorationist and as a Quaker, I have to take Joe very seriously: we are called—we have a calling, *as members of Wild Ones*—to "bear witness."

Bearing witness involves what Gary Snyder has called a "practice": a dedicated, devoted way of life. To Marshall Massey, a founder of the international Quaker environmental organization, Quaker Earthcare Witness, the ancient discipline of witness involves recognizing and taking responsibility for the truth of one's own situation and one's own complicity and guilt, changing one's own life in accordance with that recognition, and seeking to bring others to recognize the truth and therefore "change direction."

Thus, says Massey, "The fruits of witness meant spiritual redemption and social reform *both*."

What, then, is our true situation, especially with regard to this long emergency called climate change? We know already that possible consequences of climate change range from widespread disruption, devastation, suffering, and death to, in the extreme case, a collapse of civilization as we know it. Moreover, as Wild Ones, we see climate disruption within a context of the Sixth Great Extinction of species, already well under way and likely to be greatly exacerbated by climate change.

ARE WE SERIOUS YET?

We also know that despite some encouraging signs, our civilization is not yet really serious about changing direction: melting of the Arctic ice leads to new territorial claims and a race to drill for oil; the diminishing supply of easily accessible oil spawns costly and carbon-producing schemes for liquefying coal, for drilling down into the depths of ocean beds, and for tearing away the flesh of mother earth to squeeze oil from Canadian tar sands; switching to alternative fuels such as ethanol seems to create at least as many problems as it solves. Perhaps most discouraging, the fundamental objective remains, for most of us in so-called developed nations, one of preserving "*our* way of life"—not one of preserving and cherishing the creation as a whole, which, from Adelie penguins to tigers to common backyard birds to tiny invertebrates, is dwindling and disappearing before our eyes.

Terry Glavin's haunted travels across the globe, eloquently depicted in his book *The Sixth Extinction: Journeys Among the Lost and Left Behind*, disturb me deeply. Glavin writes not just about extinction in and of the wild but also extinctions of domesticated species of animals, grains, and vegetables, as well as extinctions of languages and entire cultures.

On one level, the book is a classic jeremiad—prophetic denunciation of our venality, heedlessness, profligacy. "The harvest is done," says Glavin, quoting Jeremiah, "and we are not saved." But the book is also a love story—a "Song of Solomon," if you will. It celebrates the "lovers" who selflessly work against the odds to save the beloved community, one plant at a time, one species at a time, one acre at a time.

God told Jeremiah to speak to the people and kings the terrible truth of their situation. But God also told Jeremiah to buy a field: "Buy my field which is at Anathoth. For the right possession and redemption is yours" (*Jer.* 32:8). Despite being exiles in Babylon, stay where you are. This is your place. "Plant gardens and eat what they produce" (29:5).

How are we to understand what it means to *redeem* a field, a plot of land? Surely, for Jeremiah—and for us—it has to mean more than buying and taking possession. For Jim Corbett, a Quaker who established the Saguaro Juniper Land Redemption Covenant on degraded grazing land in New Mexico, land redemption requires "knowing a homeland personally and betrothing oneself to it, through a community, as the place to practice a hallowing way of life … Land redemption is the foundation of community redemption" (Corbett, pp. 16–17). The community practice of restoration is a *redemptive* act. The practice of the Wild Ones community, restoration of degraded urban yards, is no less a redemptive action.

> What you do makes a difference, and you have to decide what kind of difference you want to make.
>
> —Jane Goodall

AN ACT OF OPPOSITION, A WAY OF LIVING IN PLACE

For Wendell Berry, gardening is "an act of opposition or protest." But more than that, it's what he calls "a *complete* action." It deals in a very practical, immediate way with the emergency situation itself—an energy crisis and a violent assault on the creation. It is, in short, a bearing of witness—to put it simply, a telling and showing of an entire way of restorative life. It is what Marshall Massey calls us to: "a healing response to some wound that another has suffered" ("Quaker Environmentalism," 1999).

Of course, Berry has in mind the planting of vegetable gardens. But what he says pertains even more to native-plant gardens and natural landscaping because they provide healing and sustenance for countless creatures *other than just ourselves.* Just as much as vegetable gardens, our native-plant gardens are what the founders of the Anathoth Community Garden in Cedar Grove, North Carolina, call "a small act of witness, a way of living in place that, if practiced, might begin to repair some of the damage we have inflicted upon our neighbors, the fertile soil, and ourselves" (Bahnson, p. 68). Our neighbors include *all* our fellow creatures, even those with roots and those that live in the soil itself.

With our acts as Wild Ones we restore a relationship, a sense of community with one another and with all our fellow creatures—with the beloved community. One yard at a time. One step at a time. And every step is peacemaking.

> If we put our minds to it, can we gardeners, with our centuries of practical experience in growing plants, help rescue species from the brink of extinction and restore ancient natural communities that have become more and more fragmented and degraded? What *is* our role, as the quintessential self-conscious species, in the greater destiny of the Earth?
>
> —Janet Marinelli,
> *Stalking the Wild Amaranth*

Fields Going Wild   Etching with drypoint and aquatint   Ladislav Hanka

"Life, given a reprieve, begins immediately to heal itself. Relaxing into that primordial rhythm, we can take solace in the original order and join in its regeneration as well." —Ladislav Hanka

A WAY OF PEACE AND NONVIOLENCE

Perhaps, writes Fred Bahnson about Anathoth, "a community garden is actually a threat to life as we know it" (p. 69). So, for me, is a native-plant garden. It too is an act of opposition and protest. In many ways it is a countercultural act, in opposition to the homogenizing and laying waste of the land and its life. Moreover, natural landscaping is indeed a *complete* action—sufficient in itself but also, I hope, witness to an entire way of life—a way of simplicity, a way of peace and nonviolence in a time of wars in which we are unwilling participants—wars within ourselves, against our fellow human beings, and against nature. It is, however modestly, "a witness to the world, of what is possible" (Massey, 1999).

Perhaps, as many of the scientists tell us, "we are not saved." The waters will rise, and havoc is come upon us. But we are nonetheless, whether we will or no, saviors. We have no choice. We are *called*, because we are lovers. To save and redeem ourselves, we must, as a community, save as much as we can of what we love. In the concluding words of Terry Glavin's loving jeremiad, "you join the epic battle with the demons that are devouring the world, and you do what you can. It's all anyone can expect of you. You do everything you can."

REFERENCES

Bahnson, Fred. "The Field at Anathoth: a Garden Becomes a Protest," *Orion*, July/Aug., 2007, pp. 62–69.

Berry, Wendell, "The Reactor and the Garden," *The Gift of Good Land: Further Essays Cultural and Agricultural*, New York: North Point Press, 1981, pp. 161–170.

Corbett, Jim. *Leadings*. Tallahassee, FL: Southeastern Yearly Meeting of the Religious Society of Friends, 1995.

Glavin, Terry. *The Sixth Extinction: Journeys Among the Lost and Left Behind*. New York: St. Martin's Press, 2007.

Hahn, Thich Nhat. *Peace is Every Step: The Path of Mindfulness in Everyday Life*. New York: Bantam, 1992.

Massey, Marshall. Materials for a workshop on "The Ancient Discipline of Witness" for the 1997 Friends General Conference Gathering of Friends.

_____. "Quaker Environmentalism," 1999. Online at www.quakerinfo.com/quak_env_shtml.

Powelka, Joe. "Climate Change: The Answer May Not Be as Complicated as You Think," *Wild Ones Journal*, May/June 2007, p. 2.

Snyder, Gary. *The Practice of the Wild*. San Francisco: North Point Press, 1990.

A version of this essay appeared as "Why Wild Ones? Why Me? And What Then?" in *Wild Ones Journal*, Sept./Oct., 2007, pp. 6–7.

31

WHAT DOES A LATTER-DAY NOAH NEED TO KNOW?

BY TOM SMALL

In wildness is the preservation of the world.
—Henry David Thoreau, "Walking"

Most of us feel that we live in dark times. Perhaps we grasp that most of what we love is at risk, and we're angry, discouraged. I am. Nancy was too. Month after month, she swore she was going to stop reading *The New York Times* every morning. But she was addicted to depressing news, just as I am to apocalyptic books. Oh, I try to shake the habit. At the bookstore, I pass by Bill McKibben's latest book detailing just how bad things are. Instead, I pick up a copy of *Yes! Magazine*, the journal of "Positive Futures." There it is, on the coffee table, displaying its positive cover and flaunting its exclamation point. Besides, the sun's out. Life is good.

Why *should* we belabor ourselves with all the bad news about mortgage foreclosures, about pelicans slimed with oil and West Virginia mountains reduced to rubble, about drowning polar bears and dying coral reefs?

Maybe I'm perverse, but those golden smiley faces have always irritated me. I know I can't live up to Thoreau's determination "to drive life into a corner, and reduce it to its lowest terms, and if it proved to be mean, why then to get the whole and genuine meanness of it, and publish its meanness to the world." Those words, however, remain for me some of Thoreau's most memorable. I can't delude myself with corporate greenwash and false hopes—not for very long anyway. I'm not persuaded that changing the light bulb, or writing a severe letter to my Republican Congressman, or rescuing a trillium from the blade of the bulldozer (all good things in themselves) is going to save us from disasters

that loom ahead—or are already upon us. And as long as we continue to colonize most of the world's living space, modest gains in alternative energy and smaller carbon footprints won't be enough to hold back the oncoming tide of species extinction.

We live in what James Howard Kunstler has called, evocatively, "The Long Emergency," an accelerating convergence of multiple catastrophes: peak oil, climate change, water scarcity, financial breakdown, habitat destruction, food shortages, soil degradation, pollution, disease, and more. Our future does indeed look dark. But if I am to play the role of an imperfect Noah in saving biodiversity, then I need to understand clearly what sort of flood is coming and why I must share my understanding with others more or less in denial. As Joanna Macy counseled in—oh, yes!—*Yes! Magazine*, "Pain for the world—the outrage and the sorrow—breaks us open to a larger sense of who we are. It is a doorway to the realization of our mutual belonging in the web of life" (Feb., 2008). The legendary Greek physician Aesclepius said only the wounded can heal.

And Walt Whitman, a nurse to the wounded during the Civil War, felt their pain:

> I do not ask the wounded person how he feels, I myself become the wounded person
> ("Song of Myself," 33, line 845.)

CLEARING THE MIND OF FALSE HOPE

So the namesake of butterfly weed (*Asclepias tuberosa*), and Walt Whitman, and even *Yes!*—they all urge me to face up to my fears, angers, and despairs if I hope to heal my own wounds, never mind those of the planet.

I return to the bookstore and buy McKibben's new book.

Over 20 years ago in *The End of Nature*, McKibben had it right about climate change. Now, in *Eaarth: Making a Life on a Tough New Planet*, he sums up, in one abrupt sentence, his view of our situation: "The earth that we knew … is gone" (p. 27).

The sociologist William R. Catton, Jr., also had it right, back in 1980. In *Overshoot: The Ecological Basis of Revolutionary Change*, Catton provided, thirty years ago, a compelling analysis, in terms of ecological processes, of what we've done to ourselves and the planet by overshooting the limits that nature ineluctably imposes on us. Back then, he offered solace: ways that we might yet avoid the worst of the consequences. But now, since we've only made matters worse in the last 30 years, he again defines our situation with a single word: *Bottleneck*. His subtitle elucidates: *Humanity's Impending Impasse*.

E. O. Wilson devotes a whole chapter in his *The Future of Life* to discussion of the bottleneck that he sees as humanity's immediate future. Planet Earth cannot sustain us at our current and still growing levels of population and wasteful consumption. In particular, says Wilson,

> The appropriation of productive land—the ecological footprint—is already too large for the planet to sustain, and it's growing larger … The constraints of the biosphere are fixed.

> The bottleneck through which we are passing is real. It should be obvious to anyone not in a euphoric delirium that whatever humanity does or does not do, Earth's capacity to support our species is approaching the limit. (Chapter II, "The Bottleneck," pp. 22–41.)

The limits we have overshot and the bottleneck we have "foolishly blundered into" (Wilson, p. 41) involve a drastic narrowing of what Catton calls "life opportunities" (p. 188)—not only for species populations (including our own) but also for genetic diversity within those populations. David Orr, discussing Wilson's diagnosis in his recent book *Down to the Wire: Confronting Climate Collapse*, has no doubt about the severity of the crisis but remains uncertain about the precise outcome:

> On the other side of E. O. Wilson's "bottleneck" we do not know … how much biological diversity will have survived, or whether stressed ecosystems will recover in time spans meaningful to humans … The earth, then, will be very different from the planet we've known. Our descendents who come through the bottleneck … will be the survivors of a close call with extinction (Orr, p. 157).

> We can anticipate, then, huge changes in Earth's ecosystems, both locally and globally.
>
> —Anthony D. Barnosky,
> *Heatstroke*

It's remarkable how suddenly, in just a few years, the sense of crisis has escalated. Consider how many recent works have analyzed the collapse of past civilizations and societies that overshot the limits of their resources, with perhaps the most notable being Jared Diamond's *Collapse: How Societies Choose to Fail or Survive* (2005). Also consider the shift in titles from earlier to more recent warnings by some of the best scientists and journalists in the prediction business.

- Tim Flannery, Chairman of the Copenhagen Climate Council: from *The Weather Makers*, 2005, to ***Now or Never***, 2009.

- James Gustave Speth, Dean of the School of Forestry and Environmental Studies, Yale University, advisor to Presidents Carter and Clinton, founder of World Resources Institute: from ***Red Sky at Morning***, 2004, to ***The Bridge at the Edge of the World***, 2008.

- Ross Gelbspan, one of the foremost environmental journalists of the last 20 years: from *The Heat is On*, 1997**,** to ***Boiling Point***, 2004, and then to "**Beyond the Point of No Return**," *Grist* (www.grist.com), Dec., 2007**.**

- Rebecca Solnit, my favorite practical visionary: from ***Hope in the Dark: Untold Histories, Wild Possibilities*** (2004) to ***A Paradise Built in Hell*** (2009).

- James Lovelock, founder of Gaia theory: from ***Gaia: Medicine for an Ailing Planet***, 2005, to ***The Vanishing Face of Gaia: A Final Warning: Enjoy It While You Can***, 2009, and finally, "**Lovelock: 'We Can't Save the Planet',**" *BBC Today*, 30 March 2010.

Enough. You get the point.

Once We Know the Worst, What Then?

Who then can help us believe that another world is still possible? What can they offer in the way of hope? What can we *do* to help our inheritors squeeze through the bottleneck and survive as a chastened, diminished, relocalized, resurgent species with a new sense of earth community? Here are three "wild possibilities."

- ***Join*** **the Dance.** In *Animate Earth: Science, Intuition and Gaia* (2006), Stephan Harding, resident ecologist at Schumacher College in Devon, England, offers a powerful dramatization of Gaia theory, the conception of Earth as an evolving, self-organizing system. He evokes the "incessant dance of existence" and "the astonishing intelligence at the heart of all things." He demonstrates, clearly and passionately, the necessity for understanding and preserving the rich biodiversity that regulates the basic processes, such as the carbon, sulfur, and phosphorus cycles, essential to the "gyring,

eddying circles" in which all life, including our own, participates. He offers us exercises and practices by which we might come to "live into the body of the Earth."

Only through this intuitional recentering of the self in "deep ecology" and the life of things can we shift, Harding believes, from a destructive way of life and a "desperate Earth" to a life in harmony with Earth's natural systems. He wants us to see the whole, but his message resonates with the mission of Wild Ones because he emphasizes the absolute necessity for a *local* "love of place" and participation in the local community of all our fellow creatures, including the very rocks and waters, the plants, and the "bacterial web."

- ***Plan*** **for Transition.** Relocalize now, advises Rob Hopkins in *The Transition Handbook: From Oil Dependency to Local Resilience* (2008). If impending catastrophes will indeed utterly disrupt both the natural processes and the complex global civilization we have come to depend upon, then only grass-roots-level, hands-on preparation for the disruption offers a way forward. Hopkins, the inspiration for the Transition movement, provides a guidebook for rebirth of local communities through a step-by-step process of "energy descent" and local self-sufficiency as peak oil, "peak everything," and climate change bring global breakdown. Finding inspiration in E. F. Schumacher's classic *Small is Beautiful* and his concept of "Buddhist Economics," the Transition movement goes one step further: "Small is inevitable."

- *Save* **Biodiversity.** In *Heatstroke: Nature in an Age of Global Warming* (2009), Anthony Barnosky, a paleoecologist, puts our current crisis—especially extinctions and catastrophic loss of biodiversity—in ecological and evolutionary perspective. Thoughtful and eloquent, the book focuses not just on loss of species but, just as important, loss of local populations and genetic diversity as well as, globally, degradation and loss of whole ecosystems. Barnosky enables us to locate ourselves at this particular moment of the immense evolutionary journey that brought us here and still lives within us, interconnected with all creatures and process-

es in the universal web of life. In his final chapter, "The Geography of Hope," he endorses saving as much wilderness as possible, thereby preserving ecological processes that can thrive *only* in the absence of significant human interference, even well-intentioned management. But he recognizes that there's simply not enough wild land left, much less a willingness to leave it alone. He therefore also endorses the "reconciliation ecology" of ecologist Michael Rosenzweig, involving the planting "of native vegetation in yards and city parks." Barnosky's whole book speaks powerfully to the natural-landscaping community and is thus more important to us than most books focused on climate change.

> Taking in traumatic information and transmuting it into life-affirming action may turn out to be the most advanced and meaningful spiritual practice of our time.
>
> —Richard Heinberg

THE GIFT THAT CAN'T BE REFUSED

So, we come full circle, back to the beginning: the daunting *gift* God bestowed upon Noah in the time of retribution and crisis: "as I gave you the green plants, I give you everything" (*Gen.* 9:3). Now, here we are at our own time for crisis and covenant—with the green world.

Of the recent books of prophecy calling to us in the suburban desert, the most cogent is not Barnosky's, nor Rosenzweig's *Win-Win Ecology* (2003), but Douglas Tallamy's modest but insistent and insightful *Bringing Nature Home: How You Can Sustain Wildlife with Native Plants* (rev. 2009).

Tallamy, a professor of entomology and wildlife ecology, demonstrates, scientifically, that "reconciliation ecology," the redesign of human habitats for the accommodation of other species, is not just vitally important; "it's the future"—if we're to have one.

Like Barnosky and Rosenzweig, Tallamy argues that there simply isn't enough protected land, actual or potential, to sustain the earth's vital biodiversity. Yet we continue, with our prosthetic machines, to convert relatively undisturbed land to human use. So, as Sara Stein argued, in *Noah's*

Garden: Restoring the Ecology of Our Own Back Yards (1993), the book that inspired the two of us to transform our own home landscape and establish a chapter of Wild Ones, "Our task is therefore nothing less than to create a new landscape." It's an emergency. Even we suburbanites must take up the task of saving species and ecosystems from the flood of extinction.

> [Tallamy's] work underscores one of the fundamentals of the Nature Principle: conserving wilderness is not enough; we must conserve and *create* nature, in the form of native habitat, wherever possible; on roofs and in gardens in our cities and suburbs. This is the road leading to natural communities.
>
> —Richard Louv,
> *The Nature Principle*

Tallamy uses research by landscape ecologists to bring home to each of us the urgent need for us to transform our gardens into *habitat*:

> Unless we modify the places we live, work and play to meet not only our own needs but the needs of other species as well, nearly all species of wildlife native to the United States will disappear forever (p. 36).

Stein emphasizes, as does Tallamy, the delicacy and intricacy of the web that we're going to have to weave—*at home*:

> The web is strong when there are many strands and their ties accordingly complex; break too

many strands and it collapses … Picture the ark of our ecosystem as gossamer. Realize that its many strands will have to be flung wide over lots, tracts, neighborhoods, and towns if it is to hold us all (pp. 96–97).

Arguing from long experience as a gardener, Stein recounts her years of effort to tame an overgrown piece of rural land into a conventional garden, only to realize that "we had banished the animals from this paradise of ours," just as Adam and Eve had been banished from Eden—only this time the cast-out creatures were innocent, and the flaming sword was a power lawnmower.

Studying his own rural property, Tallamy argues as an entomologist that planting a diversity of *native* plants is crucial to sustaining the herbivorous insects that transfer the sun's energy from plants to birds and other creatures and are thus essential to life on earth.

Both Stein and Tallamy are very down to earth. Both communicate a powerful sense of urgency. Both are dead certain that the 45 million acres of mowed lawn in the U.S. amount to little more than what Stein calls "a hole in the world." Both perceive clearly that Noah's ark, as popularly depicted, could have saved nothing: "Noah," says Stein, "could have saved the animals only if he had rolled up the whole landscape and taken it aboard." Noah couldn't do that. Neither can we. No, we must invent a new landscape: Noah's Garden. *Our* gardens.

> Every scrap of ground can serve as an ark.
>
> —Scott Russell Sanders,
> *A Conservationist Manifesto*

ECOS—The Household as an Ark: Springtime   Elizabeth Henderson

There's a difference between "having a wildflower garden" and living within the garden: pervasive native greenery, biodiversity, wildlife—an ecosystem—all around you and embracing you. This is the Ark.

Restoring a Rough Facsimile of Eden—at Home

They won't be—can't be—more than simplified simulations of the rich web of life that this immense journey of evolution gave to us as Eden. Nor can we know, for sure, what species and genetic information will come through the bottleneck of "humanity's impending impasse" and thus be the key to survival of diminished but still life-supporting ecosystems. It is precisely our uncertainty that makes it essential to preserve—to *plant*—as great a diversity of native species as your quarter of an acre, or your 20 acres, or your tiny side yard will support.

What we do know for certain is that diversity of species—plants, insects, fungi, birds, microbes, mammals—is essential to resilience: the "capacity of a system to absorb disturbance; to undergo change … without crossing a threshold to a different system regime—a system with a different identity" (Walker and Salt, p. 32). Thresholds are the tipping points or "crossing points that have the potential to alter the future of many of the systems that we depend upon" (p. 53). But we have already crossed the thresholds for several life-support systems, vital for us and all other species on earth.

According to a group of 27 internationally renowned environmental and earth-system scientists gathered by the Stockholm Resilience Centre in Sweden, there are ten "planetary life-support systems" vital for human well-being. For each system, the scientists quantified safe boundaries. If we push even one of the ten interconnected life-support systems beyond its tipping point, we have therefore crossed a threshold; we risk causing "irreversible and abrupt environmental change" that could make the earth a much less hospitable place—both for us and for most other species.

For three of the crucial systems, humanity has already overshot the safe limit: climate change due to perturbation of the carbon cycle, disruption of the nitrogen cycle, and loss of biodiversity. For each system, natural-landscaping practices are just about the most meaningful and effective contribution we can make, as individuals, organizations, and communities, to *reducing the risk* of life-threatening catastrophe.

- **Climate Change.** We natural landscapers don't use gas-powered lawnmowers or petroleum-based fertilizers and pesticides. We don't repeatedly rototill the soil, destroying its structure and releasing immense quantities of carbon. We *do* plant perennial native species with deep and massive root systems, which thus store immensely more carbon than lawns, or annual bedding plants, or even urban tree plantations.

- **Nitrogen Cycle.** Humanity's massive interference in the nitrogen cycle—doubling the amount of biologically active nitrogen on earth in just 50 years—puts us much farther beyond a safe planetary boundary than does our interference in the carbon cycle. Nitrogen pollution, according to more and more scientists, may ultimately prove a more intractable and deadly problem than carbon pollution and climate change (see Smil, pp. 200–203). So we natural landscapers don't use industrial fertilizer, the greatest contributor to nitrogen

pollution. We *do* use our own yard wastes—leaves, branches, plant residues—and let them decompose slowly so as to recycle nitrogen naturally, build soil, and feed the soil organisms vital to all life.

- **Biodiversity.** For biodiversity, the rate of loss is so great, so far over the limit compared to the other systems, that it exceeded the space available in the diagram accompanying the Resilience Centre's scientific paper. Moreover, the rate of increase in loss of biodiversity per year is such that the already dangerously high rate of extinction will be ten times greater by the end of the century, as much as ten thousand times the normal background rate of extinction. C. S. Holling of the Resilience Alliance affirms that "the world seems to be moving toward a major transformation." No matter whether you call it bottleneck, or collapse, or transformation, the process will not be "easy and gradual"; it will be "tough and abrupt" (Holling, 2004).

We all hope fervently that we and our children and theirs will come through what biologist E. O. Wilson calls "the bottleneck" with a more tempered and improved and more vital democracy. But I do not believe that to be even remotely possible without extending our boundaries of consideration and affection to include posterity and, in some manner yet unknown, other life forms.

—David W. Orr, *Down to the Wire: Confronting Climate Collapse*

Since diversity, as Michael Rosenzweig empha- sizes, results from "the adaptations that millions of species have made to exploit countless niches in their environments," therefore "the threats facing individual species and the possible ways of pro- tecting them are as unique and local as the species themselves" (Best, p. 36).

So, recognizing massive losses of biodiversity and anticipating still greater, we natural landscap- ers don't maintain, at great expense, monocultures of nonnative turf grasses that contribute little or nothing to the local community of life. We don't allow invasive nonnative plants to squeeze out and destroy the natural, beautiful, and essential diver- sity of both plants and all the creatures that depend on them. We *do* plant and foster as great a diver- sity of *native* species and *local* genetic types as we can manage, including some of the species most at risk in our local ecosystems. We *do* bear witness to our faith that the impending crisis will bring about transformation to a social system more enlight- ened than ours and ecological systems changed but still diverse enough to be cause for wonder, "full of surprises, danger, and opportunity" (Homer-Dix- on, p. 308). We *do* garden not just for ourselves but, as Tallamy insists, for "the needs of other species." **Like Noah, we have no choice.**

OFFERING A SMALL GIFT TO THE FUTURE

Hold in mind that the news is not only bad but rapidly getting worse. Lovelock and McK- ibben agree on one thing, and they're probably right: "we can't save the planet." It's too late. The relatively stable planet that we so swiftly colonized and seemingly made our own by right of conquest is gone, energized by our own success into a force that threatens not just our comforts but our sur- vival.

Nonetheless, as Paul Hawken affirms in *Blessed Unrest*, "Small things, lovingly done, are always within our reach." In fact, these small things—these wild possibilities that one can hard- ly help but love and cherish—are right outside the door and underfoot. "Every scrap of ground," af- firms Scott Sanders, "can serve as an ark."

So let us, *together*, weave as intricate and far- flung a web as we can. Let us *rejoice* in what re- mains and whatever we can restore. Above all, de- spite the morning news, despite discouragement,

Nancy always felt *grateful*. Grateful for the gift we received—our love for each other and the call- ing we shared, to participate in the work of Noah, growing arks to save whatever we can of wondrous, astonishing creatures and the green plants—the di- vine gift of *everything*. "We are so lucky," she said, over and over again.

Love the place where you are, right now; it's what the whole of your life and fourteen billion years of cosmic evolution have delivered you to. In- vest *yourself* in it, *because of* the risk, and because you love it. Save native biodiversity at home. Recruit your neighbors as fellow weavers of the web. Grow an ark as many cubits long and wide, and with as many beds for native plants, as you can manage. Trust the vast intelligence of the earth-system: something of what we save will come through. It always has. It always will. It's the best we can hope for—all we can do. And we *can* do it. Together, we are *learning how*.

REFERENCES

Best, Jason, "Like Most Conservation Scientists, Michael Rosenzweig Thinks We're in the Midst of a Mass Extinction Event," *onearth,* Summer 2005, pp. 34–36.

Catton, William R., Jr. *Bottleneck: Humanity's Impending Impasse.* Xlibris, 2009.

Heinberg, Richard. *The End of Growth: Adapting to Our New Economic Reality.* Gabriola Island, BC, Canada: New Society Publishers, 2011.

Holling, C. S. "From Complex Regions to Complex Worlds," 2004. Available on the web at www.ecologyandsociety.org/vol9/iss1/art11.

Homer-Dixon, Thomas. *The Upside of Down: Catastrophe, Creativity, and the Renewal of Civilization.* Washington, DC: Island Press, 2006.

Louv, Richard. *The Nature Principle: Human Restoration and the End of Nature-Deficit Disorder.* Chapel Hill, NC: Algonquin Books of Chapel Hill, 2011.

Lynas, Mark. *Six Degrees: Our Future on a Hotter Planet.* Washington, DC: National Geographic, 2008. One of the best books—and one of the scariest—on the range of possible consequences of climate change, what triggers them, and how likely they are.

Macy, Joanna, "The Greatest Danger," online at www.yesmagazine.org/issues/climate-solutions/the-greatest-danger (Feb., 2008).

Orr, David W. *Down to the Wire: Confronting Climate Collapse.* Oxford: Oxford Univ. Press, 2009.

Peterson, Garry, Craig R. Allen, and C. S. Holling, "Ecological Resilience, Biodiversity, and Scale," *Ecosystems* (1998), 1:6–18.

Rockstrom, Johan, et al.,"Planetary Boundaries: Exploring the Safe Operating Space for Humanity," *Ecology and Society* 14(2): 32. On line: www. ecologyandsociety.org/vol14/iss2/art32. See also www.stockholmresilience.org/planetary-boundaries.

Sanders, Scott Russell. *A Conservationist Manifesto.* Bloomington, IN: Indiana Univ. Press, 2009.

Smil, Vaclav. *Global Catastrophes and Trends: The Next Fifty Years.* Cambridge, MA: The MIT Press, 2008.

Stein, Sara. *Noah's Garden: Restoring the Ecology of Our Own Back Yards.* Boston: Houghton Mifflin, 1993.

Tallamy, Douglas. *Bringing Nature Home: How You Can Sustain Wildlife with Native Plants.* Updated and expanded edition. Portland, OR: Timber Press, 2009.

Walker, Brian, and David Salt. *Resilience Thinking: Sustaining Ecosystems and People in a Changing World.* Washington, DC: Island Press, 2006.

Watson, Elizabeth. *Healing Ourselves and Our Earth.* Chelsea, MI: Friends Committee on Unity with Nature, 1991.

This essay incorporates some material from my article, "What Do We Need to Know, and How Soon Do We Need to Know It?" in *Wild Ones Journal,* January/February, 2008, p. 4, and draws inspiration from Nancy's reviews of *Bringing Nature Home,* published in the newsletters of the Wildflower Association of Michigan and the Audubon Society of Kalamazoo, as well as from her many observations on the writings of Sara Stein.

FOR THE CHILDREN
By Gary Snyder

The rising hills, the slopes,
of statistics
lie before us.
the steep climb
of everything, going up,
up, as we all
go down.

In the next century
or the one beyond that,
they say,
the valleys, pastures,
we can meet there in peace
if we make it.

To climb these coming crests
one word to you, to
you and your children:

stay together
learn the flowers
go light

The Authors and Illustrators

The Authors

NANCY AND TOM SMALL. Nancy grew up on the Gulf coast of Texas, on the coast of Venezuela, and in Cuba, where her father managed oil refineries. Tom grew up in Colorado, on the edge of prairie and in front ranges of the Rockies. Both owe early fascination with nature to journeys with parents into wild areas.

They became colleagues in the early 1970s at Western Michigan University, where both were professors of English literature. Nancy taught Renaissance literature and poetry. Tom taught Romantic poetry and modern drama. During the last few years of their teaching careers, they team-taught the Department's undergraduate Shakespeare course. Increasingly, they realized how many interests and passions they shared in common.

Even before their retirement from WMU in the mid-1990s, they began to live, together, what they both called "their second life," devoted to saving and restoring the degraded and lost biodiversity of southwest Michigan. They were founding members of the Stewardship Committee of the Southwest Michigan Land Conservancy, for which Nancy served on the board of directors. They traveled the continent with the Friends Committee for Unity with Nature, the Quaker environmental organization for the Americas, for which Tom was the presiding clerk. They co-wrote a column, "Leadings," for FCUN's newsletter, *Befriending Creation*, as well as writing for other environmental journals and newsletters. Both peace activists, they had campaigned against wars, from Viet Nam to Iraq. Together, they strove to counter humanity's violence against nature.

Soon after their marriage at Kalamazoo Friends Meeting in 1995, Nancy and Tom began transforming their conventional yard into wildlife habitat, with Michigan native plants. In 1999 they co-founded and became co-presidents of the Kalamazoo Area Chapter of Wild Ones, a national organization devoted to natural landscaping, and Nancy began educating people about the beauty and the benefits of native plants. She developed slide shows on native plants and, with Tom, presented them throughout the area, along with guides and plant lists that she developed. Out of all this grew the vision for a book, to include many of her writings, some of Tom's, and more that they wrote together. When she died from cancer in late 2009, she left the book almost completed, and Tom promised her to complete and publish it. This is the book.

The Illustrators

Nancy Halliday was attracted to nature from childhood, and as a budding artist always drew what interested her. When her zoology and botany professors in college asked her to illustrate their scientific reports, she was able to combine the best of both worlds. The University of Oklahoma granted her bachelor's degree in zoology in 1962. Later, she returned to school to earn a master's degree in geography and environmental studies from Northeastern Illinois University in 1988.

Nancy has worked for the Museum at Michigan State University, the Museum of Northern Arizona, the Smithsonian Institution, and the Florida State Museum. While at the Smithsonian, she joined other staff illustrators to form the Guild of Natural Science Illustrators in 1968, now an international organization. When the Guild published its Handbook of Scientific Illustration, Nancy wrote the bird illustration chapter. Her work for the popular press includes several stamps for the National Wildlife Federation and 13 plants for the field guide Mammals of North America, by R. Kays and D. Wilson. Nancy began teaching scientific illustration in 1977 and regularly offers classes at the Morton Arboretum and the Chicago Botanic Garden.

A descendant of German immigrants to the Chicago area, Nancy returned to the midwest in 1984, where she is active in several environmental organizations, including an appointment as Natural Resources Commissioner (one of five) in her village of residence—Glenview, Illinois. She enjoys birdwatching, bicycling and canoeing.

Ladislav R. Hanka (web.me.com/ladhanka) makes prints and drawings in Kalamazoo. His work appears in approximately 100 public collections on all continents.

"I once asked my father why grown men shave and mow lawns though they all claim to abhor doing so. When I grow up, I was told, I would understand. In 1987 I bought a house and converted the yard to quasi-native status. Unsure of when a naturalized plant with edible or medicinal qualities had earned a green card, I slowly settled into accepting the many plants that grow here without much imposition of my own will. I keep bees, pull up the native poison ivy, eat the non-native nettles, enjoy the goldenrods, raise some vegetables, and marvel at the diversity of insects that has moved into my yard by letting it go wild. At 58 I am still awaiting a grown-up's enlightenment on the shaving issue.

"As an artist I am formed by my use of nature—that which takes me out the door every day. I love to walk, forage, fish, and gather mushrooms. I cannot get enough of ancient trees—the way their asymmetries bring me back to a place of profound stillness. The very idea that trees alive today were seeded at the birth of the old kingdom of Egypt and are thus as old as the written word, sets me free. And yet what do I do with that freedom? Some of us respond with prayer; others organize marches, found conservancies, or craft legislation. I draw pictures. I do so not only because nature is the mirror in which I find my own existence most meaningfully reflected, but also because moving past self-reflection and recognizing intrinsic value in the other is more fulfilling—an extension of one's consciousness beyond utilitarian perspectives—an opening of one's self and thus an act of grace."—Ladislav R. Hanka

AMELIA HANSEN (www.ameliahansen.com) has been a freelance illustrator since 1989, specializing in nature and natural history subjects for books and interpretive exhibits. She has a BFA degree in watercolor from Western Michigan University. She's a member of the Guild of Natural Science Illustrators and the Society of Children's Book Writers and Illustrators. One of the children's books she illustrated, It's Raining Cats—and Cats!, by Jeanne Prevost, won an ASPCA Henry Bergh Children's Book Award for Fiction in 2008, as well as a KIND award from Humane Society Youth.

Amelia illustrated several books by the Michigan naturalist John Eastman, including The Book of Field and Roadside, The Book of Swamp and Bog, and The Book of Forest and Thicket. Nancy greatly admired and often consulted these books, and it was through them that both Tom and Nancy came to know and love Amelia's work as an artist and illustrator.

"Illustration is about taking an idea and making it visual. Sometimes the image serves to support text; sometimes it's a powerful communication tool on its own that speaks more clearly than words. As an illustrator, the ideas I most like to explore involve 'nature' — more specifically, the connections and relationships between people, animals, plants, and the earth. I feel it's my role to direct people's attention to the natural world. Whether it's by explaining an ecological process, pointing out the seldom seen, or exploring the mysterious, I hope to introduce the natural world to those who are unfamiliar with it and celebrate it with those who love it as I do."—Amelia Hansen

ELIZABETH HENDERSON (wagtail@chartermi.net) happily works and lives with her husband, David Posther, in Kalamazoo, Michigan. They have two wonderful kids, Adam and Marin, and a great daughter-in-law, Rebecca. Liz is helped in her work by their orange cat, Niko, and pink dog, Rooey. Pen and ink, pencil, scratchboard, charcoal, colored pastels and pencils are Liz's main media of choice.

Liz illustrated two books by Nancy and Tom's friend and mentor Emma Pitcher. It was through Nancy's admiration of these books, Ramblings: Reflections on Nature and Of Woods and Other Things, that Tom came to know and admire Liz's work as an illustrator.

"I figure it's not easy to draw something exactly the way it looks or the way something makes you feel, so whatever I draw is usually realistic enough to recognize and has been changed by the way I feel about it."—Liz Henderson

NANCY STROUPE, a painter and printmaker living in Kalamazoo, has been a very important longtime friend to Nancy and Tom.

"Someone once said that the humblest and happiest of life's intuitions is a child's connection to the Earth. I was fortunate enough growing up in Iowa to form such a connection, and it has nurtured me throughout my life—a life that has been blessed with marriage to a fine man, with three fine sons, two fine grandchildren, and many fine friends—certainly one of the finest being Nancy Small. I try in my art to express gratitude for that fineness, for the beauty of simple things, and above all to suggest devotion to the loving Presence that insists on giving us life.

"*Holding Turtle Island* is an attempt to symbolize that Presence and the care She gives to our life together—even, and maybe especially, when we ourselves forget to care. Nancy Small was one who did not forget. In so many ways she, like that Presence, held Turtle Island for us, calling our attention to the beauty and the fragility of all that surrounds and sustains us, reminding us of our connection to the Earth—reminding us that we are here to share in the holding."—Nancy Stroupe

The Designer

LINDA K. JUDY, a newly retired graphic designer at Western Michigan University, worked most of her 29+ years at the Medieval Institute and the Institute of Cistercian Studies as a book designer. She is now embarking on a new life as a free-lance designer/artist, and is a student at the Center for New Media at Kalamazoo Valley Community College. Life-long learning is her greatest passion, especially in the arts. She has earned a B.S. in painting and an A.A. in graphic design (pre-computer), and has studied photography, pottery, painting, and sculpture at the Kalamazoo Institute of Arts. An avid gardener, especially interested in herbs and ornamental grasses, she completed the MSU Master Gardener program a number of years ago. Linda also enjoys studying Spanish, reading, movies, music, bicycling, and hiking with her dog Ivy.

"I first met Nancy and Tom in the early 1970s as a student and secretary in the English Department at WMU. Our paths have crossed many times over the years. In addition, I have had the pleasure of knowing a number of the other people involved in the production of their book.

"I am so grateful to have been given the opportunity to be part of producing Nancy and Tom's timely and important book project. Working with Nancy and Tom's powerful, informative, and passionate essays, and with the variety of illustrations by artists I have long admired, respected, and been inspired by, is a gift and a privilege."—Linda K. Judy

ILLUSTRATION CREDITS

NANCY HALLIDAY

192, 193, 194, 195, 196, 213, 215, 216, 217, 234

LADISLAV R. HANKA

ii, xvii, xviii, xxi, xxiii, xxiv, xxv, xxvi, 4, 7, 8, 16, 26, 36, 65, 68, 73, 96, 98, 104, 119, 120, 130, 164, 165, 169, 173, 177, 178, 180, 183, 185, 186, 187, 190, 196, 200, 208, 217, 218, 219, 221, 222, 230, 234, 238, 239

AMELIA HANSEN

iii, v, vii, viii, ix, xv, xix, xxiii, 5, 9, 15, 17, 19, 20, 24, 25, 27, 30, 31, 33, 37, 38, 39, 41, 42, 45, 46, 50, 51, 52, 53, 54, 55, 56, 57, 58, 61, 63, 65, 68, 69, 70, 71, 72, 73, 74, 76, 77, 78, 79, 80, 81, 82, 83, 84, 85, 86, 87, 88, 89, 90, 91, 92, 93, 98, 100, 101, 102, 103, 105, 107, 108, 109, 110, 111, 113, 114, 115, 117, 118, 121, 122, 123, 124, 125, 126, 127, 131, 133, 134, 135, 137, 139, 140, 142, 145, 147, 148, 149, 152, 153, 155, 156, 159, 160, 161, 163, 167, 174, 179, 184, 197, 198, 199, 205, 206, 231, 233, 235, 236

ELIZABETH HENDERSON

xi, 54, 55, 58, 59, 67, 83, 85, 90, 128, 129, 131, 132, 136, 143, 155, 158, 170, 175, 176, 179, 182, 201, 203, 204, 209, 211, 212, 223, 228, 232, 233, 235

JANA PYLE

171, 172

NANCY STROUPE

166, 236

Scriptum herbarum   Etching   Ladislav Hanka

Scriptum arborum   Etching   Ladislav Hanka